Philip French has for many years been a ￼ ￼ ular
film criticism: perceptive, well-informed, alert to the visual as well
as the literary, concerned about film as industry and as art, unpretentious and particularly good at communicating the immediate
experience. Witty, too, with his celebrated titles and puns. This
personal selection from among his essays, book reviews and lectures
– dating from 1964 to 2009 – contains some of the best of his longer
pieces, a cellarful of vintage French: on movie cities and movie
people; on books in films and films in books; on assorted occupa-
tions – including journalism, boxing and racketeering – according
to cinema; plus impassioned and embattled essays on the ups and
downs of British film and the cultural importance of film criticism.
French with tears and French without tears. And a classic April Fool
involving Orson Welles, Leonard Bernstein and the National Film
Theatre. *I Found It at the Movies* is the first of three collections. I
can't wait for volumes two and three…

SIR CHRISTOPHER FRAYLING

Philip French has been there as long as anyone, maintaining a tough,
adoring attitude to the movies… No one at the *Observer* or the
various other places he writes has said so much so regularly about
the important, odd, difficult, daring films that occasionally come
along.
DAVID THOMSON

Philip French knows the canon, and he loves it. He can place new
work in a tradition, but he's also the first to recognise when it's
genuinely new.
DAVID HARE

It's very rare that you find someone who manages to find a way of
writing that expresses the essence of the emotional experience of
watching a film and Philip manages to do that beautifully and
succinctly.
NEIL JORDAN

Philip is one of the monuments of our culture.
A.S. BYATT

PHILIP FRENCH was born in Liverpool in 1933, and after service as an officer with the Parachute Regiment in the Middle East he read law and edited *Isis* at Oxford before going on to study journalism at Indiana University. For over thirty years he was a producer for BBC Radio, specialising in programmes on the arts and American affairs. From the early 1960s he has been a regular contributor to numerous magazines and newspapers ranging from *Sight & Sound* to the *Times Literary Supplement*, and from the *Financial Times* to the *Observer*, where he has written a weekly film column since 1978. His books as author or editor include *The Age of Austerity* (1963), *The Movie Moguls* (1969), *Westerns* (1973), *Three Honest Men: Edmund Wilson, F.R. Leavis, Lionel Trilling* (1980), *Malle on Malle* (1992), *The Faber Book of Movie Verse* (1993), *Cult Movies* (1999) and *Westerns and Westerns Revisited* (2005). He served on the jury at the 1986 Cannes Film Festival, was a Booker Prize judge in 1988, was given a life achievement award by the Critics Circle in 2003 and received an honorary doctorate from the University of Lancaster in 2006. In 2008 Philip French became the first critic to be made a Lifetime Honorary Member of BAFTA, and in 2009 he was named Critic of the Year in the National Press Awards.

Philip French

I Found It at the Movies
Reflections of a Cinephile

CARCANET

First published in Great Britain in 2011 by
Carcanet Press Limited
Alliance House
Cross Street
Manchester M2 7AQ

A CIP catalogue record for this book is available from the British Library

ISBN 978 1 84777 129 2

The publisher is grateful for the support of Peter Thompson for the
publication of this book and other titles in the Carcanet film series

The publisher acknowledges financial assistance
from Arts Council England

Typeset by XL Publishing Services, Tiverton

Printed and bound in England by SRP Ltd, Exeter

Contents

Foreword

Over the past nearly 50 years, in addition to writing and editing a number of books, I've churned out millions of words on films, theatre, fiction, non-fiction and related cultural matters for newspapers and magazines, or to be delivered on the air or as lectures and in symposiums. This is the first of three collections of these occasional writings, which have all been produced with as much care and thought as I've put into anything intended for publication between hard covers, though usually with deadlines hanging over my head. The third volume will contain portraits of literary figures written during my time working in BBC radio, alongside material pertaining to the cinema, but the others are entirely concerned with the movies. The second will feature film reviews and obituaries, while this first one is devoted to essays and articles on broader, more general themes, some relatively long and discursive.

The subjects of these articles were either suggested to me by editors, were based on ideas of my own or arose out of discussions. None was undertaken as a chore. The essential criteria for their selection have been that they throw light on the times during which they were written, appear to have some enduring interest and continue to surprise and amuse me.

I have been a regular moviegoer since the age of four, though not until I left home for the army in 1952 was I able to go as often as I wished. A 1950 letter in *Picturegoer* attacking political bias in newsreels was the first piece of mine to get into print. The next was a 1955 review of Hugo Fregonese's *The Raid* in the Oxford undergraduate weekly magazine, the *Isis*, which I edited the following year. My output since then has been moderately substantial if not – by Fleet Street standards – exactly prolific.

For only part of my life, however, have I been a full-time writer. The first occasion was the six months I spent in 1958–59 as a reporter with the *Bristol Evening Post*, during which time I contributed a staggeringly unfunny humorous column and a

covertly satirical weekly piece on male fashions under the pseudonym Philippe Sartor. The second occasion I lived solely by my
pen (an antiquated phrase suggestive of frantically dipping a quill
into an inkwell) was the 12 months in 1967–68 when I was the *New
Statesman*'s theatre critic, a job I combined with being joint chief
book critic for *The Financial Times*, film critic of the *London Magazine*, reviewing TV films for the *Observer* and contributing regularly
to *Sight & Sound* and other magazines. The third has been these past
20 years, when my principal job has been film critic of the *Observer*.

Otherwise, between the age of 25 and 57 my day job was as a
producer for BBC radio where the only absolutely mandatory
writing was letters, memoranda, *Radio Times* billings and on-air
announcements to be read by the presentation staff. The job itself
largely involved putting ideas to potential broadcasters, considering
subjects they proposed for my consideration, convening suitably
interesting collections of folk for live or recorded discussions,
producing talks and conversations in the studio or elsewhere, and
editing texts or transcripts. An additional task, and the occasion of
much anxiety, amusement and embarrassment was the constant
consultations with colleagues, senior figures in the BBC hierarchy
and the legal department about good taste, libel and obscenity.

Of course, from quite early on and like a good many BBC
colleagues (the place was full of novelists, playwrights, poets, biographers, historian and humorists), I wrote in my spare time. If you
intended publishing anything while a BBC employee you had to
seek permission, always adding in the memo that 'the work will be
done in my spare time, will not mention my employment by the
BBC without permission, and will not deal with topical political
issues or touch on matters of Corporation policy unless submitted
for prior scrutiny'. I recall a particular note from one of my superiors rejecting my application to write a column on television, as
this time he broke into verse:

> Alas and alack,
> You'd get the sack.
> You can do Roger Vadim
> But not Kenneth Adam.

Kenneth Adam was then the head of BBC television.

From the early 1960s onwards I published something somewhere most weeks, and in 1978 I received permission to review films weekly for the *Observer* for a year, an arrangement that continued without further explicit discussion for 12 years until my early retirement from the BBC in 1990. Much therefore of what appears in this book is the product of moonlighting, a happy hobby, pieces written out of joy, a compulsion to assuage my puritanical conscience by turning what might be simple pleasure into some sort of work.

The pieces appear for the most part in chronological order, the earliest written in 1963, the latest in 2009. Each is dated and its source given. Nothing has been changed other than to remove obvious errors or particularly egregious grammatical formulations. Occasionally I have added a note of clarification and commentary at the end of a piece. There are, I am aware, some repetitions of phrases, references and stories but this is not surprising in essays written over such a long period. To have removed them would have weakened the pieces in which they appear and only someone reading the book cover to cover in an ungenerous spirit is likely to be offended. So I've left them in.

It has been my pleasure to work with a number of sympathetic and encouraging editors over the years, the earliest as far as this book is concerned being the late Richard Findlater at *Twentieth Century* and Penelope Houston at *Sight & Sound*, the most recent Jane Ferguson on *The Observer*. My greatest thanks, as always, go to my wife Kersti, whose careful and critical reading of everything I've written over the past 50 years has helped improve not only my books, essays and reviews, but also my notes to the milkman.

I am grateful to the various journals in which these pieces first appeared over the past 45 years, and with whose permission they are reprinted here, and to their editors. The journals' names and the dates of first publication are given at the foot of the first page of each article. The book begins with a tribute to a writer and critic who had a special influence on me at a crucial point in my career.

My Mentor (2001)
An Obituary

David Sylvester, the British critic who died last week at the age of 76, was a large, imposing presence. Clean-shaven when I first knew him 40 years ago, subsequently heavily bearded, he resembled a cross between Luciano Pavarotti and Zero Mostel. He wrote mainly about the visual arts (which included carpets and postage stamps as well as painting and sculpture) and was one of the great curators of exhibitions. But he also wrote about films in *Encounter*, cricket and football for the *Observer* and both classical music and jazz. One of the last cards I had from him thanked me for describing him in this paper as 'our best critic of the arts' rather than as an art critic. I've always thought of him as one of the most original minds in post-war British writing.

We first met when I was a young producer of the BBC Home Service programme *The Critics*, which attracted a couple of million listeners every Sunday lunchtime, and he was one of its most illustrious contributors. He took me under his wing, and meeting artists with him and accompanying him to exhibitions, films, plays and jazz clubs provided me with some of the education he had given himself (he'd left school at 16 and subsequently turned down a scholarship at Cambridge), and which I had never really received. He showed me how to look at pictures, individually and together, to relate one art form to another, to question other people and myself, to see art in a context yet not to be affected by sentimentality or consciously influenced by ideology, class or political conviction, to formulate ideas, to question the idea of art itself. When I began reviewing films for the *Observer*, he insisted I read drafts of my pieces to him over the phone.

'My Mentor' first appeared in the *Observer*, 23 June 2001. I have added comments from my tribute at a Tate Modern memorial event in February 2002.

Hearing in 1963 that I was preparing an essay on westerns, he phoned to say that Anthony Mann's *The Last Frontier* was showing at a back street cinema in South London (the long defunct Grand, Camberwell) and suggested in his characteristically commanding manner that we see the film together. It was showing in a continuous double bill, and I arrived just before the film started. When the lights came up there was David sitting a few rows away, and in another part of the large, dilapidated auditorium was the painter and critic Andrew Forge, who'd also been summoned to attend. We repaired to a nearby pub, took our drinks to a corner table and prepared for David to conduct a discussion. I had anticipated that it would start with Mann's compositions and his use of the crane shot, something David had once remarked on with great enthusiasm. Instead he asked Andrew and me very seriously how different the film would have been had Marlon Brando played the central role of the trapper rather than Victor Mature. Would this, he proposed, have turned *The Last Frontier* from a merely excellent film into a masterpiece?

He was never so certain about his positions that he couldn't bring himself to revalue aspects of artists he extolled such as Moore, Bacon and Giacometti. But he never backed away from championing the new. In 1962 he saw Bridget Riley's first exhibition of smallish black-and-white kinetic abstracts at the now defunct Gallery One, when it had only the last week of its short run left. 'Tell Victor Musgrave [the gallery's owner] that we'll discuss the show on *The Critics* if he'll keep it on for another week,' David said to me. Musgrave extended the run for a fortnight, and his gallery received an unprecedented number of visitors. The following year, weeks before William Mann wrote his famous 'What Songs the Beatles Sang' for *The Times*, David proclaimed on *The Critics* that the Beatles were the most original musical phenomenon of the Sixties, and attracted much undeserved abuse by comparing them with Monteverdi. The same year we spent an evening discussing voyeurism in *From Russia With Love* prior to his writing the first major study of Bond pictures for *Encounter*. Earlier he had become a friend of Stanley Kubrick (another eccentric, middle-class, self-educated Jew with a passion for originality) and a guest on the set of *Lolita* as a result of his early piece on *The Killing* and *Paths of Glory* for *Encounter*.

David was an intensely serious (but only occasionally solemn) man, and highly comic. He could hold his own in the company of philosophers and keep his end up on the terraces of Highbury and White Hart Lane. He loved taxonomy, forever thinking up new categories for art and artists, and was a playful, ludic man who liked watching games, and creating them. He once proposed the idea that everyone, irrespective of his origins, was either Roman, Greek or Jewish. (C.P. Snow was a Roman pretending to be a Greek.) David, in debate with John Berger, invented the term 'kitchen sink school', which he first used in a 1954 article in *Encounter*.

He had a marvellous hearty laugh. But he also had a ferocious temper, though rarely would that beautifully modulated voice change while expressing his white-hot anger. I remember him once turning his vast back on a fellow speaker on *The Critics* (no mean feat at a round table) and telling the other participants: 'I'd like to continue this conversation with people seriously interested in the arts.' The subject under discussion was Francis Bacon's 1962 retrospective at the Tate. But he had a conspicuous fault known among producers as 'the Sylvester Pause'. He sustained pregnant silences in discussion until he'd made up his mind, and eventually this went beyond a rhetorical device to become something that excluded him from conventional broadcasting involving participation with others. Eventually, after trying to explain the situation, I could no longer employ him in regular programmes and this led to an unhappy hiatus in our relationship.

David disliked fashion and affectation and always wanted to know just why you liked something. He admired S.J. Perelman, who, I think, represented something especially Jewish to him in his fastidiousness, mixture of styles and idioms, wry humour, and singular ability to look the world right in the eye. His single-minded perfectionism once got the better of him one evening hours into overtime on the eve of an exhibition of Persian rugs he was organising at the Hayward Gallery. Characteristically he turned to one of the workmen and asked if he thought the layout right. 'Well, perhaps a couple of inches more to the left, Dave,' the man said sarcastically. David paused for a few moments, and said, 'Yes, you're right.' So everybody was at work for another hour or so until well after midnight.

Some years ago David was diagnosed with cancer and expected to die. Then after a period of remission his condition was declared terminal. He cancelled a succession of major projects and in a cheerful spirit undertook just one small, final show. This was a modest exhibition at the Serpentine Gallery in Hyde Park of the working drawings of Ken Adam, the production designer on the Bond movies and *Dr Strangelove*, who had been a pre-war school friend. David asked me to write the main catalogue article, and for months we spoke almost every day. He was one of the greatest of telephone talkers and had a long flex that allowed him to walk around the house and sit on the loo. When I turned in my piece to the gallery's director he insisted upon negotiating the fee on my behalf and obtained the largest sum I'd ever received for such an essay.

At this same time I co-authored a book with my son Karl on cult movies, but thinking David might consider it somewhat frivolous, I didn't have a complimentary copy sent to him. When he heard of this omission he was very annoyed, so I dispatched one with my apologies and an explanation. He wrote back claiming that D.W. Griffith's *Intolerance* could not be regarded as a cult film, and pointed out that in *Farewell My Lovely* Moose Malloy describes his lost lover Velma as being 'cute as lace pants', not 'lace panties'. I acknowledged my error, but claimed that all silent films except for a few comedies were now cult movies. He then sent me a list headed 'David Sylvester's Twenty Cult Movies', a carefully annotated document, and what was fascinating was that virtually all his choices were works in some way unfinished or mutilated, among them Eisenstein's *Que Viva Mexico*, Jean Renoir's *Une Partie de campagne*, Josef von Sternberg's *I Claudius* and Orson Welles's *The Magnificent Ambersons*.

David will live on in different ways: in his writings and the transcriptions of his seminal interviews, in portraits of him by Bacon and Giacometti, as characters in novels by David Storey and Shena Mackay, in his brother-in-law Frank Marcus's play *The Formation Dancers*, and as the flamboyant, egocentric art critic in Barry Humphries's *Barry Mackenzie* strip cartoon in *Private Eye*, which David didn't much like. I'll never forget him as a mentor and as a friend. He was the best teacher I ever had, the worst timekeeper I ever encountered. 'No wonder they hate us – critics, I mean,' he once said apropos of his colleagues' patronising reception of Arnold Wesker's *Chips With Everything* on *The Critics* in 1962. His remark produced a shocked silence around the table, and after a pause he gave a brief, cogent analysis of the play's meaning, establishing immediately the indispensability of good criticism.

The Right Kind of Englishman (1964)

It has always seemed to me that the archetypal screen Englishmen are Naunton Wayne and Basil Radford, And nowhere did they appear more so than in their first joint appearance as supporting actors in roles created by the screenwriters Frank Launder and Sidney Gilliatt in Alfred Hitchcock's 1938 movie *The Lady Vanishes*, a film that is as popular today as when it was first shown.

Radford (tall, plumpish, straight-faced, moustached) and Wayne (slight, quick-tongued, nervously smiling) together constituted a formidable team proffering a solidly middle-class, invulnerably insular front to the challenges of social change and foreign intrigue. There they were as Charters (Radford) and Caldicott (Wayne) in Hitchcock's political thriller set at the time of Munich on the fringe of an international explosion, worrying only about the score of the Test match at Manchester. Told that they'd have to share a room with an attractive Middle European maid, their embarrassment is acute. One of them complains to the hotel manager that they should have been given two, and immediately assures the other that he means rooms, not maids; their concern is mainly over whether they'll have to dress for dinner out in the corridor. Yet when the chips are down they are ready to meet the challenge. Wayne can handle a gun with coolness and accuracy; Radford dismisses a wound as a mere nothing. They are buffoonish, of course, and audiences laugh at them, then as now, but indulgently, as if to say: 'Yes, we British are funny, but at the same time sound and sensible, if diffident and slightly eccentric; no wonder that foreigners don't quite understand us and invariably underrate our capacity to rise to the occasion.'

Radford and Wayne went on to make a series of films as leading players. But their main role was always as points of reference for the

'The Right Kind of Englishman' first appeared in *Twentieth Century*, Autumn 1964.

filmmaker and the audience. When Thorold Dickinson wanted to end his wartime propaganda movie *The Next of Kin* with a brief scene bringing home to the general public the central message of the picture (the necessity for security), they were called into service as Charters and Caldicott to enact the roles of national symbols. In Launder and Gilliatt's celebration of life on the home front during World War Two, *Milllions Like Us*, they appear from time to time as a pair of chorus figures commenting on a changing Britain. Sometimes a slightly different context would call for a variation on their roles, in for instance the two key 1949 Ealing movies of national discontent, *Whisky Galore* and *Passport to Pimlico*. In the former, Radford appears alone as the establishment figure protesting against the islanders hijacking the wrecked ship's potent cargo. (He also appeared alone the following year as the factory owner in Bernard Miles's well-meaning but muddled study of labour relations, *Chance of a Lifetime*.) In *Passport* they both turn up as civil servants baffled by the outrageous conduct of the would-be Burgundian separatists. But the key line in *Passport to Pimlico* is spoken by the old lady who shouts from the window, correcting a tendency towards genuine insurrection: 'Of course we're British – it's because we're British that we're standing up for our right to be Burgundians.' It is evident that this is licensed anarchy; Radford and Wayne are our better selves to whom we shall return, just as surely as Peter Pan will come back for his shadow.

Not only did Radford and Wayne over a period of 20 years play an important part in representing all that was best in the English character, but the values they embodied form the central core of the majority of serious and comic films concerned directly or obliquely with the British. They are, for example, the humorous counterparts of the serious war hero. Thus in *The Way to the Stars* (1945), while Michael Redgrave goes off to die and John Mills and Trevor Howard keep 'em flying, there is Basil Radford with the ground crew teaching the transatlantic visitors the mysteries of cricket and in turn learning to master the technicalities of baseball. And much later the qualities of Radford-Wayne, slightly soured, form the basic assumptions about the young man in Joseph Losey's *The Servant*, just as Ian Carmichael in the Boulting Brothers' comedies is Radford-Wayne robbed of social confidence.

The Radford-Wayne character in fact represents the perennial middle-class Briton, frequently embattled, normally complacent, but always capable of facing up to the vicissitudes of life and seeing it through. He is a modest man, respecting the established order but anti-authoritarian, little troubled by problems of sex or politics or religion. If his life is incomplete, it is not that he is waiting for Samuel Beckett's Godot or Clifford Odets' Lefty, but merely for Lassie to come home. Or for the Thunderbolt to take him to Titfield.

Leslie Howard embodied these qualities in a highly serious form in a number of roles, and most obviously in *The Scarlet Pimpernel* and *Pimpernel Smith*, which he wrote himself. In both of these movies, the French revolutionaries and the Nazis having been put in their place (quietly and with stylish diffidence), Howard makes his way back to England quoting patriotic verse − in the first proclaiming John of Gaunt's speech from Shakespeare's *Richard II* and in the second reciting selected passages from Rupert Brooke's 'Grantchester'. It is not surprising that Howard should be Shaw's essential Henry Higgins and his debonair, more flamboyant counterpart Rex Harrison the Lerner and Loewe version. Howard as Mitchell, the inventor of the Spitfire, in *The First of the Few* is to his straight Higgins in *Pygmalion* what Harrison as Vivian Kenway in *The Rake's Progress* is to the singing Higgins of *My Fair Lady*. They are both fellow clubmen of Basil Radford and Naunton Wayne.

That this should be the view of British cinema is hardly surprising. Though the majority of those who pay the piper may not be middle class, the piper himself is. And he plays his own tunes, albeit that on occasion he may dedicate them to his betters or invite the lower orders to dance to them.

In recent years there has been in Britain an attempt to break out of this tight, middle-class web in which the bourgeois mythology had been spun. I doubt if Roger Manvell would write so confidently now as he did in 1955 (*The Film and Society*):

> The best actors and actresses are the embodiment of the characteristics of their own people. Who are more American than Spencer Tracy or Henry Fonda or Marlon Brando? Who more Italian than Anna Magnani? … Who more British than Michael Redgrave, John Mills or Laurence Olivier? Yet these and many other actors and actresses have revealed on the international

screen of the world's cinemas the finer qualities of temperament and feeling and thought and spirit proper to the nations to which they belong.

The cinematic expression of 'these finer qualities of temperament' began to fall into general disrepute in the later 1950s, though it would be seriously underrating their strength to suppose that they have been more than temporarily displaced.

The principal impetus for this change has come through the stage (or more precisely the English Stage Company at the Royal Court), television, the working-class novel, and the Free Cinema documentary movement of the late 1950s. The result has been such feature films as *Room at the Top*, *Saturday Night and Sunday Morning*, *A Kind of Loving*, *Loneliness of the Long Distance Runner*, *The L-Shaped Room*, *This Sporting Life*, *Nothing But the Best*. Some of these pictures evidenced a visual imagination rare in the British cinema, but all involved a conscious revolution against Radford-Wayne. The central character of these films came to be known as 'the Albert Finney part' after Finney had played Arthur Seaton in *Saturday Night and Sunday Morning*. 'Who is going to play the Finney part?' became the casting question. Finney's services were actually sought for many of these pictures, and such was the detachment from the essential subject matter that producers became conscious of their similarity. Consequently Stan Barstow's Yorkshire novel *A Kind of Loving* was switched to a Lancashire setting for the screen in order not to be confused with *Room at the Top*; David Storey's Arthur Machin became *Frank* Machin in the film of *This Sporting Life* to prevent identification with Sillitoe's Arthur Seaton.

This new character, the working-class rebel, was trapped by the inadequacies of working-class life, reacting with varying success to the age of affluence with its apparent, but not real, opportunities. It is odd that he should have become briefly the dominant image of contemporary Britain at this time. But he was soon replaced or at least accompanied by the carefully tailored film version of Ian Fleming's James Bond. (Strangely enough, Sean Connery who plays Bond was, I believe, one of the actors considered for the lead in *This Sporting Life*.) This screen Bond emerged as a semi-classless figure – equipped with a Scots or mid-Atlantic accent, the consumer tastes of the A-B group of newspaper readers and routine sex fantasies. He came at the end of a line of avenging, displaced-bourgeois thriller heroes that had run through our cinema since the end of World War Two, from the former commandos fighting the spivs in *Noose* (1948) to the seedy ex-officers robbing the state in *League of Gentlemen* (1960) and the commercial traveller tracking down the racketeers who stole his car in *Never Let Go* (1960). Bond was back attacking an *external* enemy rather than the forces that had been eating away at the middle class. He was at peace with his own society.

Still, whatever the shortcomings of this group of working-class films, and they are considerable, they were a genuine attempt to reflect the life of a section of the community hitherto largely ignored or patronisingly kept where they belonged – on the actual or figurative lower deck. An interesting example of the earlier attitude is expressed by one of the makers of the 1947 Ealing working-class picture *It Always Rains on Sunday*, when he wrote in a book about the production of the film that the changes made in the adaptation were 'an attempt not to glamorise the story or the people, but to make them more typical. The novel is somewhat brutal.'

Some makers of the later films became highly conscious of the drift towards the 'typical' – the idea that the films contained a joint hero for our times. And Lindsay Anderson wrote of his first feature film:

> Throughout *This Sporting Life* we were aware that we were not making a film about anything representative. We were making a film about something unique. We were not making a film about a 'worker' but about an extraordinary (and therefore more significant) man, and about an extraordinary relationship. We were not, in a word, making sociology.

But so possessed did Anderson apparently become with the idea that he was not making a mere film about the working class, that David Storey's highly individual but credible football player became a lumbering giant in the movie, whose appearance and motivation was as convincing as a Hammer Film monster, a central weakness in an otherwise impressive picture.

While I would agree with Lindsay Anderson that good films are about unique people, individuals, there does not seem to be any reason why they shouldn't at the same time present valid representatives of something or other. (I doubt if Anderson would disagree that the characters in, say, *La Règle du jeu*, *The Tokyo Story* or *The Leopard*, are both unique and representative.) Indeed there are good reasons why they should be, whether the director seeks to have the audience identify with his characters or not. But the majority of films appeal to comforting stereotype notions of behaviour, for good commercial reasons or bad artistic ones. This goes for the working-class films as well, though most filmmakers must be aware that the middle-class image presented is less true than the working-class one, for the latter is generally based on a remote acquaintance with the world of Donald McGill postcards or the sincere though misguidedly sentimental notions of middle-class intellectuals, who have read their Opie, Hoggart, Orwell, etc. The working class is somehow seen as more 'real'. I cannot but recall a favourite *New Yorker* cartoon that depicts a demure middle-aged spinster sitting in a publisher's office. The publisher, fingering a thick manuscript on the desk, is saying to her blandly, 'Generally speaking, your novel is quite good, but everyone here feels that the New Orleans bordello scenes lack authenticity.'

Nevertheless in recent years the range of experience reflected in British films has been greatly extended, and permanently, though it remains doubtful whether this extension represents a real increase in self-criticism. One thing, however, is certain: that the old Hollywood view of the British will never be able to reassert itself with the strength it had in the past, despite the huge popularity this reassuring picture of Britain once enjoyed. These films made with largely British casts (C. Aubrey Smith and Dame May Whitty smiling benignly in the background, with professional Englishmen or honorary citizens like Douglas Fairbanks Jr in the foreground), often based on 'authentic' British sources like *Cavalcade* or James Hilton novels, glorifying immortal institutions like Lloyds and the Grand National, served for many years to present the national image of this country at a time when the British film industry was at a low ebb. A number of the most memorable 'British' films of the 1930s were made by American directors in this country: MGM's famous pre-war trio for instance, Jack Conway's *A Yank at Oxford*, King Vidor's *The Citadel* and Sam Wood's *Goodbye Mr Chips*.

A Yank at Oxford was a great success because, although it allowed Robert Taylor of Cardinal College to triumph in the athletics meeting with Cambridge and stroke his crew to victory in the Boat Race, the initially brash American was won over to the traditional understated decencies of British life. The flattering American vision of Britain corresponded for a long time to our own, and due to its essential purity and the superiority of its expression the films embodying it easily pushed ours aside. Siegfried Kracauer has pointed out that except for a few period pieces, Hollywood laid off this country in the immediate post-war years as a consequence, he suggests, of the American difficulties over a socialist Britain. But the American vision of Britain is by no means dead nor, let it be said, is our capacity to respond to it – Mr Jack Le Vien's television tribute to Sir Winston Churchill and his compatriots, *The Finest Hour*, sees it flourishing still, and almost as popular as ever.

On the other hand when René Clément came over here in 1953 and let a French Don Juan (Gérard Philipe) loose on London in *Knave of Hearts*, his film got a very cold reception. Now this was a quite remarkable movie for its time. It made striking use of London locations, and in a series of seductions of a variety of British girls it demonstrated a maliciously precise knowledge of English character. 'A story about a French wolf who comes over to prey on our girls' ... 'so shabby' ... 'vulgar morals and no point' ... 'a tedious young roué and his colourless victims' ... 'an expendable and nasty piece': these were a few of the British critics' outraged comments. The film won Clément the best director prize at the Cannes festival! It's not that easy to take criticism from outside, and the more accurate it is the more likely it is to provoke a defensive reaction.

That is ten years ago, and I fancy Clément's film would now be received with less hostility. Nevertheless it was only a couple of years back that *Bachelor of Hearts*, with a German at Cambridge to replace a Yank at Oxford, showed that old ideas die hard, though a little more sex and a little less rowing indicated a move in the right direction. We do after all like our foreigners to be less knowing than M. Philipe's Don Juan, to move – like the Russian engineer in Anthony Asquith's *The Demi-Paradise* (1943) or the American factory worker in Val Guest's *Miss Pilgrim's Progress* (1949) – from bafflement and impatience to acceptance and admiration in a few easy reels.

There is a telling scene in Billy Wilder's *Sunset Boulevard* in which a girl tries to cheer up an out of work screenwriter by informing him that one of his rejected scripts seems to her true and moving. 'Who wants true? Who wants moving?', he asks bitterly. Certainly Wardour Street would agree with T.S. Eliot that 'human kind cannot bear very much reality'. But the question of reality is one of the most difficult and widely discussed aspects of the cinema, both as it relates to films themselves and to the audience's response to them. Which, if either, was the more 'real', *The Miniver Story*, with Mr and Mrs M. in 1950 contemplating emigration after soaking the garden of their Thames-side villa ten years before with their blood, sweat and tears, or *Passport to Pimlico*, which allowed a symbolic outlet for middle-class revolt? Certainly critics and audiences alike rejected *The Miniver Story* very decisively.

Then again, which films are more 'true', those made on location or those largely produced in studios? If it were the former kind, then surely the real insight into the British character would be found in the documentary film, especially in the pioneer school of the 1930s. But today those pictures, with the exception of Robert Flaherty's study of primitive life, *Man of Aran*, have less to say about the people with whom they deal and much more about the educational and propaganda interests of their makers. As Roy Boulting said in a recent radio programme:

> I think all filmmakers owe a tremendous debt to the documentary movement; at a time when our feature films were concerned principally with a romantic fantasy world that had nothing to do with reality, the documentary movement really brought us face to face with the excitement of reality, but it was a reality that dealt with things rather than people, by and large.

Now anyone who came to this country for the first time would recognise familiar landmarks that he has seen in a succession of films. Since British producers started making extensive use of location shooting, there can be few areas of the country that have not figured in feature films. But the visitor would be ill advised to expect to meet any of the characters, colourful or colourless, that he has seen in most of these films. This is of course true of practically any national cinema. As I have indicated, what he sees in the films are the notions that people have of themselves.

It is instructive here to compare two very different pictures, both of which set out to engage in social criticism and both made in this country by foreigners. Sidney J. Furie, a Canadian, recently directed *The Leather Boys*, a picture about young married life in the working class. I myself found the film unconvincing in almost every aspect, and I suspect that those who did find it convincing did so because it was shot largely on location, and the cafés, the Butlin's camp and the workplaces in which the action took place were undeniably the genuine article. The film's failure to touch off much of a response despite the plausibility of its story line was because it neither corresponded to accepted ideas about people, nor substituted a consistent vision of reality for these stereotypes.

On the other hand, Joseph Losey's picture *The Servant*, stylised in its treatment and made largely in a film studio, contained for many of us a basically truthful and convincing image of contemporary British life. The story of a young upper-class man gradually corrupted by his servant and eventually turned into a slave seemed not only 'real' – despite or because of the rejection of naturalism by Losey and his screenwriter Harold Pinter – but also to offer a critical comment upon, for instance, class relations and the sterility of British tradition, and to relate the small event it depicted to wider issues such as the nature of power. Because *The Servant* was real, it could also be symbolic; the apparent uniqueness of the situation did not rob it of its possibilities of being representative. The same is true of Losey's immediately preceding British films, *The Criminal* (1960), a thriller set in the underworld and jail, and *The Damned* (1961), a piece of political science fiction. Both represent a re-ordering of reality to produce a personal image of society. You don't have to agree with Losey's view of the contemporary scene to acknowledge the validity and consistency of the world he creates.

There is an important distinction to be drawn between films that present a personal vision of society and those basically conceived in terms of what a society thinks about itself. And this extends to criticisms of society as well. While it is usual to flatter the audience's self-esteem, there are also the stereotyped faults in a society that filmmakers feel free to criticise. Thus the Boulting Brothers' series of tilts at various institutions are never really concerned with what any serious critic elsewhere sees as the real problems. Though a popular audience has accepted the pictures as powerful satires, they are in fact no more relevant than *Carry On Sergeant* or *Carry On Teacher*, which were obviously and deliberately conceived as farces based on stock responses.

So what *appear* to be rebellious films are often directed not against experienced reality itself but against the enduring clichés. At a serious level, for instance, the Borstal governor (played by Michael Redgrave) in *The Loneliness of the Long Distance Runner*, is a projection of the stereotype of such a person. This may well have been the intention of course, though the general level of sophistication in the film hardly sustains this view, and even if this were so it would hardly change the situation. At another level there is *French Dressing*, the first feature film of Ken Russell, a TV director. The theme of the picture, I take it, is the revolt of young people against the stifling, 'anti-life' society of provincial, bourgeois England. A deckchair attendant, supported by his American girlfriend and the local council's entertainment manager, sets about bringing a Cannes-style film festival to an English seaside resort. It rains every day; not surprisingly the beaches are empty; when a crowd does turn up it behaves in the sheep-like manner of an adman's dream; the mayor and alderman are shown as moronic, inhibited, sex-mad automata ready to do anything that will attract people to their town or starlets to themselves; the atmosphere is totally joyless save for the *joie de vivre* of the young lovers. True, the film is intended to be a farcical comedy, though presumably one based upon the observation of character, and we are expected to have some feeling for the lovers' plight. But this staggering picture of British life is a mixture of Donald McGill and the most ancient of hoary French jokes about the English. Ironically enough, when we reach the point of final rejection, Mr Russell and his colleagues have it both ways. The mayor and corporation, together with the group of naked bathers they're ogling, are struck by lightning, while the hero, heroine and friend (in a scene that like many others seems to strive after the lyricism of *Jules et Jim*) prance down the promenade, the men liberated from the shackles of bureaucracy, the girl saved from the dread fate of deputising for a French starlet and bathing in the nude – though the opening of the nudist beach had been seen as quite natural for the starlet. So where does this leave us? – the young people feeling free, though in fact trapped by their insularity, and the townsfolk struck down for either being themselves or trying to be different. Perhaps I dwell too long on *French Dressing*, but it does seem to me that for all its apparent attempts at freshness, it is as much informed by complacent, inhibited middle-class notions as any earlier British films of the kind that its makers would surely despise.

In this it is quite unlike *Tom Jones* (1963), the great commercial success of which surprised many people. Albert Finney's performance and John Osborne's script, I suggest, offered a fresh and valid national image of life and behaviour quite unlike that of previous costume pictures, and this brought an unusual response from the British public. (The popular 'black' costume movies of the mid-1940s, such as *The Man in Grey* and *The Wicked Lady*, were deliberately escapist, though the brutal, sensual leading men as played by Stewart Granger and James Mason were a reaction against the traditionally effete, reserved hero, and perhaps prefigured the more realistic, virile protagonists of the late 1950s who preceded *Tom Jones*.) Osborne seemed to have found in Fielding's novel, and in eighteenth-century England, the positive side of national qualities that, earlier on, he could reflect only negatively. Jones as played by Finney embodies certain traits of charity and generosity, an ebullience and vigour that one can identify as essentially English but which seem to have gone partially underground in our national life since the beginning of the Industrial Revolution and never made their appearance in British films.

Indeed the characteristics of Jones and of his England, despite its frequent brutality and its basically hierarchical nature, are those that have previously been associated in films with the French, the Italians and to a lesser extent the Americans. More so than any other films, I fancy, *Tom Jones* has aroused a deep response to a new and acceptable national image of character and conduct.

It is, however, part of the commercial nature of the cinema that whatever other merits films may have, even good ones will tend to reflect a rather dated image: what their makers think the audience wants to see or is prepared to see. If I have mentioned very few pictures of real distinction in terms of their assumptions about the British, then this is because they *are* unique experiences, reflecting the personal views of their creators; their excellence is unconnected with 'the British way of life', whatever that is. But for commercial reasons, and technical reasons too, the British cinema in general is likely to lag behind the theatre, the novel and even television in its response to changing ideas about society. Still, if one of Wardour Street's doomed Dakotas (now, of course, a jet) were to crash in the

Shepperton jungle or the Elstree Alps, its passenger list would need to range more widely and sympathetically over the social spectrum than it has done in former years. Phyllis Calvert, or her heir, would still be needed as air hostess, and Michael Redgrave or James Donald would still be at the controls. Margaret Rutherford and Wilfrid Hyde White and David Tomlinson or Ian Carmichael (as natural successors to Radford and Wayne) would still be aboard. The role of the hysterical foreigner would now probably go to a cool Jean-Paul Belmondo or Alain Delon. But seats, and no longer back ones, would have to be found for Albert Finney, Sean Connery and, most likely, Rita Tushingham – and maybe for a pop singer as well (though come to think of it, Marty Wilde did get on to one such flight a few years ago). It should also be less easy to guess in the first reel who would rise to the occasion and rally the survivors.

Two recent international co-productions – the Anglo-German *Station Six – Sahara* and the Anglo-American *Dr Strangelove* – indicate the way things are going at the moment. They are both excellent films, skilfully directed and intelligently scripted, but quite different from each other in character. In Seth Holt's *Station Six – Sahara*, two Britons, a middle-class Englishman and a working-class Scot, are running an oil pipeline station in the Sahara with two German engineers. Into their midst is flung a young American blonde. The spineless Englishman continues living in his fantasy world with his pathetic memories of the war and his dreams of future upper-middle-class acceptance. The coarse Scot with a social chip on his shoulder blunders in his advances to the blonde intruder. The girl goes from one cool, laconic German to the other, before being knifed by her husband. The film ends with life at the station returning to normal, the Scot dragging to his hut a girl from a mobile brothel and the Englishman retiring with his new batch of mail from home. The movie in effect deals pretty ruthlessly with both principal types of current screen Brit.

In Stanley Kubrick's *Dr Strangelove* there is only one British character, Group Captain Lionel Mandrake. He is played by Peter Sellers as a version of Radford-Wayne, and of course Mandrake is here a national representative. In a film where virtually all the characters are mad, he is merely eccentric. He tries desperately to make the paranoid General Jack D. Ripper recall the wing of H-bombers unleashed against Russia; then, when Ripper has committed suicide, the Group Captain has another fight to persuade a second deranged American, Colonel 'Bat' Guano, to let him call the US president and pass on the recall code. Once again apparently the Englishman has come through, late but still triumphing against the odds. Yet the names in *Dr Strangelove* carry a built-in comment on the characters – Strangelove himself, President Merkin Muffley, General 'Buck' Turgidson, Major 'King' Kong, Ambassador de Sadesky etc. – and Mandrake is part of this pattern. So we recall the traditional superstition about the mandrake, whose forked root 'was thought to resemble the human form, and was fabled to shriek when plucked up from the ground'.

The above piece for Twentieth Century *(which in some way anticipates what I was to say a couple of years later in* The Alphaville of Admass*) was the first of numerous articles I wrote over the next 30-odd years in which my contribution to symposiums was the theme's title with the addition of 'and the cinema', whether it be Raymond Chandler or Marriage. The one that follows was also for* Twentieth Century, *an outstanding quarterly edited by Richard Findlater. It paid small fees while letting you write at length, which in retrospect seems preferable to magazines that pay well, screw up your copy and leave you feeling frustrated.*

Violence in the Cinema (1965)

The cinema is a peculiarly violent form of entertainment, developed in and catering for what we have come to think of as an age of violence. Undoubtedly one of the reasons that we think of our time as a violent age is because of our vivid vicarious experience of destruction and brutality in newsreels and feature films. One can have lived the quietest of lives and yet feel that through the cinema one has looked upon the face of war and civil disruption, participated in bank robberies, committed murder and witnessed a hundred gunfights and brutal assaults. Of all aspects of the cinema, the treatment of violence is perhaps the most complex, controversial and in many ways central. It is only equalled as a controversial issue by the often closely related question of sex. The extreme views of its effects are on the one hand those of certain social observers, who see it as one of the principal causes of crime and delinquency, and on the other those of psychologists who believe that it plays an almost essential cathartic role in diminishing aggression.

A not untypical reaction is that of an ex-secretary of the British Board of Film Censors, who has been quoted as saying that 'anyone who prolongs scenes of violence is only doing so to titillate a small unhealthy section of the audience'. This generalisation might find wide acceptance, but it does not stand up for a minute to close scrutiny. To begin with, a mass medium does not persistently set out to please small sections of its audience, so if an interest in violence is unhealthy then it is one that is pretty widely shared. Furthermore the most obviously prolonged scene of violence ever made is the appalling carnage on the Odessa Steps in *Battleship Potemkin*, the most celebrated single sequence in the history of the movies. Although it is deliberately prolonged beyond the actual time the real event would have taken, few would accuse Eisenstein

'Violence in the Cinema' first appeared in *Twentieth Century*, Winter 1964–65.

of titillation. The view of the popular audience, which is too rarely heard in these matters (it votes with its feet at the box office), is no doubt expressed for them by Sammy Davis in the gangland comedy *Robin and the Seven Hoods* (1964). As he dances around a gambling den he's wrecking with a submachine gun, he celebrates the outrage with a mischievous song:

> I like the fun
> Of reaching for a gun
> And going, Bang! Bang!

This is the true spirit of the unselfconscious groundlings breaking through the rational carapace of our nervous times.

Cinematic violence can be approached in terms of two closely linked questions: Why is there so much of it? How much of it is justified and on what grounds? Naturally some of the answers take one straight into the field of sociology and psychology, and where it seems better for these matters to be expanded by sociologists and psychologists I shall break off and leave it to them. There are already far too many film critics sitting in the stalls and treating the screen as if it were society on the couch. But those questions can only be posed against a historical background. There never has been a time when the movies have not been preoccupied with violence. (One of the earliest films of the Edison Company in 1893 was a one-and-a-half-minute film for Kinetoscope viewing called *The Execution of Mary Queen of Scots* – the doomed lady walks to the block, an axe swings, a head rolls in the dust.) Before the end of the century it became apparent that the movies would take over the theatre's role of providing violence and spectacle, although the theatre's immediate response to the challenge was a vain indulgence in greater realism, more elaborate spectacle. But of one such attempt, the chariot race in a 1898 dramatisation of *Ben Hur*, a contemporary critic observed: 'The only way to secure the exact sense of action for this incident in a theatre is to represent it by Mr Edison's invention.'

If one is looking for the origin of the public opprobrium that is attached to movie violence, this too can be found in the 1890s. Terry Ramsaye, who lived through the period and was the American cinema's first serious historian, places it around 1897, two years after the invention of the movie projector. Faced with the limitless

possibilities of the new medium, the American pioneers could think
of nothing better to do than record prize fights round by round. Of
the consequences of this obsession with the ring, Ramsaye observed
in his book *A Million and One Nights* (1926):

> One marked effect of the Corbett-Fitzsimmons picture as the
> outstanding screen production of its day was to bring the odium
> of pugilism upon the screen all across Puritan America. Until that
> picture appeared the social status of the screen had been uncer-
> tain. It now became definitely low-brow, an entertainment of the
> great unwashed commonalty. This likewise made it a mark for
> uplifters, moralists, reformers and legislators in a degree which
> would never have obtained if the screen had by specialization
> reached higher social strata.

The history of the cinema has since had running through it a
continuous battle between the 'uplifters, moralists, reformers and
legislators' and the practitioners in the medium, its greatest artists as
well as its most blatant commercial exploiters, and the battleground
has usually been the treatment of sex and violence.

The cinema was not exactly slow to realise its power, though at
first a trifle vague about its dramatic uses. When Edwin S. Porter
filmed the first important dramatic close-up, it was of a menacing
bandit firing his pistol directly into the camera. But he stuck it onto
the end of *The Great Train Robbery* (1903) almost as an afterthought,
and the Edison catalogue of the following year, while recognising
that 'the resultant excitement is great', suggested to exhibitors that
'this scene can be used to begin or end the picture'.

Subsequent filmmakers became more knowing in every way as
they came to understand the new medium and as the society in
which they lived grew increasingly sophisticated in its appreciation
of the nature of violence. Since the turn of the century violence has
been a constant factor, and I fancy that such evidence as there is for
periodic increases has been exaggerated. It is the form and intensity
of violence that has changed rather than its quantity. This is a
minority view, and a more generally accepted one is that the
German cinema was particularly violent in the 1920s, the American
cinema in the early 1930s and the French cinema in the 1950s.
Socio-political reasons – the atmosphere of the Weimar Republic
in Germany, the post-Prohibition early-Depression era in America,

the national confusion and colonial unrest in France – are usually suggested. What these backgrounds may have done is to give a unifying character to the bodies of films (i.e. German Expressionist pictures tend to look alike, American gangster films share similar characteristics), and the violence may have had a more jarring effect through its repetitive, contemporary character. (Whereas paradoxically the repetitive, formalised violence in an established genre, the horror film, say, or the western, has the opposite result, making it almost cosy.) Yet if we look closely at the work of someone like Fritz Lang, we see in the style and the treatment of violence a continuing personal development that links his German movies of the 1920s with his American ones in the following three decades.

As it happens there has never been a time when some critic hasn't been spotting a new upsurge of violence (and sex). There are at least four major instances in the case of the American cinema. First there was the outcry in the 1920s that brought into existence the infamous Production Code. (This followed an alleged cycle of violent movies that included DeMille's popular success of 1919, *The Cheat*, where Sessue Hayakawa branded his adulterous wife with a red hot iron, a sequence considered barbarous at the time but recently regarded as sufficiently innocuous to be presented during a sycophantic tribute to DeMille on peak hour television.) A second outcry came in the 1930s with the gangster films, which contravened – directly or obliquely – almost every section of the Production Code, and yet a third in the mid-1940s, immediately after World War Two. At this point an anonymous 'Film Critic' contributed an article to *Penguin New Writing* (No. 30, 1947) called 'Parade of Violence', which contained the following lament:

> Gone completely the sophisticated and adult attitude of American film melodramas such as *Laura*, *The Maltese Falcon*, *Mask of Dimitrios* etc.; instead we have the purposeless parade of violence for its own sake: physical violence unrelated to any known form of life and apparently catering for a supposed audience of sadistic schoolchildren.

Several of these pictures too are considered fairly innocent fare now that they have eventually reached the television screen, and a handful of them are thought minor classics – including two by Fritz Lang, which 'Film Critic' compares unfavourably with those

German pictures of the 1920s that had been accepted as so dangerously prophetic by the adherents of the heady thesis advanced in
Siegfried Kracauer's *From Caligari to Hitler*.

It is easy enough now to see these post-war pictures as expressing
the black mood of the time and reflecting Hollywood's belated
discovery of abnormal psychology. The psychopathic villain had
arrived, soon to be joined by the psychopathic hero, and both
remain with us. Still, 'Film Critic' was in good company and was
talking about what G. Legman described as 'Hollywood's New
Violence' (in his 1949 book *Love and Death*), quoting 'a working
abridgment' of the Production Code coined by an American Jesuit:
'No tits – blood'. Legman's well-known theory about the suppression of sex leading to an increase of violence in all media, although
taken much too far, has a certain validity. Clearly the Catholic
orientation of American censorship leads to a toleration of violence
and an intolerance of sexual frankness which, coupled with the
inescapable violence of American life, makes pictures from the
United States the most violent in the world.

Still, within less than ten years of Legman's and 'Film Critic''s
assumption that the situation could hardly get worse, there was an
article on censorship in *Sight & Sound* asserting as a fact scarcely in
need of support that 'The ferocity of American films has undeniably increased'. And in the same issue (Spring, 1956) the magazine's
associate editor devoted a long essay to the 'instinctive rebellion that
finds its expression in meaningless acts of violence', that seemed to
her to characterise the most significant of recent US social protest
pictures. Again one must observe that there wasn't a real increase in
violence but merely that it was more disturbing on account of its
confusion with insoluble social problems – *Rebel Without a Cause*
(1955) is a case in point. At its best it could even be the result of a
desperate honesty.

Now, eight years later, we seem to be involved in a similar
debate, and it concerns movies from all over the world, including
– since the success of the James Bond pictures – our own film
industry. From this we can draw some obvious conclusions. The
most apparent is that yesterday's excess is today's restraint. When
the searing brutality of *Barabbas* struck London, there were those
who looked back to the good taste of *Quo Vadis*, forgetting that it
was from this earlier film that many people, including a leading

Labour MP, had walked out in protest against its sadistic arena scenes. A 1955 reviewer of *Les Diaboliques*, the film which started a cycle of sick thrillers, recoiled with the observation that 'rarely if ever has such a wallow in the sickeningly macabre been passed for distribution in this country'; five years later Hitchcock's *Psycho* made Clouzot's picture look almost like a production of the Children's Film Foundation. *Psycho* caused several critics to quit the press show in disgust. Though it is still going the rounds and scaring the pants off appreciative audiences, many now regard it as a black comedy.

Another obvious conclusion is that just as screen violence needs to keep getting more intense to compete with preceding shocks – especially where it is only the impact that matters – so there is a lag between national tastes. Where, say, Sweden is some years ahead of us in the tolerance of sexual frankness, so America is ahead in the tolerance of violence. Thus our censor cuts sex scenes from most Swedish pictures and can spot Eva Dahlbeck's nipples behind a screen better than Ingmar Bergman (who had to run this sequence from *Smiles of a Summer Night* through several times before glimpsing them). While the censor is rarely troubled in this way by imports from the United States, around two out of three American films leave on his floor a few hundred feet of violence of a kind that would scarcely disturb a sensitive youth in Dubuque, Iowa.

Violence on the screen tends, I have said, to take its character and form (if often obliquely) from the mood of the time and place in which it originates. This operates in two ways. On one level is the creative artist responsive to the undercurrent of the society in which he works and reflecting it in his personal vision. On another level is the skilful producer of films intended to meet what he divines to be in contemporary taste. Naturally there is a good deal of middle ground here. Some directors, Hitchcock for instance, have ideas that usually and happily (in commercial terms) match the public mood, while others, such as Luis Buñuel, rarely do. Thus Joseph Losey, although he has worked in this country for over ten years, still has the personal approach to violence evident in his American pictures, though these at the time (late 1940s, early 1950s) seemed very much of their period and place. The three James Bond films, however, are deliberately thought out in terms of exploiting current tastes, and as they get more certain in touch they become more decadent in treatment. If, then, you wish to see how violence is dealt with in a personal way, you might go to a Losey film, but if you want to see the way in which the industry thinks the public want it serving up, *Goldfinger* is the better guide.

It might be interesting, therefore, to look at the opening sequences of a recent Losey picture, *The Damned*, and of the third Bond movie, *Goldfinger*. Both pictures contain a great deal of violence but represent quite different approaches to it, and a comparison between the two will bring us on to the further consideration of the questions posed earlier about the amount of violence in the movies and its justification.

The Damned opens with the credit titles presented against the background of pieces of sculpture outside an artist's studio on a deserted cliff. The scene quickly shifts to the promenade of a quiet south coast resort where a motorcycle gang are swinging on a statue of George III and singing a rock song. An American visitor is then lured down a side street by the gang leader's sister to be beaten up and robbed. A few minutes later, battered and bleeding, he is carried into a nearby hotel and meets a civil servant (head of a secret atomic research establishment situated beneath the nearby cliffs). 'I never expected something like this to happen to me in England,' the American says and receives the reply: 'The age of senseless violence has caught up with us too.'

The opening sequence in *Goldfinger* goes something like this. The setting is apparently a Caribbean republic – we see a seagull swimming on the water, which turns out to be the head of James Bond as he surfaces in a frogman's outfit. With the aid of a rope fired from a dinky little gun he climbs a wall, kicks a Latin American guard in the teeth and plants a time bomb in a huge gas tank. He then peels off the rubber suit to reveal a white tuxedo, in the buttonhole of which he places a carnation, and arrives at a nightclub just in time to be relaxing at the bar when the bomb goes off. (A semi-audible line is muttered which suggests that the factory had been, I think, the HQ of drug traffickers.) Mission accomplished, Bond adjourns to the room of a dancing girl. While kissing her he sees the reflection of an assassin in her eye and uses her to receive the blow intended for him. During the ensuing fight the would-be assassin falls into a bath and, while attempting to reach for Bond's gun which is hanging over the tub, is electrocuted by an electric fire (equipped with a conveniently long flex) that 007 hurls across the room. After the obligatory wry crack from Bond we at last get the credit titles – some fancy design of a gunman firing through an eye-socket against the background of a golden body.

The chief difference between these two sequences is that in *The Damned* every shot is related to themes and incidents that occur later in the picture, while the introductory episode in *Goldfinger* is wholly gratuitous – it exists as a film in its own right, and its only function is to excite and amuse, to establish a mood. Both pictures work in terms of what its audience knows and understands, but the aim of *The Damned* is to explore violence, that of *Goldfinger* to exploit it. (But I don't wish to condemn violent entertainment *ipso facto*, and *Goldfinger* is nothing if not entertaining.)

Take the characters in the two films. In *The Damned*, the American visitor is immediately recognisable as the two-fisted adventurer (the part is played, incidentally, by an actor associated with private eye and western roles), a suggestion of the perennial movie hero who usually carries a gun or a sword and seems not merely prepared for violent encounters but positively to will them, though in this case deliberately thrown into a situation he cannot comprehend. There is the teddy boy gang – traditional figures of group menace, creations of social and psychological unrest, but here set against the atomic scientist and *his* uniformed team, men associated with a new destructive force too hideous to contemplate. In *Goldfinger*, Bond is played as a fantasy figure, totally in control of his world, surrounded by stock figures – the loyal American, the sinister Oriental, the treacherous Latin American, the brilliant but deadly German – and when atomic science comes in, it does so as part of an action plot, a contemporary gimmick.

Then compare the treatment. In *The Damned*, a sudden outburst of violence in a peaceful setting; the attack shown in brutal close-up, sado-masochistically presented from the point of view of both attackers and victim, disturbing and difficult to enjoy; and in the pick-up which precedes the assault there is the suggestion of an underlying erotic implication. From the very first frame of *Goldfinger*, on the other hand, we are disarmed – it is all a huge joke. The violence is rapid and perfunctory (rarely lingered over as in the Fleming books), the association with sex is not implied but hammered home in knowing collusion with a pseudo-sophisticated audience, which is never genuinely involved in it. *The Damned* may be deliberately manipulating conventional material in its schematic way and operating at a symbolic level, but it is set in a real world where people get hurt, contaminated; *Goldfinger* is set in a fantasy world, with elaborately dazzling sets, and even the actual locations are made to seem unreal. The tradition in which it works is that of the violence of slapstick farce and of those sadistic cartoons where animals get squashed flat or have their fur blasted off, only to reappear instantly, ready for further humorous punishment.

Finally, note the verbal exchange quoted above between the American and the scientist in *The Damned*; it's a trifle portentous, certainly, yet indicative of a serious awareness of the problem of violence on the part of the filmmaker and assumed by him in his audience. *Goldfinger*, of course, is equally self-conscious and assumes in its audience a shallow knowledge of psychology, but this self-consciousness takes the form of deliberately sending itself up, of protecting itself against any serious charge by ensuring that no one likely to make such an accusation could take the film seriously.

These films represent the two poles of contemporary screen violence. Superficially they have a great deal in common. They also share another quality that is not so superficial: no other medium could have presented what is contained in these initial scenes so rapidly or with such impact – before, in fact, we had any knowledge of the characters or the story other than that which we bring from other films.

I have dealt at such length with these two pictures because they highlight many of the ways in which violence is handled in the contemporary cinema, and because they help explain why there is and has been so much violence in the movies. The first reason is squarely faced by *Goldfinger* – there is a vast international public for such exercises in brutality, and the cinema is dependent upon the support of a mass audience. Indeed, the cinema (with the recent low-powered assistance of television) now bears the main burden of satisfying this legitimate and enduring need. Secondly, as *The Damned* illustrates, serious artists are attracted by violent themes, perhaps today more than ever before, because of the urgent social issues involved, the extreme experiences it entails, and (it must be acknowledged) the 'terrible beauty' violence has in itself.

There is a sense in which the cinema by its very nature is drawn towards violence. In writing on 'Film Aesthetic' many years ago,

Sir Herbert Read spoke of the camera as 'a chisel of light, cutting into the reality of objects', and it can be maintained that the flickering passage of 24 frames per second through the projector, the vertiginous movement of the camera, the continuous shifting of viewpoint, the rapid change of image in both size and character, the very idea of montage, make films – irrespective of their subjects – a violent experience for the audience. Undoubtedly the technique of film is employed in this way. An obvious and conscious example is Alain Resnais's *Muriel*, where banal, undramatic material is deliberately presented in a violent and shocking manner primarily through its style of editing. In a far more obvious sense, however, the cinema – as the best description of it, 'motion pictures', suggests – tends towards violence. It is concerned with movement, with the telling of stories, the conveying of sensations, the sharing of experiences, the expression of ideas, primarily in terms of the changing relationships of people and objects. True, sound effects, words and music have since come to play an important part in a medium that was developed without them, but their role is essentially ancillary; when the word dominates, as it too often does, the result is usually disastrous as either art or entertainment. The movies are predominantly about things happening, and the extreme form of things happening is violence. As everyone knows, the final word before shooting a scene is symbolically the director's call for 'Action'. Not surprisingly, to the moviemaker and the moviegoer the words 'action' and 'violence' as relating to the content of a film are virtually synonymous.

This natural violent bent of the movies as art and entertainment has been compounded by the scenes of violence in the actual world that it has been the lot of the newsreel to record. And when one comes down to it, the task of distinguishing between the nature of newsreel material and that of the feature film is no easy one. We usually rely upon the context to do it for us, yet such is the basic similarity that the images of the two blend easily in our minds and are frequently mixed in films. Occasionally there is an outcry when illegitimate use is thought to be made of documentary footage. For one thing it can be used to propagate falsehood – the Italian 'documentary' *Mondo Cane* (where the individual scenes of violence and degradation were undeniably 'real' and 'true' in themselves) is an obvious and rather complicated example. And a few years back there were strong objections to actual combat shots of dying marines being inserted into an 'entertainment' film, *Sands of Iwo Jima*, despite (or perhaps because of) the fact that few people could have told which were the real deaths and which the simulated ones.

The Oxford Dictionary defines the primary meaning of violence as 'the exercise of physical force so as to inflict injury on or damage to persons or property', and this, the generally understood meaning in everyday life, is the sense in which I have been using it here. It shows how close the cinema is to violence in real life, that one can discuss the widest possible range of films in these terms. In most other media, however, it is necessary to extend this meaning. In the series of discussions on Violence in Society and the Arts staged in 1964 at the Institute of Contemporary Arts in London, categories were devised to give as much (or more) prominence to violence in analytical cubism and the work of Fontana, Appel and Mondrian as to a painting like *Guernica*, which is after all about violence, if not an act of violence in itself. (It is significant that the short movie *The Reality of Karel Appel*, which shows the artist at work, is truly violent in a way that one of his completed canvases isn't. As Mary McCarthy said of Harold Rosenberg's theory of action painting: 'You cannot hang an event on the wall, only a picture.')

In Martin Esslin's ICA lecture on violence in the theatre (reprinted in *Encore,* May–June 1964) only one of the five categories he created – his first, 'violence that occurs between characters in the play' – fits the dictionary definition and actually relates to the dramatic action itself. And even here Mr Esslin was concerned primarily with psychological violence. Physical violence within the play he considers to be 'relatively unimportant', and it's almost with a sigh of relief that he records that 'this most primitive aspect of the theatre has devolved almost entirely on to the other media'. But the uses to which violence is put in the cinema are far wider than they ever were in the theatre, and of course Mr Esslin's other categories (violence of the author towards his characters, a rallying call for violence from the stage, violence directed against the audience, violence developed by the audience towards the characters on the stage) are also found in the cinema. They all apply to *Battleship Potemkin*, for instance.

One must admit, however, that most violence in the movies, notwithstanding the calculation and the frequent skill in presentation, must be deemed primitive in its ultimate provenance. For every sequence like the one in which the architect in Antonioni's *L'Avventura* expresses all his self-disgust and professional disappointment through the simple act of spilling a bottle of ink over a young student's drawing board, there are a thousand meaningless gunfights, knifings and bar-room brawls. The distinction here is primarily a moral one. Gunfights, knifings and bar-room brawls are among the things we go to the cinema for. As both art and entertainment they can be justified in themselves and of themselves, whereas the scene I've mentioned from *L'Avventura* has its moral and artistic significance only in terms of the film as a whole. I stress this because it leads on to the justification of violence in the movies. And part of the case must be concerned with what we seek in them. Certainly no one goes to the theatre for physical violence any longer, and the Grand Guignol has at last sadly had to shut its doors in the face of the overwhelming competition from two generations of horror picture producers. Unless handled in a stylised way or with a considerable build-up (and even then its use must be sparing), violence no longer works in the contemporary theatre and can never be the *raison d'être* or principal ingredient of a dramatic work.

Violence in the cinema can be justified in terms of its necessity to the overall moral and artistic conception of a work, or merely in terms of the artistry with which it is executed. Many of the principal genres in the movies – the thriller, the western, the war film, science fiction, the gangster picture – endure by virtue of the violence they contain but have their own rules about its use. If one accepts the validity of making these types of film, then one is necessarily condoning that violence. Merely to make the films well is then sufficient justification. But to work against the prescribed rules, to challenge the basic conventions, often results in an intensification of the violence. The most determinedly anti-war pictures, other than those that get bogged down in verbiage like *The Victors*, are more violent than the general rule – as was, for instance, Robert Aldrich's *Attack*, with its close-up of the hero having his leg severed by a German tank track.

Westerns that take a more realistic view of character and of the pioneering experience often tend to dwell on wounding (Anthony Mann's films), sadistic humiliation (Brando's *One-Eyed Jacks*) and unheroic viciousness (Henry King's *The Bravados*). This kind of break with convention has perhaps been too rashly applauded. On behalf of the traditional western, the late Robert Warshow, in perhaps the best article yet written on the subject, argued that 'it offers a serious orientation to the problem of violence such as can be found almost nowhere else in our culture'. Warshow in the same context touched upon a similar problem in the gangster picture and voiced a feeling that I have long had myself, when he observed:

> Some of the compromises introduced to avoid the supposed bad effects of the old gangster movies may be, if anything, more dangerous, for sadistic violence that once belonged only to the gangster is now commonly enlisted on the side of the law and thus goes undefeated, allowing us (if we wish) to find in the movies a sort of 'confirmation' of our fantasies.

It is for this reason that the cycle of gangster pictures in the late 1950s, which dealt with the careers of Prohibition and post-Prohibition mobsters, were a good deal healthier than the cycle of vicious private eye and police movies that preceded them, despite the obvious commitment to characters outside the law. It produced two outstanding films, Budd Boetticher's *Rise and Fall of Legs Diamond* and Don Siegel's *Baby Face Nelson*, which, partly through their close attention to period detail, had about them, for all their violence, a kind of balletic purity.

It is easy enough to talk about justifying films on moral and aesthetic grounds and approving of perhaps only a small number of pictures. By these standards one would reject, for instance, the bridge being blown up at the end of *The Bridge on the River Kwai*. Destruction is popular, as Cecil B. DeMille profitably discovered, and it makes for a splendid conclusion in a visual medium to have mighty edifices totter and fall. It was into this twofold cinematic trap that the producers of *Kwai* fell, changing the end of Pierre Boulle's novel and thus ruining the ironic moral comment that the picture was seeking to make.

Already into this consideration of justification has slipped the second and frequently conflicting category – the type with which the censor is concerned. Broadly speaking, censors will pass that which is harmless (or not positively harmful) to society, and that which is very obviously in the public interest. What they *consider* to be so, that is. (Newsreels have never been subject to the British

Board of Film Censors' approval; but we must remember that most pictures are produced with the known requirements of their national censors in mind and often in consultation with them, and the British censors have regularly made their opinions known to the American industry.)

The result of censorship in practice is frequently to pass violence that is artistically indefensible because it is socially harmless (which is fair enough) and to ban or demand cuts where the violence is totally justifiable on artistic grounds. Thus ineptly handled or meaningless 'entertaining' violence (i.e. the kind that the censor feels cannot be taken seriously) is permissible while say, the realistic rape and murder sequences in Visconti's *Rocco and His Brothers* and Bergman's *The Virgin Spring* were severely cut, despite their essential role in the films' overall conception. Meaningful or realistic violence is usually disturbing in its intensity and therefore considered dangerous. But the result of cutting (or of prior consideration of what the censor will allow) can make what appears on the screen have the titillating effect the director intended to avoid, thus making enjoyable and bearable what was intended to be painful and shocking. In a similar way the sexy scene can usually get by, is almost encouraged to do so, while sexual frankness is generally suspect.

Few films with violent scenes are banned outright in this country, though many are elsewhere, in Sweden for example. But some have been banned because of the danger that they might be misunderstood. The best known is perhaps *The Wild One*, refused a certificate here on the grounds that though incontrovertibly a serious study of the causes of violence, it did not punish clearly enough the depredations of the motorcycle gang and might therefore lead to their conduct being emulated. The film paid the price of its own understatement, of the refusal to admit an easy solution to the problems it posed. Another less well-known example is Samuel Fuller's recent picture *Shock Corridor*, a complex allegory about violence in America. This is a fascinating if not entirely successful film about a reporter who poses as a lunatic in order to investigate an unsolved murder in an asylum. The witnesses to the crime are three inmates – a demented nuclear scientist, an ex-POW defector to the Chinese, and a Negro deranged by his experiences as the only coloured student of a Southern university. An extraordinarily violent film, it deliberately sets out to disturb and, to judge from the censor's decision, only too obviously succeeded. One would guess that the real objection was that *Shock Corridor* did not make positive points about mental health.

Sometimes, admittedly, the overall seriousness and social desirability of a work will result in the censor passing a brutal scene that might be objected to on artistic grounds. I am not suggesting for a minute that it should have been cut, but the beating that Marlon Brando takes in the final reel of *On the Waterfront* strikes me as largely gratuitous and detrimental to the film's ultimate effect. It represents another example of an intelligent director falling into the trap of the slam-bang, upbeat conclusion. (When Budd Schulberg later wrote the film as a novel, his ending was quite different, though less powerfully dramatic.) Its success in terms of impact on the audience confirmed and encouraged a cinematic tendency to administer emblematic physical punishment to the hero, that we have seen employed with varying degrees of justification in many films, including such British pictures as *Room at the Top* and *Saturday Night and Sunday Morning*.

For those in search of further descriptive and synoptic material I cannot do better than commend the special issue in February 1963 of the British film magazine *Motion*, a 'Companion to Violence and Sadism in the Cinema'. Like the recent programme at the Institute of Contemporary Arts, it raises the question of the intellectual's preoccupation with violence that is worth an essay in itself. Under 'D' alone the Companion lists 'Dark Side of the Light Fantastic, The'; 'Dassin'; 'Deaf Aid, Torture by'; 'Dentures, Death by'; 'Disease'; and 'Doctor No'; and under 'F' the editors choose their 'Favourite Movie Scars'. Even a cursory perusal of this document should save many a busy person the experience of sitting through a large number of tedious if not actually corrupting pictures. As the old saying goes: 'The movies have ruined a lot more evenings than they have morals.'

I was struck the other day by the way the author of an advertisement for a recent horror picture touched in striking fashion on a fundamental aspect of screen violence. The film is called *Strait-Jacket*; it's described as 'Entertainment Plus', and the poster depicts a screaming Joan Crawford, together with another photograph of her swinging an axe, above which is the slogan: 'Keep saying to yourself, it's only a film – It's Only A Film – IT'S ONLY A FILM!'

The escalation of the Vietnam War and the riots and demonstrations across Europe and America during the second half of the 1960s led to a tsunami of interest in violence, and my Twentieth Century *essay was reprinted in two American anthologies aimed at student readers:* Sight, Sound and Society *edited by David Manning White and Richard Averson (1968) and* Violence in the Mass Media *edited by Otto Larsen (1969). The British censors eventually lifted their ban on* The Wild One *in 1968 and on* Shock Corridor *in 1970, and the 1970s began with a further brouhaha over cinematic violence, principally centring on Ken Russell's* The Devils, *Don Siegel's* Dirty Harry, *Sam Peckinpah's* Straw Dogs *and Stanley Kubrick's* Clockwork Orange. *Not long after the appearance of my essay I learnt from John Lehmann, the founding editor of the by then defunct* Penguin New Writing, *that the article on 'Parade of Violence' was by Julian MacLaren-Ross, who had died in 1964. It was signed 'Film Critic' because the prolific author already had a piece in that issue. It has since been reprinted in MacLaren-Ross's* Bitten by the Tarantula and Other Writing *(Black Spring Press, 2005). That collection also contains his pioneering essays from the mid-1940s on film noir and Alfred Hitchcock.*

The Alphaville of Admass
Or, How We Learned to Stop Worrying and Love the Boom (1966)

Coming to New York from the muted mistiness of London as I regularly do, is like travelling from a monotone antique shop to a Technicolor bazaar.

(Kenneth Tynan, *Holiday*, December 1960)

Ancient elegance and new opulence are all tangled up in a dazzling blur of op and pop ... In a once sedate world of faded splendor, everything new, uninhibited and kinky is blooming at the top of London life.

(*Time* magazine, April 1966)

The first of these comments coincided with the London première of *Saturday Night and Sunday Morning*, the second appeared just after the New York screening of *Morgan*. Between the two films, as between these two assessments of London, there is a world of difference and a whirl of indifference. Something has changed in a country and its cinema. As an admirer of *High Noon* said when he saw *Born Free*, a funny thing happened on the way to the Foreman.

The word 'renaissance' is freely bandied about at home and abroad. The British cinema is 'undergoing a renaissance', Alberto Moravia told *Time* magazine, and Miss Pauline Kael, no irresponsible anglophile, wrote a couple of months ago that 'even in England there has been something that passes for a renaissance'. Yet one resists the term as far as one can. Partly because it catches in the throat in the same way that the label 'New Elizabethans' gummed up the lips in the 1950s; partly because a term that has sufficed for one three-century period in the visual arts has been invoked every

'The Alphaville of Admass' first appeared in *Sight & Sound*, Summer 1966.

couple of years about some national film industry since the war.

British film critics are indeed forever proclaiming a renaissance, and this time they must be heartened at finding that for once they're not standing alone. Yet each impending new birth has usually turned out to be a hysterical pregnancy. Whenever the cautious are tempted into optimism, they usually live to regret it. During 1962 for instance, Penelope Gilliatt had seen no sign of a rebirth and picked only one British film (*The Loneliness of the Long Distance Runner*) among the year's ten best. Yet she felt *something* stirring and wrote (and I would forbear from quoting her, were it not for the fact that her end-of-the-year comments are preserved between hard covers):

> I'm looking forward to the thrillers we are going to produce next year; directors like Cliff Owen (who made the pungent *A Prize of Arms*) are pulling them up by the bootstraps. I'm longing to see Lindsay Anderson's *This Sporting Life* and Joan Littlewood's *Sparrers Can't Sing*, and I can't wait for the movie of *One Way Pendulum* … The ice-floe of the British cinema really is breaking up.

In a sense the icefloe of the British cinema did begin to break up in 1963, though not in the way Mrs Gilliatt anticipated. The thaw began and, to move the political metaphor a little further East, the time was ripe for a thousand flowers to bloom. That they would be lilies of the field no one could have anticipated at the time, any more than one could have seen that these lilies would spin money. If the British films of the previous four years appeared to have been guided by the editors of the *New Left Review*, Richard Hoggart and the Opies, then those of the three years that followed looked increasingly as if they had been made under the personal supervision of the Regius Professor of Applied Camp at the Royal College of Art.

1963 then can be seen as a turning point on the crooked road from the wheelwright's shop to the boutique. It was the year in which the drift North of the moviemakers was arrested, and in which they began to do a social as well as geographical about-face. The future historian might see the move enacted in symbolical terms in *Billy Liar*. In retrospect the highpoint of the picture is that *nouvelle vague*-ish promenade through the Northern high street by Julie Christie as Liz, harbinger of short skirts, discothèques, op art, the pill and what you will. (One almost expected to see Arthur Seaton, bearded and carrying a scythe, disappear over the nearest slagheap.) And when Liz caught the midnight train to London at the end, the camera may have remained to follow Billy on his lonely, elegiac return to the family semi-detached, but spiritually the filmmakers had a one-way ticket to ride south with Miss Christie.

Actually the provincial realism of the 1959–63 period had its zenith fairly early on with Karel Reisz's *Saturday Night and Sunday Morning*, still far and away the best feature film in a realistic vein made in this country. It had also reached its nadir in *A Taste of Honey* or, as some would have it, *The Loneliness of the Long Distance Runner*. If you think that what was fundamentally wrong about the films of this period was their phoney lyricism, then it was the former; if however you consider it to be the callowness of their social and political thinking, it was obviously the latter. Or maybe it was just a matter of heavy-handedness.

Whatever way you care to look at it, Tony Richardson takes the prize; and he was the first off the mark in 1963 with *Tom Jones*, the film that played a crucial part in shaping the 'new' (or 'nouvelle' new) cinema. A number of people (including myself) greatly over-rated this picture when it appeared, through a combination of chauvinism, surprise, a desire for something fresh and a regard for John Osborne's screenplay. Although the picture opened some months after *Dr No*, its initial impact was much greater and actually has more in common with the later Bond pictures than the curiously diffident beginning of that cycle. *Tom Jones* certainly seemed a liberating picture at the time but instead has proved to be a prison, albeit one without bars. Its lack of form, its air of slovenly improvisation, its tasteless eclecticism, its inchoate and inappropriate social comment – these have been the hallmark of the modish British cinema ever since.

The other film of 1963 that showed the way things were going was *This Sporting Life*. This ambitious but far from successful attempt to dig in up North, to use the experience gained from the previous five or six years, was the beached whale left when the first English 'new wave' retreated, just as the delayed British Lion films (kept waiting until 1964–65 to get on the circuits) were the stranded minnows. Lindsay Anderson had written in 1957 about the porters in his Covent Garden documentary *Every Day Except Christmas*:

These good and friendly faces deserve a place of pride on the screens of their country; and I will fight for the notion of community which will give it to them.

By 1963 however his views had changed somewhat:

Throughout *This Sporting Life* we were aware that we were not making a film about anything representative; we were making a film about something unique. We were not making a film about a 'worker' but about an extraordinary (and therefore more deeply significant) man, and about an extraordinary relationship. We were not, in a word, making sociology.

Indeed he was not. If the earlier pictures suggested Mass Observation, *This Sporting Life* was delving into abnormal psychology. It was almost Krafft-Ebing in a rugby shirt, or Wakefield Trinity with Richard Harris playing all three parts.

The not wholly unexpected commercial failure of *This Sporting Life* and the surprise success of *Tom Jones* were to determine the future development of British pictures decisively. As *Time* magazine wrote in the summer of 1963 (before *Tom Jones* had been shown in the States, and in an article that bracketed Richardson with other 'inspired pioneers' of world cinema including Buñuel, Antonioni, Ray, Resnais and Fellini):

Moviegoers are getting a bit bugged by the same scummy old roofscape and the eternal kitchen-sinkdrome. They sometimes find it a bit hard to believe that things are really all that bad in Merry England. Yet at their best the British protest pictures have served up great juicy hunks of local colour.

It is still possible for Americans to respond to the exotic British hinterland, and one notes that this very month an American publisher is advertising a new book as 'a brilliant, bawdy novel, the wildest yet to come out of the steaming back streets of working-class England in a decade of literary revolt'. Generally speaking, however, they have found the product of the last couple of years more palatable, being more attracted by people *from* a working-class background than *in* one (this goes for the British too); and the chance one once saw of Americans developing a permanent taste for a new genre, 'The Northern', now seems remote. There had been a pretty obvious clash between the conventional picture of the British (via received ideas and the British Travel Association advertisements – the so-called 'thatch-roofed Spitfire' image) and that which the proletarian movies conveyed. But it did help to prepare them, directly and dialectically, for those that followed, as did life itself and particularly those three key events of 1963, the Profumo Affair, the Great Train Robbery, and the Beatles. Now in April 1966, *Time* magazine writes:

> There is not one London scene, but dozens. Each one is a dazzling gem, a medley of checkered sunglasses, and delightfully quaint pay boxes, a blend of 'flash' American, polished Continental and robust old English influences that mixes and merges in London today.

And if you think that this sounds less like the London we love, loathe and live in than one of a number of British films, you would of course be right. For *Time* magazine goes straight on to say:

> The result is a slapdash comedy not unlike those directed for the screen by Britain's own Tony (*Tom Jones*) Richardson or Czech émigré Karel (*Morgan*) Reisz, and filmed by director Richard (*Help!*) Lester, a fugitive from Philadelphia.

As Dr Johnson might have said, a man who is tired of London is tired of *Life*. But what London is this? Not the London of Karel (*We Are the Lambeth Boys*) Reisz or Tony (*Momma Don't Allow*) Richardson; nor should one have to invoke the London of Edward (*Saved*) Bond to redress the imbalance created by James (*Goldfinger*) Bond.

In *Time* magazine's conjunction of London and the British cinema we have something that goes beyond the normal ideas of life imitating art. Here we have a curious interplay (not to say confusion) between art and a sort of life with which we have recently become acquainted, though to which we have not yet necessarily become accustomed. Robert Rauschenberg's dictum 'I act in the gap between art and life' is perhaps the most frequently quoted of any contemporary artist. But now we must ask: what art? what life? It is increasingly difficult to establish just what is that area of reality upon which a film seeks to impose form and back to which, in terms of our own experience, we can refer it. It is the kind of problem that faces us when we turn the pages of a colour supplement and only with difficulty distinguish between the editorial content and the advertisements. Artists work for ad agencies, produce art that draws on the techniques and iconography of advertising and then, like Peter Blake (for Wills cigars), are drawn back into advertisements that are indistinguishable from Lord Snowdon's colour magazine photographs.

Still, that London is 'a swinging city' (*the* swinging city) and that British films are an expression of it is, however factitious it may seem to more temperate natives, no mere aberration of *Time* magazine. It is as widely acclaimed abroad as it is accepted at home. Accepted of course does not necessarily mean the same as believed, and it certainly doesn't mean experienced. Yet it is not my purpose here to consider the origin or significance of this weird phenomenon other than as it affects the British cinema. The movies are, for reasons not entirely economic, peculiarly at the mercy of the zeitgeist. Naturally a good artist will resist it or put it to his own use if he can, and if he is aware of it. But currently a large part of our cinema and the 'swinging scene' are almost inseparable.

There are a good many people who have a vested interest in the continuing success of the present vogue, in the notion of London as the Alphaville of Admass. In the sense that everything from Mary Quant dresses through to James Bond's Aston Martins to *Darling* affects the balance of payments situation, we're all affected. National prestige and economics are very much bound up in this, and not for the first time. (Oddly enough, though, the direct expression of chauvinism, which declined with the falling off of British war films, is now found only in spy movies: e.g. the elevation of Bond over the CIA, the shooting of the interfering American agents in *The Ipcress File*; and it is little more than harmless compensation fantasy.) A chilling instance of a previous occasion when national prestige was at stake can be found in a *Sequence* editorial of 1948:

> Mr. Harold Wilson was recently recorded by Gaumont-British News in the act of presenting Miss Margaret Lockwood with a heavy, silver-plated ornament, thus bestowing official sanction to the British people's judgment that Miss Lockwood is their finest actress. Indeed, as Mr. Wilson smilingly remarked, this comes to the same thing as saying 'the finest actress in the world'. 'For [*as*

near as makes no matter we quote his own words] there is no doubt
that the British film industry today is first and foremost among
the film industries of the world.'

We are all acquainted with what happened to British cinema in
the years that followed. The basis of the industry is scarcely sounder
today than it was then. So it is with some alarm that one reads in an
Evening Standard editorial (19 April 1966):

By winning an Oscar as the best actress of 1965, Julie Christie has
added yet another jewel to the crown which the British film
industry has been so assiduously making for itself over the past
few years.
   For if any country is setting the pace in the highly competitive world of filmmaking, that country is Britain ...
   As Julie Christie and her colleagues collected their awards ...
the applause which roared for them was a tribute to the whole of
the British film industry.

Let us look at some of the gems in the bejewelled crown that this
pace-setting industry is said to be wearing. It is difficult to deny that
the new pictures are in the main far better made than most British
films of the past. There is a feeling for the medium, a drive, a sense
of style, a freewheeling vigour for which there are few previous
parallels. These qualities are not to be despised. Yet at the same time
these gains can be seen as unassimilated, or only partially understood, influences from the younger French directors and the *cinéma
vérité* movement, as well as from TV commercials, on which most
British directors spend the greater part of their time. The feeling for
the medium is often only a concern for stylishness and fashion, the
vigour a desperate energy that seeks to conceal a lack of content
behind a battery of tricks.

Whereas the British cinema from 1958 to 1963 evinced a
conformity of subject matter, now it is one of treatment. This
undoubtedly reflects the predominant movement in our society
itself, which has been from statement to style, from what people
stand for to how they stand and what they stand in. It is probable
that the interest of the filmmaker now would be centred not upon
what Jimmy Porter said but upon the shirts that his wife was ironing.
This ascendancy of the visual over the verbal has social, psycholog-

ical and even economic roots and consequences.

The shortcomings of the current cinema can be seen in three of its most lauded products of the past year – *Darling, Alfie* and *Morgan*. Together they sound like a rather staid firm of solicitors, and in a way of course, though far from staid, they are brazenly soliciting our interest in their eponymous central characters who, as presented on the screen, are among the most tedious ever inflicted upon an audience. There is a considerable discrepancy between the talents that have produced these pictures: Karel Reisz is a far better director than John Schlesinger, who in turn is infinitely superior to Lewis Gilbert. Nevertheless all three films illustrate the way a uniform style has been imposed upon disparate material. They resemble middle-aged men trying to squeeze into Mod clothes. This is more cause for sorrow than anger, though a recent stage musical, *On the Level*, provoked the drama critic of the *Times* to thunder that 'the sight of middle-aged showmen clambering on the bandwagon of youth is one of the most contemptible the theatre has to offer'.

Whatever individuality these films might have had has been consciously or unconsciously ironed out. Each has been furnished with cool music, which in the case of the John Dankworth scores for *Darling* and *Morgan* is not inappropriate; *Alfie*, however, needs Sonny Rollins on the soundtrack about as much as a Whitehall farce cries out for incidental music by Stockhausen. This is one aspect of the similar packaging and is actually the reverse of the once normal commercial procedure whereby identical goods are made to appear different through individual presentation.

In its original form *Alfie* was a 1962 radio play called *Alfie Elkins and His Little Life*. It took place over a period of years from the early days of World War Two until about the late 1950s and concerned the meetings between a North Country narrator (an obvious stand-in for author Bill Naughton) and Alfie (born *c*.1916). It was a study of working class Don Juanism seen against the background of a changing society, and the device of Alfie bringing the author up to date on his life was a workable convention, a bit old-fashioned perhaps but in keeping with the traditional morality that all Bill Naughton's work seeks to establish. The film on the other hand takes place in no discernible span of time and has no form to replace the original narrative style or sustain a moral theme, which now seems laboured, tacked on. Alfie's method of addressing the audience is inconsistently maintained – sometimes he is talking directly, sometimes he is giving a running (and predictive) commentary, and sometimes he is not there at all. But when he is absent we are given a caricatured view of married life consistent with his view and consequently in contradiction to Naughton's. The result is that his final rejection has no meaning at all: Alfie has not aged (unless the point is that you are past it in your early twenties), and there is no adequate view opposed to his, other than a sentimentally contrived glimpse he has of the christening of an ex-mistress's child. Yet in the *mélange* of advertising colour, the slow motion pursuit of his little son in the park, the hip music, the putting on of airs and the slipping off of clothes, the ingratiating, button-holing narration, who is to notice?

Darling likewise has an unconvincing form (the heroine supposedly confiding her memoirs to a women's magazine) and much grander pretensions to social comment. Once again no time seems to pass for any of the characters, though what the film seeks to capture and invites you to come behind the façade of, is a society in crucial transition. As the film opens, the advertisements for Diana Scott's memoirs go up over an Oxfam poster, and there is some legitimate if coarsely handled fun at the expense of a fund-raising party. The effect of this is no more than a fashionable gesture. Where *Darling* aims at verisimilitude, its success is intermittent (which is admittedly more than one can say of the London sequences of *Life at the Top*), and its often astutely chosen locations serve to emphasise rather than conceal the general air of fantasy of its riches-to-riches, poor little princess story. Now this is odd, though unfortunately typical of the current cinema, for one would have predicted that the shift in attention from the provincial working class to the metropolitan middle class would have seen the filmmakers once more operating within the terms of their own experience. Apparently not so.

Unlike *Darling* and *Alfie*, which finish up that way, *Morgan* actually sets out to be a fantasy. Or at least the film does. The play, however, didn't. In David Mercer's 1962 TV comedy *A Suitable Case for Treatment* (now the film's subtitle), Morgan Delt was 35. But like the fortyish Alfie, so aged a Morgan would have been almost an *Umberto D* figure by the mid-1960s. As played by David Warner in the film he is, one would guess, in his early twenties.

In the play Morgan is a working-class novelist divorced by his upper-middle-class wife for habitual adultery so she can marry a literary agent, and he finishes up in the arms of a sensible telephonist. In the movie he is a painter, divorced for mental cruelty; the wife's boyfriend has become an art dealer, and Morgan is ultimately committed to a lunatic asylum. Underneath the frenetic bravura style is a strange marriage of two types of theatre. Some indication of what it is can be seen in the fact that David Warner plays Morgan much as he interpreted Valentine Brose in Henry Living's farce *Eh?* at the Aldwych, while Nan Munro plays the mother-in-law exactly as she performed her equivalent in the Royal Court revival of an earlier Aldwych farce, *A Cuckoo in the Nest*. (These two productions opened the same week in autumn 1964.) One's objection to Morgan is not the mixing of different conventions; this has after all become an accepted method nowadays (*Shoot the Pianist* is one of several highly successful examples). It is rather that in the confusion, control of the movie has been lost. If everything in the film is fantastic, why should anyone object to Morgan's conduct in particular; when the whole film is a fantasy then what is the reality to which his fantasies relate? In a sense *Morgan* is a paradigm of the present British movie scene.

Equally, Morgan's youthfulness makes nonsense of the sociopolitical situation of which he is supposed to be a victim. In the play he was around ten at the time of the Spanish Civil War, while in the film he would scarcely be older than that when the Hungarian uprising took place. It is hardly surprising that the towering political figures (Marx, Trotsky et al) which the film invokes are reduced metaphorically and actually to figures in a Pop painting.* Somewhere between people in their sixties (Morgan's mother, the die-hard Stalinist) and those in their early twenties (Morgan himself) there is a missing generation. It is this generation that is behind the cameras.

From a variety of critical stances then, *Darling*, *Alfie* and *Morgan* have been reduced to the same final point – a celebration of the

---

* Morgan's car is actually got up to look like one of Peter Blake's Pop doors. The film itself is being advertised with a Pop art poster by Barry Fantoni, host of the TV teen show *A Whole Scene Going*. Ironically enough, when the stage version of *Saturday Night and Sunday Morning* eventually arrived in London, the poster for it was designed by Derek Boshier in the style of Roy Lichtenstein.]

personal presence and ambience of Julie Christie, Michael Caine
and David Warner. A celebration, not an examination or analysis.
They have become objects, and as such the treatment of them is
analogous to the way in which the Bond films consciously dwell on
objects of ingenuity and concupiscence. In effect the pictures are
advertisements, and what they are advertising is themselves and their
central characters. Like *Nothing But the Best* and *What's New
Pussycat?* they have become one with the non-world or half-world
upon which they comment. Their implicit criticism has been viti-
ated by a process of stylistic and cultural homogenisation. Existing
outside time, divorced from the past, denied the conditions through
which experience can be obtained, their characters wander through
a world in which it is an eternal 12 noon on a Saturday morning in
the King's Road, Chelsea.

Time magazine was right in a way about the films and about
London, when it wrote of the curious mixture of the old and the
new. For oddly enough many of the characters in the new cinema
could happily co-exist with those of the pre-*Look Back in Anger*
1950s. There is for instance a striking resemblance between the
policeman (or rather bobby) playing hopscotch in *Morgan* and the
bishop dancing to the magic piano in Julian Slade's musical *Salad
Days*. In the wake of the theatre of non-communication we see the
return, under a new guise, of a Peter Pantheon of people congeni-
tally incapable of forming adult relationships or articulating their
situation. ('I simply involve my people in the consequences of their
stupidity and then give them brains so they can suffer,' wrote
Stendhal; you are not halfway towards *Le Rouge et le noir* by fulfilling
only the first of these conditions.) Morgan Delt is almost a stock case
of regression into infantilism, and he is buttressed by a traditional
English feyness masquerading as disaffiliation. The recrudescent
fascination with animal imagery probably stems from the 'bears and
squirrels' relationship of the hopelessly mismatched Jimmy and
Alison Porter, whose final curtain dialogue has opened the gates of
a veritable Whipsnade of whimsy. People call each other Pussycat;
Joe Lampton envies the freedom of homing pigeons (and like them
returns to his *Life at the Top*). Diana Scott in *Darling* carts around the
goldfish with which she is identified; Alfie at the beginning and end
is seen and eventually comes to see himself as a lovable mongrel dog;
and as for *Morgan*, the whole picture is based on an endless associa-

tion of animals from zebras to gorillas.

In the early 1960s no British film was complete without a sequence set in a funfair. One might say that the funfair was the objective correlative of the moviemakers' attitude to the working class. It was ambivalent of course – a combination of disgust with what they took to be an impoverished mass culture (the overwhelming impression given by Lindsay Anderson's 1954 documentary *O Dreamland*) and an admiration for the uninhibited vulgarity and *joie de vivre* of the masses (*Saturday Night and Sunday Morning*). Its overall tone was democratic, brash, provincial, unselfconscious. What has replaced it as the significant locus of the new cinema is the private art gallery. Here the characteristics are quite the reverse – exclusive, cool, metropolitan, sophisticated. Just the place for Joe Lampton to be initiated into London life or Diana Scott to visit on her social round, or for Morgan, with speeded up camera, to chase his rival about in. If this is the objective correlative of the new attitude, it too is ambiguous – on the one hand a mild repugnance for the fashionable world of modern art, on the other a scarcely disguised infatuation with this very milieu. In terms of High Camp, the most amusing and aware expression of this ambivalence is to be found in *Modesty Blaise*: the op art headquarters of the villainous Gabriel and, especially, the mock torturing of Modesty with a piece of jagged iron sculpture.

Stylistically there is an interesting parallel between recent developments in the cinema and the visual arts. In a review of an exhibition of David Annesley's painted sheet-metal sculpture, Norbert Lynton remarked perceptively:

> When avant-garde taste requires the image to be human and the surface to be expressionistic you have little option but to dive into the sorrows and burdens of human existence: when circumstances invite you to work in entirely abstract forms, to colour your sculpture and to keep it very clear-cut, the result is likely to be gay and decorative.

Now *mutatis mutandis* this is the phase that our cinema has entered, and it is one closely related to a significant strain in the prevailing cultural climate of Britain. It is not a phase conducive to the creation of important works of art, or for that matter of entertainment that seeks to treat its subject in any kind of depth. It is for

this reason that the style I have been describing works for Richard
Lester in *A Hard Day's Night*, *The Knack* and *Help!*, but not for most
of his contemporaries. Lester's aim is to celebrate the present, to
capture it or that part of it which attracts him, which is principally
and unashamedly the adman's, visitor-to-London's 'it's all
happening' world of the youth revolution. He is temperamentally
suited to it and has no larger claim upon the material than the instant,
ephemeral and expendable use to which he puts it. For Lester the
style *is* the subject, the medium is the message.

Lester too has been fortunate in having for two of his films the
real Beatles, who have an incontestable right to the hairstyle that
bears their name and the nexus of attitudes they represent. One
might question the appropriateness of similar haircuts (or wigs) for
Evelyn Waugh's Denis Barlow in the Tony Richardson film of *The
Loved One*, for the painter Morgan Delt, or for the psychiatrist
played by Peter Sellers in *What's New Pussycat?*. This no doubt is all
part of the joke. Anything goes, but *anything*. If in the light-headed
mid-1960s London has become the Cockaigne of the Western
world, then the film industry's bejewelled crown, of which the
Evening Standard wrote, is in reality the cap and bells of a jester's
motley worn over a Beatles wig.

One imagines that this is a passing phase – it can scarcely be other,
although it could be argued that the coming of colour television
might well provide it with an added lease of life. What it will give
way to is anybody's guess. The need is still, as it always was, for
personal films made in a style congenial to their makers and consistent with their subject matter. Why so few British directors seem
capable of achieving this and utilising the freedom they presently
enjoy, but may not have for long, is a question that puzzles me and
to which I have found no satisfactory answer. 'Is it the chromo-
somes,' asks Morgan Delt plaintively, 'or is it England?' One begins
to wonder. That the most personal films on important themes made
during the last seven years have been the work of Joseph Losey,
whatever shortcomings some of them may have, is undeniable. That
directors as varied as Polanski and Lumet, Kubrick and Truffaut find
this country a satisfactory place to work in is not without significance. Maybe they don't feel the pressures experienced by our
native filmmakers. Perhaps, like Irish writers in the past, it was
necessary for the two greatest directors England has produced to

leave home in order to realise themselves. I refer of course to Hitchcock and Chaplin.

In 1958 when Jack Clayton made the honourable, pioneering
Room at the Top, it seemed as if a new range of techniques and subject
matter had been made available to the British cinema. This has
proved largely, though not entirely, an illusion. At least, as after the
opening of Pandora's Box, hope remains. If the rough-hewn *Room
at the Top* makes us think of Pandora's Box, the films of the past
couple of years bring to mind nothing so much as David Bailey's
Box of Pin-ups. As for the renaissance: well it is true that the
emperor *has* got new clothes, but should emperors shop exclusively
in Carnaby Street?

*Perhaps I should explain the title 'The Alphaville of Admass', which seemed
so obvious at the time. Alphaville is of course the desolate dystopian future
of Godard's realistic science fiction fantasy. 'Admass', a once popular but now
little used term, was coined by J.B. Priestley in the 1950s to describe the
rootless homogenised culture created by advertising, the media and mass
society. The idea for this article arose during discussion with Penelope
Houston, the editor of* Sight & Sound, *and her deputy, Tom Milne, and
it was intended to be a controversial work on the lines of François Truffaut's
aggressive polemical 'On a Certain Tendency in French Cinema' published
by* Cahiers du Cinéma *in 1954. We hoped that it would spark a debate
in forthcoming issues, and several of the filmmakers mentioned were invited
to reply. Clearly, however, I had gone too far. Not only did everyone except
Lester and Losey refuse, most of them were angry and abusive, and some time
passed before I was again on speaking terms with Karel Reisz, Lindsay
Anderson and John Schlesinger. It had, however, excited considerable interest
among moviegoers, and I was particularly pleased by some favourable
comments from Dwight MacDonald, one of the American intellectuals I most
admired, in the film column he was then writing for* Esquire. *Commenting
on* Morgan *and the Swinging London business, he wrote: 'The summer
1966 issue of* Sight & Sound *has a very trenchant, and, for that all-too-
bland journal, a refreshingly critical survey of this phenomenon by Philip
French.'*

*This piece was published at a crucial juncture of British cinema, and the
worries expressed about the future were soon realised and rapidly followed by
a devaluation of the pound in 1967, a major nail in the coffin of Swinging*

London. Shortly thereafter the Hollywood companies, then seemingly entrenched in Britain, packed up and moved out after it became evident that the British New Wave was exhausted. After that it was no longer possible for a director to have a sustained career in the British film industry or create a consistent oeuvre here. Most of the new British filmmakers launched in the 1970s by David Puttnam rapidly gravitated to the United States, and the 1980s saw the rise and fall of Goldcrest, the last major home for a successful, stable film industry in Britain.

Goodbye to all What?
On Giving Up Film Criticism (1966)

I was talking the other day to a former critic, who after nearly a decade of writing on films had changed jobs and scarcely been to the movies since. He was, he said, utterly worn out and found it an almost insuperable effort even to drag himself along to those occasional films that fall into the sorry category of 'conversational necessities'. Naturally I was a little depressed to hear this, but not in the least surprised. For I know several people, untroubled by either failing eyesight or advancing years, who served longish periods as movie reviewers and now go to the cinema about as often as they say their prayers.

What is more, there is no shyness about their abdication, no sense of guilt about not keeping up with the art that once consumed so much of their attention, no feeling that they might be missing something. On the contrary, the attitude is one of almost blessed relief from what in some cases seemed a well-nigh intolerable burden. And giving up film criticism is often the occasion for a farewell article that combines a confession of being washed out with a ritual washing of hands. As this phenomenon seems as common among critics of the cinema as it is rare (or almost non-existent) among those of other arts, it might be useful to examine some of these valedictory pieces to see the reasons offered.

The most recent is of course 'Tynan's Farewell', as it was advertised on the front page of the *Observer*'s Weekend Review for 29 May 1966, and I was particularly struck by the fact that it appeared on the anniversary of similar though much longer articles by two other well-known critics. In 1946 Wolcott Gibbs wrote 'The Country of the Blind' in the *Saturday Review of Literature* after ten months of film reviewing for an unnamed 'magazine of modest but

---

'Goodbye to All What?' first appeared in *Sight & Sound*, Autumn 1966.

genteel circulation'. In 1956 Harry Schein brought his eight years of criticism for the Swedish monthly journal *BLM* (*Bonniers Litterära Magasin*) to an end with a final article called with devastating simplicity 'Trött på film' ('Tired of Films').

Kenneth Tynan's 'valediction as a critic of the cinema' was actually fairly brief, and perhaps the most significant thing about it is precisely that he should have chosen those words to describe it. Maybe (some would say 'no doubt') he will return, but it had been clear that the cinema was providing him with rapidly diminishing stimulation. He made three points, however, as he hurried through the foyer. The first was that unlike a play 'which is still a living organism capable of change and alteration', a film was fixed long before a critic saw it and so 'cannot be modified by what he says'. From this he devised tests for a good play ('its ability to respond to different interpretations') and a good film ('cannot be other than what it is'), which start a number of hares that we needn't pursue here.

Tynan's second point concerned the critic's limited influence upon the audience for a current film – that he 'can sometimes unearth an audience for a minority movie but he cannot compete with the vast advertising techniques that ensure a mass audience for a majority movie'. This led him on to his third point, which was that even if a critic wished to influence the character of future big-budget films (he placed the lower limit at £250,000), what chance would he have? About as much chance, he suggested, as asking General Motors to build helicopters instead of cars.

After these snappy clinching points (in baseball parlance: three balls, no strikes), there followed a little italicised note at the foot of the column to the effect that I would be the *Observer*'s guest critic for a couple of weeks. 'My God,' many readers must have felt justified in saying, 'how can he be bothered to do it?' Yet Tynan's lament is really as nothing compared with the varied reflections and animadversions of Gibbs and Schein.

Wolcott Gibbs is best known in this country as the author of some of the outstanding *New Yorker* profiles of the 1930s, most notably those of Alexander Woollcott and Henry Luce. He had joined the magazine shortly after it started and helped shape its urbane, slightly condescending character. For many years he was the *New Yorker*'s theatre columnist, and on his death in 1958 he was succeeded by Kenneth Tynan as guest critic for a couple of seasons. It was a contribution to the war effort that he wrote on films from December 1944 until the following September, and his witty notes on that experience are to be found in his book *Season in the Sun*.

Not a man given to equivocation, Gibbs made a few self-deprecating remarks about the influence of his writing and came rapidly to the point:

> The purpose of this essay is to explain, as clearly as I can and while certain memories are still green, why it seems to me that the cinema resists rational criticism almost as firmly as a six-day bicycle race, or perhaps love ... It is my indignant opinion that ninety per cent of the moving pictures exhibited in America are so vulgar, witless and dull that it is preposterous to write about them in any publication not intended to be read while chewing gum.

By implication one supposes that it was all right to review plays in a magazine intended to be read while drinking Beefeater gin, and I doubt if Gibbs found the Broadway seasons that straddled his period as a film critic much more rewarding. But for the record: in 1944–45 he might have seen, among other not un-noteworthy films, *The Southerner*, *They Were Expendable*, *Hail the Conquering Hero*, *Meet Me in St Louis*, *Spellbound*, *A Tree Grows in Brooklyn* and *Double Indemnity*. The highlights of the Broadway season of 1944–45 were *The Glass Menagerie* (which very nearly folded in Chicago), Arthur Miller's *The Man Who Had All the Luck* (which closed after four performances), Helen Hayes in *Harriet* (a biographical play about the author of *Uncle Tom's Cabin*) and the Pulitzer Prize-winning *Harvey*.

During the 1945–46 season Mr Gibbs and the critical fraternity came in for one of those counter-attacks from playwrights which are such a recurrent feature of the theatrical scene but so rarely occur in the cinema. Maxwell Anderson took large advertisements to defend his poetic drama *Truckline Café*, and Orson Welles weighed in with a vigorous defence of *Around the World*, a musical on which he collaborated with Cole Porter. There was, I believe, no reaction from the industry to Gibbs's film piece, but then he mentioned no film or filmmaker by name. Anyway, back to the article.

Gibbs made a couple of exceptions to the remarks I've quoted – the occasional good picture with a slight element of reality (one or two a year at most, and they invariably lose money), documentaries, and 'frank melodramas which have nothing to do with life and therefore are exempt from criticism'. Most pictures were bad because they were necessarily aimed at people of low intelligence, had to appeal to such a heterogeneous international audience and were at the mercy of every kind of pressure group.

Having outlined this situation, Gibbs went on to describe the 'small but fascinating literary comedy' involved in a conscientious reviewer's attempt to write about films costing more than a million dollars (the same sum by pre-devaluation rates that Tynan cited). 'He writes, you might say, rather the way Henry Wadsworth Longfellow used to look', claimed Gibbs, is driven to debase the language by frequent recourse to 'a very special vocabulary' ('luminous', 'taut', 'haunting', 'lyric', 'brave', 'tender', 'compassionate', 'poignant', etc.), develops a remarkable talent for inflating 'non-existent plots' and for suggesting the presence of, but not elucidating, symbolism. This highfalutin' vagueness extended to the critic's remarks on direction and photography; in the case of the former because 'the mass mating of minds in any Hollywood picture makes it impossible for the layman to tell who did what', in the latter because it is 'an insanely complicated, endlessly refined, and wickedly deceptive technical process about which it is reasonable to assume he knows about as much as he does about the inner workings of a seismograph'. By 'correct' or 'striking' compositions the critic invariably means 'those that most closely resemble the paintings on sale in department stores'. And 'he is a perennial sucker for the studiously telling details ... that are all part of a sort of primitive shorthand used by films to trap the unwary'.

Modestly Gibbs concedes in conclusion that all this must have occurred to anyone who has thought at all about the cinema. But it took him 'ten months of physical discomfort and mental confusion' before he appreciated 'the whole absurdity' of what he was trying to do – 'to write, that is, for the information of my friends about something that was plainly designed for the entertainment of their cooks – and before I realised that I had no intention of doing it again'.

Now just at the moment when Gibbs was seeing the light and making his separate peace, some four thousand miles away in Stockholm a youthful, enthusiastic Harry Schein was preparing to embark upon a critical career. He was already an astute businessman and in the process of building up a considerable fortune in the field of chemical engineering. Schein's position was an enviable one. *BLM* is Sweden's leading intellectual journal, in appearance something like *Encounter*, but more literary and less political, and one meets few Swedes interested in the arts who don't read it.

Obviously the rewards of writing for such a periodical are immense (in terms of professional satisfaction this is, not financial), but it imposes a strain on a critic. For though he doesn't have to review (or indeed even see) every film that comes along, he is likely to feel eventually that he has had his say on the general themes he has the time and space to tackle. Further, he is writing for a broadly based readership rather than one with a particular commitment to the cinema. And after eight years Schein was 'tired of films, fairly tired of looking at films and very tired of writing about films. I have long since said all I am able to say about films.'

These prefatory remarks set the tone of Schein's piece; and unlike Tynan (by implication) and Gibbs (explicitly) he does not go on to suggest that the practice of film criticism is impossible or worthless. In fact he pays tribute to several Swedish critics who, miraculously 'still write with an impressive enthusiasm, a youthful vitality, which cannot simply be due to the ability of superior writers to make a better job of hiding their fatigue'. Incidentally, when I first met Schein seven years after this article appeared (I hadn't read it at the time), I found him totally unwilling to discuss any aspect of film criticism other than its possible fatuity, though he'd talk endlessly about the cinema itself. Not that there was any ill feeling; indeed I believe it was in the course of a very friendly dinner party that his wife, the actress Ingrid Thulin, told Jacques Doniol-Valcroze that she had cancelled her subscription to *Cahiers du Cinéma*.

The fundamental cause of his tiredness with films, Schein thought, was not merely that he had said everything he had to say, but that everything he had thought in his initial enthusiasm for the medium had been said years before, when 'the film industry was in its infancy and the discoveries were real'. And that what was 'new in filmic development is in fact the emergence of new generations of film critics rather than the rejuvenation of an artistic medium'.

Over the years, too, he had noted that he had begun thinking too much in relative terms, something he had intended to avoid, and to suspend his critical faculties in favour of the kind of relaxed enjoyment that is 'strictly for teenagers – for whom the cinema really seems to exist'. (A decade, one notes, has brought us from cooks to teenagers.) The film industry he knew was 'probably largely unaware of the existence of the magazine', but he had to put up with a good deal of abuse from readers as a result of his critical attitudes, which seemed to worry them more than the films themselves.

Schein was further tired by what seemed at the time a general levelling up and down of the product – 'not only the peaks have been lost but also the lowest depths', which was perhaps good from a social point of view but bad for the art. This had been reflected in the state of Swedish film criticism, where the overall standard of daily reviewing had improved but serious public discussion had ceased to exist, other than of an academic kind among the new generation of critics who 'appear paralysed by their own knowledge'.

It becomes clear that it is criticism Schein is tired of, and the fact that 'there are too few films of such interest that they at all merit a serious analysis before qualified but unspecialised readers'. A number of his concluding observations concern the situation of the film industry and film appreciation; and here he is, if not sanguine, at least not in despair. After giving up his column he began to examine what might be done about the cinema and eventually came up with an influential study of the relationship between the state and the arts called *Can We Afford Culture?* The suggestions outlined in this book he pursued publicly, and legislation followed. That extraordinary and far-sighted organisation, the Swedish Film Institute, was set up with Schein at its head.

In 1962, the year Schein published *Can We Afford Culture?*, *BLM* printed another valedictory. The author of this was Jörn Donner: it was called 'Tired of Films II' and dedicated to Harry Schein. Donner had been a critic in Finland for most of the 1950s, was *BLM*'s film critic 1959–61, and had just resigned after 15 months as principal reviewer for Sweden's leading newspaper, the liberal daily, *Dagens Nyheter*. And he asked himself the question: 'I wonder what it is that can make a critic so tired of film?'

Much of what he had to say concerns the loss of his early vitality after helping to pioneer criticism in Finland, and the low standard of reviewing he found in Sweden. He also suggested, only half-humorously, that some of his fatigue was due to 'the watchful eyes of distributors and press agents' obliging him to 'observe a forced state of wakefulness'. He also believed that regular reviewing in the press too seemed to be corrupting his style. Furthermore, critics over the years had done nothing to alter the deplorable state of the industry; in terms of ignorance there is little to choose between the two. In the course of 15 months he had found 'only ten films at the outside that one would really like to remember in the way that one remembers a good novel or a good play', and he began to ask himself in his weariness 'was it really true that I had considered this art form the most interesting, most rewarding of all?' He was filled with 'disappointment over thousands of missed opportunities'.

After giving up criticism Donner moved into the cinema himself and is currently shooting his fourth feature film. But I do not think it adequate to say that his dissatisfaction was simply that of a frustrated would-be filmmaker, any more than it would be to say that Tynan and Gibbs were 'natural' theatre critics wandering off course, or that Harry Schein was cut out to be an administrator, however more satisfactory they have found these roles. Equally I do not think it sufficient to say of all four that the fact that they wrote for general readers rather than film specialists was a principal cause of their unhappiness, though it would be impossible to disregard it as a factor. As I said at the outset, the fugitive film critic is a recurrent figure. I have chosen this quartet because of the span of years and countries, because they are people of exceptional talent, and because between them they put up such a formidable range of personal and general arguments against the craft they were abandoning.

I've seen my main purpose here as noting the prevalence of this phenomenon, for it appears to have escaped the attention not only of the people I have quoted but also of those who have acted and written similarly. I don't wish to tackle their arguments individually or to argue the case for the function of criticism in general or of film criticism in particular. A great deal of what they say seems to me eminently reasonable (in some aspects even self-evident) and I cannot altogether discount the possibility that they might be right. Yet as this is not my own valedictory article, it can be assumed that at the moment I do not accept their conclusions. I should like, however, to make some tentative observations about the phenomenon itself.

The most obvious point is that the four people quoted do not question the practice of criticism in general, and it is a matter of experience that we are not regularly regaled with the sight of dramatic and literary critics throwing in the towel and questioning their erstwhile vocation. Yet as I have indicated in the case of Gibbs, and as can be demonstrated in the other instances, current theatre and literature in the periods in question offered nothing better than the cinema, and maybe something less attractive. Critics of other art forms, however, are fortified by sustaining traditions. They do not need to find their pleasures in the latest productions in their field, though certain pressures operate upon them to at least try. Anyway, no critic expects to find a dozen important new symphonies or novels or plays every year, let alone one a week.

Doubts can even be expressed as to whether a whole decade will enrich a particular art, and historical precedent exists for extending this judgment to a much longer period. This is not however true of the cinema. Not merely is it a young art, but one of which a tremendous amount has come to be expected. Fifty years ago it was regarded as a mere passing fad. And though this is no longer felt, there has always been a sense of urgency, as if it were all to come to an end very soon. Unable to attend on evolution, critics have demanded revolution. Back in the mid-1940s, for instance, James Agee argued that it was vital for the movies to take advantage of the next half dozen years before they were eclipsed by television. This pressure has been compounded by the speed of technical development and innovation within the industry itself.

Yet the very fact that the cinema *is* an industry and can scarcely operate on any other basis is obviously one of the factors that tend to undermine the confidence of the critic. Unlike the other arts, most films are not being produced for *him*, for the limited section of the community of which he feels himself a part. They are being made for that mass society from which he himself is alienated and by an industrial complex, usually indifferent to his praise and strictures, that by its every word and action seems to express a hostility towards the values he himself espouses. (This is of course a gross exaggeration about the situation, but not about the way critics customarily feel.)

Despite this and contrary to all the evidence, the critic nevertheless believes that at any moment the cinema is about to 'come of age'. Thus we are confronted with the appalling image of a tarted up harridan forever on the point of celebrating her majority. There are other reasons too why so much is demanded of the cinema. Film

has had so overpowering an effect in shaping the range of experience and consciousness of life of two generations that most of us
carry with us an ideal concept of film, and an existential notion of
living within a film, that nothing we actually see can fully measure
up to.

A couple of other points about the role of the film critic as against
critics of other media occur to me. One is that a critic feels he must
see everything new that is offered – that he ought to be an expert
on the movies of all countries in an infinity of fictional and documentary genres. The alternative can appear to be seeing nothing.
Equally, instead of accepting the diversity of what is offered, some
critics still seem to be after a general, all-embracing approach to film.
Lawrence Alloway recently suggested for instance that 'a unified
theory' is badly needed and put forward 'an approach to a descriptive criticism of the film, one that does not set out to exclude the
popular movie'. But this, in stressing the typical movie, makes the
viewing of everything obligatory and can only reinforce those
voguish, intellectual memory games so brilliantly, and perhaps
definitively, satirised in Wallace Markfield's novel *To an Early Grave*.

The other point is one stressed by Wolcott Gibbs – the incompetence of film critics. Generally it is only the mindless tipster in the
popular press who is never touched by thoughts of his own possible
incapacity. Most film critics from time to time must wonder exactly
what their qualifications are for their job, or indeed what such qualifications should be. (One is not helped in this matter by examining
the judgment over the years of the Academy of Motion Picture Arts
and Sciences.) These doubts rarely assail the critics of the other arts
in the same degree, which is not surprising when unimpeachable
academic or quasi-academic credentials can be produced to validate
their function.

What it all comes down to, I suppose, is that the film critic operates in a permanent state of personal insecurity, subject to peculiar
stresses, doubts and anxieties. No wonder that so many of them seize
the opportunity to escape and purge themselves with public recan-
tation. Those who press on in the uneven struggle, and for whatever
reason, might well bear in mind the words of Scott Fitzgerald. 'The
test of a first-rate intelligence', he wrote, 'is the ability to hold two
opposed ideas in the mind at the same time and still retain the ability
to function.' The sentence comes in his essay 'The Crack-Up'.

All the Better Books (1967)

Dore Schary: 'I want to tell the audience the narration is from the book. A lot of people don't know this is a book. I want to be blunt with them. Put them in a more receptive mood. I want to tell them they're gonna see a *classic, a great novel.*' (Quoted by Lillian Ross in *Picture*).

Hollywood has not on the whole set out to woo the reading public. As an industry it was established to provide entertainment for the semi-literate urban masses. To buy a book in Hollywood meant to acquire the film rights, at which point it became a 'property' presenting problems that had to be 'licked'. When studios hired writers they were generally reduced to lowly regarded (if highly paid) cogs in the production machine. Within movies themselves a bespectacled book-lover was traditionally a person without a Saturday date, lonely and frustrated – eventually either to be left in the lurch or to throw away book and glasses for more rewarding pursuits such as making love or money. If, as Dorothy Parker said, men seldom make passes at girls who wear glasses, women rarely gave second looks to men who read books. Not that books were totally disregarded – merely that they belonged in anonymous leather bindings on the shelves of the rich. Only a few licensed eccentrics, like Leslie Howard, were allowed to take them down.

In a vague sort of way books were respected for their prestige (as authors were before they signed studio contracts) provided they didn't have to be read. 'I would rather take a fifty-mile hike than crawl my way through a book,' wrote Jack L. Warner, head of production at Warner Brothers, in his autobiography. This ambivalence is caught in William Inge's play *Picnic*, when the footloose Hal is 'impressed' (the word used in Inge's stage direction) by the pretty

---

'All the Better Books' first appeared in *Sight & Sound*, Winter 1966–67.

heroine's unhappy younger sister having read 'a *whole* book in an afternoon', and says: 'I wish I had more time to read books. That's what I'm going to do when I settle down. I'm gonna read all the better books – and listen to all the better music. A man owes it to himself.' The part of Hal in the film was of course taken by William Holden, who a few years before had played the embittered screen-writer in *Sunset Boulevard*, and as the intellectual journalist in *Born Yesterday* had donned horn-rimmed spectacles to give Judy Holliday a crash course in civics.

This nexus of attitudes has by no means been confined to Holly-wood; on the contrary it is a reflection of the working assumptions of those functioning in the mass media throughout the world. Currently, however, European films are full of references to other arts, to books, paintings, plays and music. Some are significant and personal, others merely modish – or meaningless. This tendency is a product of many factors: the general drift of our culture; the kind of people who make films; the strata of society with which movies now deal and toward which they are targeted; the decline in straight narrative cinema and the consequent emphasis upon individual rather than generalised décor; the growing acceptance by audiences of the unexplained and the elliptical.

One cannot point to a particular date when this tendency first began to show itself, but in retrospect and in view of their subse-quent influence, the appearance of both *Breathless* and *L'Avventura* in 1960 is worth noting. In the former, Godard includes a specific if rather tangential discussion of Faulkner's *The Wild Palms*, the events and themes of which have much in common with his film. This was but one of many references to literature, music, art and other movies. *Breathless* was the beginning of a personal culture collage that has preoccupied Godard and, especially in *Une Femme mariée* and *Pierrot le fou*, even to form the infrastructure of his movies.

In *L'Avventura*, Antonioni also referred to an American novel. But its function in the film can be more easily isolated. It occurs when a copy of *Tender Is the Night* is discovered along with the Bible in the luggage of the missing Anna. Naturally her father seizes upon the Bible as an indication that she has not committed suicide. The audience however has been made aware of his lack of understanding of her situation, and Fitzgerald's novel is surely a clue to the state of Anna's mind through her identification with the neurotic spoilt rich girl, Nicole Diver. At the same time there are obvious parallels between the career of the film's ruined architect Sandro and the novel's corrupted psychiatrist, Dick Diver.

One would neither demand nor expect this level of sophistication from the straight commercial cinema, yet something has begun to percolate through. In his chapter on Hollywood and the novel in *Waiting for the End*, Leslie Fiedler asked: 'How many scenes involving books remain in the memory out of the films of the last 30 years, excepting those shelves of meaningless books in libraries, obviously bought by the gross like furniture?' But then, Fiedler added: 'Who, for instance, can imagine the great figures who survive from movie to movie reading a book? Think of … John Wayne, Steve McQueen or Mickey Mouse entering a library or standing before a bookshelf with any serious intent in mind.' For that matter one might ask just how much time Captain Ahab or Huck Finn spent haunting libraries.

Dr Fiedler, however, raised these questions in 1964 and regretted that no American director used books the way Antonioni had done. As a leading investigator of the arcane processes of cultural osmosis, he would no doubt appreciate the irony of Steve McQueen withstanding a deadly knife assault in the western *Nevada Smith* by having a copy of *McGuffey's Practical Reader* concealed beneath his shirt. Equally he might note with approval the well-stocked shelves of George and Martha in the film version of *Who's Afraid of Virginia Woolf?* (not to mention the fact that the title wasn't changed to *Campus Fury*). No random job lot of 'meaningless books' here: the complete Thomas Mann, well-thumbed, behind the bed, Günter Grass and David Storey in the living room, *Paris Review* on the coffee table, and so on. It might indeed be … well, Dr Fiedler's own house.

One doesn't want to make too much of these films, but they are instances from big-budget studio productions of books operating on the one hand (albeit pretty crudely) on a functional level, on the other hand in terms of décor. The theme of *Nevada Smith* is the way in which a man survives to carry out a self-appointed task through his willingness to learn. In this light the reading primer is not only a device to preserve him (which might have been a snuffbox or a medallion) but also an emblem. In the case of *Virginia Woolf* the books are only fine set decoration. I say 'only', but the rightness of the choice is an instance of the care that can be taken over such matters.

Naturally one might be wrong about *Virginia Woolf* – maybe
every one of those books has some dramatic meaning beyond that
of providing a convincing setting for a university couple. It is not a
problem we have in the theatre, where we just see crowded bookshelves. On the stage, when George reads aloud from a book (a
scene omitted in the film), many critics assumed it was a passage
from Spengler, whereas it was an invention of Albee's. (Similarly,
many people thought that singing the title of the play to the tune
of 'Here We Go Round the Mulberry Bush' was intended to evoke
Eliot's *The Hollow Men* when in fact it was done to avoid infringing
the copyright in the original music of 'Who's Afraid of the Big Bad
Woolf?' held by Walt Disney.) In the film we would have had to
see the book from which George was reading.

Only from the front rows of the stalls can stage décor be scruti-
nised in any detail, and only when the production is extremely dull
does one inspect it with care. Thus in the West End production of
The Owl and the Pussycat boredom drove me to examine the hero's
bookshelves and to wonder how this San Francisco intellectual
happened to possess so many English book club editions and why
all his postcards came from the Tate Gallery. Unimportant perhaps,
but it can break the mood, as in an even more striking way did a
curious anomaly in the Denver hospital sequence in Stanley
Kubrick's version of *Lolita*. How had Humbert Humbert come by
a copy of the Penguin edition of *Portrait of the Artist as a Young Man*
(with Not for Sale in the United States and Canada on its jacket) in
the Rocky Mountains? From a branch of the same store perhaps that
sold Lolita's mother the dark green British-style Gordon's gin bottle
in New England.

In the movies everything is brought up before our faces, and in
the higher reaches of the cinema, ever since audiences emerged
from *Citizen Kane* reeling after raking every frame for the identity
of Rosebud, we're often inclined to see significance where none is
intended. As a comment on the increased visual awareness and
sophistication of cinemagoers it might be pointed out that many
people back in the early 1940s searched for Rosebud in vain. Far
off indeed seem the days when critics could state with admiration
that the wedding scene in *Greed* was so compelling that no one
noticed the discrepancy between the turn-of-the-century interior

and the 1920s life going on outside in the street.

These references to the other arts raise a number of important points about the cinema. Initially there is a distinction to be drawn between those that are self-contained and those that refer one outside the film. This can only be a rough distinction, because even in the most obvious cases there is always some outside reference where a specific work is used. When Clive Donner accurately places a David Hockney on the rising executive's office wall in *Nothing But the Best*, it is not necessary to recognise the painting to appreciate its effect. It has no personal meaning for Donner of the kind that, say, Renoir and Velázquez have for Godard in *Pierrot le fou*. But before going further I'd like to mention and dispense with the three categories of film that actually concern artists.

The first of these is where works of identifiable authorship are attributed to fictional characters. Elizabeth Frink's sculptures attributed to Viveca Lindfors in Losey's *The Damned* raise no issues that go beyond the immediate thematic context of the film. When Ray Walston 'composes' little known Gershwin songs in *Kiss Me, Stupid*, we are amused and charmed. In the film version of *The Horse's Mouth*, however, our view of Gulley Jimson's genius is conditioned by our own response to the paintings of John Bratby; we react quite differently to the first-person narrative of Joyce Cary's novel.

In the second category, where real work is produced by actors portraying artists in biographical films, our main attention is given to the extent an actor measures up to our notion of the artist he portrays, and the conviction he brings to the circumstances of creation. Thus Charles Laughton conveys some idea of the identity of Rembrandt; Cornel Wilde falls rather short of suggesting the sensibility of Chopin, etc.

The third category is where fake works are turned out by fictional characters. For example the ghastly paintings that supposedly make Dick Van Dyke the toast of Paris in *The Art of Love* are obviously less carefully planned (though no less indicative of the maker's intentions) than Richard Macdonald's paintings (sort of instant Josef Hermans) run up for Hardy Kruger in Losey's *Blind Date*. In the case, say, of a fictitious novelist the burden of convincing the audience falls entirely upon the film actor – he must *be* a novelist in a way that no author in real life is obliged to.

These films however raise problems that I'm not particularly concerned with here. Rather, my interest centres upon the use of identifiable works, where what is at stake is neither the nature of their creation nor the personality of their creators, but the use that directors make of them.

The risks of misunderstanding, as I've already suggested, are immense. Let me give a couple of illustrations of what I mean. The first of these does not actually concern a work of art, though it brings up the same point. The critic of the *Guardian*, in a general slating of *Cul-de-sac*, took Polanski to task for a reference to 'Vince's shirts'. This critic cited as evidence of the fact that Polanski was not as au fait with current Carnaby Street fashions as he might think. Now it is possible that the situation had changed since Polanski wrote the script, or that Polanski *did* realise the present standing of Vince's and consequently intended that the girl should be provincial and out of touch. It is equally feasible that the girl ad-libbed the line on the set. Whichever way you look at it, it seems singularly unimportant and would always have little meaning of any kind outside a very small section of London life. But I say this because my knowledge of fashion is rather limited; the natural tendency is to discount the significance of references to fields of which we have little knowledge.

My other illustration follows on from this and is a good deal more important. It concerns the meaning Antonioni attached to Hermann Broch's *The Sleepwalkers* in *La Notte*. Ian Cameron in his valuable monograph on Antonioni refers to it as 'a vast egghead volume'. But I doubt if the director intends that we should see Valentina (Monica Vitti) merely as the sort of girl who sits around ostentatiously reading books at parties. On the contrary, I imagine that he is a great admirer of Broch, and that he has been influenced by this Austrian writer with whom he has certain affinities. It would seem that Valentina is intended to share Broch's beliefs in – if I understood it correctly – a metaphysical redemption from social problems rather than any possibility of their resolution. She is thus a person of superior awareness of her situation, who has come to terms with alienation. This would tie in with the visit that Giovanni (Marcello Mastroianni) makes at the beginning of the film to a dying friend, whose last work is an essay on the German Marxist critic T.W. Adorno, who greatly influenced the writing of Thomas Mann's *Dr Faustus*. It would be possible, however, to come to the same conclusion about Valentina without being in any way acquainted with Broch. Certainly Antonioni could count on very few people recognising *The Sleepwalkers* – far fewer than those who would know *Tender Is the Night*.

The obvious difference between playing a piece of music or exhibiting a painting and showing a book is that the former is the thing itself, and the latter can only have a meaning if the spectator knows it. Whatever may be said about Buñuel's use of Handel in *Viridiana*, no one would suggest that the choice of music was obscure. In the case of only a very few books can the general audience be expected to recognise the director's meaning immediately and relatively unambiguously. The Bible is perennially one of them; others vary with time and place. In the 1940s for instance there were numerous occasions (e.g. *Dear Octopus, Passport to Pimlico*) when an easy laugh was obtained by having someone unpack a case that contained James Hadley Chase's once notorious *No Orchids for Miss Blandish. Lady Chatterley's Lover* or *Fanny Hill* would presumable serve the same purpose today.*

With other books the director needs to take account of the possibilities of non-recognition, or of the variable subjective responses of his audience. One assumes that in *Some Came Running* Vincente Minnelli believed the audience would accept Dave Hirsch (Frank Sinatra) as a novelist in the main tradition of twentieth-century fiction, when he shows him taking from his valise the Viking Portable Library anthologies of Fitzgerald, Hemingway, Faulkner, Steinbeck and Wolfe. Minnelli certainly missed the irony intended in the original novel, where James Jones stresses that this is not Hirsch's opinion of himself but that of his sister, who had given him the books. Likewise, the subsequent publication of Hirsch's story in *Atlantic Monthly* will only seem a matter of abiding significance to those who regard the magazine as an important arbiter in literary matters.

I don't mean to suggest that the cinema should stick to invented books and periodicals, for while it cannot be denied that a director has much greater control over his material if he does so, it's doubtful if this gain compensates for the loss in verisimilitude. Confected titles rarely carry conviction. For instance, when Hitchcock shows

---

* A few days after writing this I saw Knud Leif Thomsen's Danish film *Gift*, in which the Bible and *Fanny Hill* are manipulated dialectically as ideological counters in a way that I assume would be intelligible to audiences throughout the Western world.

Sean Connery in *Marnie* reading psychiatric textbooks with titles like 'Frigidity in Women' and 'The Mentality of the Criminal Female', one suspects that Hitchcock or his screenwriter invented these titles (or *would* have done if they didn't exist). While the titles serve his simple purposes well, there is something inevitably banal or naive about this sequence. In a very real sense the presentation of the books reflects the shallowness of the psychology in the film as a whole.

It is interesting that this cinematic fascination with books should occur at a time when the ideas of Marshall McLuhan are gaining widespread currency, and that the cinema's greatest display of books in recent years should be in François Truffaut's *Fahrenheit 451*, which as Truffaut himself pointed out has more literary references than all of Godard's pictures put together. *Fahrenheit* is not only a total rejection of the cinema's traditional attitude to literature but is also by implication a counterblast to McLuhan. In Ray Bradbury's novel very few books are mentioned by name. Inevitably in the movie we have to *see* the books, and, in ways that are sometimes obvious and sometimes extremely subtle, Truffaut achieves an extraordinary power and resonance by his selection and manipulation of titles.

There is a rather touching scene in John Frankenheimer's *The Manchurian Candidate*, that much underrated expression of 1960s angst, in which Frank Sinatra's intellectual confusion is revealed by setting him in a room littered with works of 'contemporary significance' through which he has vainly sought the light. In *Fahrenheit 451* Truffaut has taken us beyond this crisis of literacy to McLuhan's 'electronic global village' and revealed its nightmare qualities. In the first three-quarters of the film he builds up a situation in which we accept books as characters, and then leads us into his poetic final scene in which characters become human walking books.

Paradoxically enough too, this rash of references to other arts and other films comes at a moment when everyone is celebrating the notion of pure or autonomous cinema. It is now necessary (or useful) to know far more about the other arts than it ever was in the past, when movies really were self-contained. How can one properly appreciate Jacques Rivette's *Paris nous appartient* without having read *Pericles*, or recent Bergman films without understanding Bach? And not only that, but working out what the play and the composer mean to Rivette and Bergman. The relationship between *Pericles* and Rivette's film is somewhat more complex than that between *Othello* and *A Double Life*, or *The Taming of the Shrew* and *Kiss Me Kate*.

Not that this has anything to do with what is pejoratively referred to as 'literary cinema', which is generally taken to mean movies that correspond formally to the well-made play or orthodox novel. The term has however always had a note of falsity about it: Richard Brooks's somewhat free film version of *Lord Jim* is 'literary cinema', while a more faithful adaptation of Conrad's novel would have resulted in a movie that strongly resembled *Citizen Kane*.

Finally it must be observed that the complexity of a film is not necessarily an indication of its importance, nor the amount of exegesis it demands an index of its quality. While writing this article I have several times thought of the full-page advertisement for an American book club that appeared in popular magazines a few years ago. It depicted the club's advisory panel (the formidable triumvirate of W.H. Auden, Jacques Barzun and Lionel Trilling) sitting at a table facing an empty chair, on the sturdy leather back of which were the words, 'This place reserved for a man who prefers books to automobiles'. Aesthetically and commercially the cinema has usually preferred automobiles. Godard and Truffaut would find it difficult to state their order of preference.

This essay on books in the movies was included in a 1970 anthology for film students called Film and the Liberal Arts, *edited by T.J. Ross in 1970. It appeared in the section on 'Film and Literature' and was followed by a series of suggestions for exercises. I once read that Budd Schulberg discovered that his alma mater, Dartmouth College, had his novel* What Makes Sammy Run? *on the syllabus, and he had trouble answering an examination question put to students – 'What* did *make Sammy run?'. I have a little problem with questions put by Professor Ross: 'What is the significance of the last sentence in French's essay? Do you find it to be an effectively concluding "punch line"?' The book club, incidentally was the Readers' Subscription, later renamed the Mid-Century, and an anthology of pieces by Auden, Barzun and Trilling from its monthly magazine was published in 2001 as* A Company of Readers. *Among the essays was an enthusiastic review of a collection of Ingmar Bergman screenplays by Trilling, who admitted to never having seen a Bergman movie.*

Incitement against Violence
The American Crime Film (1968)

The simultaneous appearance of Arthur Penn's *Bonnie and Clyde* and Roger Corman's *St Valentine's Day Massacre* has given a new lease of life to what many of us had thought a dead or dying genre – the classic gangster movie. Their popularity, and particularly the runaway success of the former, means that in all likelihood we're in for a further cycle of gangster films. Already, while Hollywood prepares the goods – the present production situation makes the immediate exploitation of a paying trend less easy than in the past – a British distributor has rushed out a double bill of *Al Capone* (1959) and *Dillinger* (1945), whose eponymous heroes are described in the new advertising as respectively 'The Number 1 Underworld King' and 'The Most Notorious Killer of Them All'. They are also said to be 'Together for the first time' – hardly surprising, as Dillinger was in a state prison during the ascendancy of Capone, and Capone was in a federal penitentiary while Dillinger enjoyed his short-lived notoriety. This opportunistic programming has been rewarded by audiences larger than either film attracted on first exhibition, and a return of other old favourites seems inevitable.

The double revival parallels and overlaps in several ways *St Valentine's Day* and *Bonnie and Clyde*, without of course in any way matching their quality. The murder of seven associates of George 'Bugs' Moran's North Side gang by agents of Al Capone on the morning of 14 February 1929 is a feature of *Al Capone* and numerous other gangster films (including *Some Like It Hot*). It is part of the social history of the inter-war years, and the ambience from which it springs has been used as a political analogue by, among others, Brecht in *The Resistible Rise of Arturo Ui*. (But, as Martin

'Incitement against Violence' first appeared in *Sight & Sound*, Winter 1967–68.

Esslin comments, 'Brecht knew Hitler; he knew very little about Chicago.') Bonnie and Clyde as dimly remembered historical figures belong to the same crime wave as John Dillinger, and *Bonnie and Clyde* as a movie is not unrelated, as we shall see, to the screen *Dillinger*, appalling as that film is when viewed in isolation.

My purpose here is less to review *Bonnie and Clyde* and *St Valentine's Day* than to relate the hard, objective, anti-mythical, anti-heroic character of Corman's film and the wry, romantic, mock-heroic character of Penn's picture to the development of the gangster genre on the one hand and to certain currents in American life on the other. Let me say now that I consider *St Valentine's Day* and *Bonnie and Clyde* the high-water marks of the two divergent streams of the gangster movie to which they belong. Furthermore, they serve to clarify these streams as no other gangster films have previously done, and in consequence each achieves its apparent aim – which is, I take it, to transcend the genre and create useful images of American life. As their superficial trappings – colour, meticulous décor, period costume, vintage automobiles, easy violence, blazing machine guns, biographical data and the rest – have tended to lump them together (to the inevitable detriment of *St Valentine's Day*), let me indicate a few important distinctions between the two.

First, *St Valentine Day's Massacre*. The time is the 1920s just before the Wall Street Crash, the setting exclusively urban and static. The characters are recent immigrants, mainly Italian and Irish and predominantly Catholic. They are organised and professional, their actions planned and purposive; they are successful and reflect success in their way of life. Violence may be endemic but it is directed towards specific ends.

Bonnie and Clyde is quite the reverse. The time is the 1930s after the Depression has bitten deep, and the setting is rural. The central characters are always on the move and own nothing, not even their cars. They are largely of white Anglo-Saxon Protestant stock, disorganised and unprofessional, and none of their actions is planned or purposive. They are failures, their violence unpremeditated, a form of gesture. Bonnie Parker and the Barrow brothers are reacting against their sense of dispossession, while the Capone mob embody a perversion of a national dream of success. The organised urban mobster belongs to a carefully delineated underworld which closely corresponds to the general structure of respectable society; Bonnie and Clyde belong not to the under*world* but to the under*side* of American life, their careers having neither shape nor pattern. Both films are after a kind of truth, and it is this search that has determined their style.

Forty years have now passed since the first major gangster film, Sternberg's *Underworld*. The screenwriter Ben Hecht tells us in his autobiography how he conceived it. An experienced Hollywood producer had informed him of the peculiar rules that had to be observed for depicting heroes and heroines, and then:

> An idea came to me. The thing to do was to skip the heroes and heroines, to write a movie containing only villains and bawds. I would not have to tell any lies then … As a newspaperman I had learnt that nice people – the audience – loved criminals, doted on reading about their love problems as well as their sadism. My movie, grounded on this simple truth, was produced with the title *Underworld*. It was the first gangster movie to bedazzle the movie fans and there were no lies in it – except for a half-dozen sentimental touches introduced by its director, Joe von Sternberg.

But it was the coming of sound that same year which made possible the first gangster cycle. Without a soundtrack to capture the screech of tyres, the chatter of machine guns and the rasping dialogue, *Little Caesar* (1930), *Public Enemy* (1931), *Scarface* (1932) and their endless imitators would have been unthinkable. Reflecting the mood of their time, these movies were harsh, cynical, angry and above all ambivalent in their attitude towards their protagonists. These years from 1929 to 1935 – from the Wall Street Crash to the middle of Roosevelt's first term, with the waning Prohibition overlapping the Depression and the bland Herbert Hoover giving way to the New Deal – were a confused period in which America seemed to be falling apart at the seams, ripe for revolution.

The gangster films of this period are clearly the ones that Robert Warshow had in mind when he wrote the article 'The Gangster as Tragic Hero' in 1948 (reprinted in *The Immediate Experience*), and it was not surprising that he found it difficult to accommodate more recent films to his thesis.

The subject of these movies was the organised urban mobsters who had thrived as a result of Prohibition. The archetype was Al

Capone, an Italian immigrant who had risen since 1920 from hired gunman and brothel bouncer to multimillionaire head of the Chicago underworld, public celebrity, controller of judges, politicians and policemen. He was a legend in his lifetime and remains so after his death: it is no accident that a lithograph of the 'Big Fellow' is to be seen on the wall of the British gang boss's sitting room in *Robbery*. From the activities of Capone and his association with the Unione Siciliana and the mafia springs the organised criminal network, the Syndicate, which runs the length and breadth of America today. *The St Valentine's Day Massacre* is in my view the first feature film that has begun to make sense of the complicated relationships between these different groups; other films have ignored them or oversimplified them beyond comprehension.

Capone himself was the inspiration of the early gangster films – W.R. Burnett's *Little Caesar* is based on his career, Ben Hecht drew on personal knowledge of Chicago crime and used the familiar nickname for *Scarface*. And sitting in the audience when these movies appeared was another group of criminals or potential criminals from different backgrounds, their names soon to become notorious, nearly as familiar as Capone's: John Dillinger, Lester Gillis (alias George 'Baby Face' Nelson), the Barker family, Charles 'Pretty Boy' Floyd, Alvin Karpis, George 'Machine Gun' Kelly, Bonnie Parker and the Barrow brothers.

Whereas the urban gangsters, as I've previously suggested, were members of immigrant minorities, grotesquely parodying the Horatio Alger myth and consciously in search of social status, this latter group were fourth or fifth generation Wasps from rural communities of the Midwest and Southwest. All of them had minor criminal records and had served the inevitable periods in state reform schools. Then suddenly they took off on the most extraordinary and widely publicised crimewave in American history in the years 1933–35. They robbed filling stations and banks and staged kidnappings in colourful, reckless ways. They loved guns, were enthralled with images of violence, were compulsive exhibitionists. Rarely attempting to conceal their exploits they positively proclaimed their identity, boasted of their achievements to victims, took photographs of each other and wrote to the press. John Dillinger, for instance, first achieved notoriety by leaping over a bank counter in imitation of Douglas Fairbanks, delighted in snapping pictures of cops from his car, and was shot down in 1934 when emerging from the Biograph cinema in Chicago where he'd been seeing the gangster movie *Manhattan Melodrama*.

In effect, these pathetic psychopaths were more like the cinematic image of the big-time gangsters than the real gangsters that inspired the films. As Robert Warshow says of his 'tragic hero':

> The gangster's whole life is an effort to assert himself as an individual, to draw himself out of the crowd, and he always dies *because* he is an individual; the final bullet thrusts him back, makes him, after all, a failure. 'Mother of God,' says the dying Little Caesar, 'is this the end of Rico?' – speaking of himself thus in the third person because what has been brought low is not the undifferentiated *man*, but the individual with a name, the gangster, the success; even to himself he is a creature of the imagination. (T.S. Eliot has pointed out that a number of Shakespeare's tragic heroes have this trick of looking at themselves dramatically; their true identity, the thing that is destroyed when they die, is something outside themselves – not a man, but a style of life, a kind of meaning.)

This posturing, this narcissistic self-awareness, was seen in extreme form in the real-life Bonnie and Clyde and is caught accurately in the movie. The photographic poses they strike during the fraternal reunion at the motor court are exactly based on the pictures captured by the Kansas police after the gang's hasty departure from the Joplin garage apartment in April 1933; the Bonnie Parker poems used are also authentic, with their self-conscious myth making, their references to Jesse James and their explicit death wish. Yet while they were the most self-conscious, the Barrows were also the most ineffectual and pathetic. 'They're just a couple of cheap filling station and car thieves,' was the contemptuous comment upon them by 'Machine Gun' Kelly's partner, Albert Bates, and John Toland in his study *The Dillinger Days* describes them as 'not only outlaws but outcasts'.

Although the cinema influenced their style and the image they had of themselves, Hollywood was not responsible for starting these doomed young men and women on their lives of crime. They were creatures of a footloose, muddled era and were enabled to pursue their brief careers through the availability of fast cars and the inefficiency of local law enforcement agencies. Also, it might be said, they survived as long as they did – which was briefly – through their very lack of planning, their psychopathic unpredictability.

Tracking them down was the finest hour of the emerging FBI, which then and since has proved singularly ineffective in countering organised crime. Quite deliberately the law is excluded from *St Valentine's Day* except as patrons of speakeasies and potential acceptors of bribes in the North Clark Street garage (the irony here is that the bribes are not accepted precisely because the officers are gangsters in disguise). In *Bonnie and Clyde* the FBI's role has been omitted and the pursuers characterised solely as vindictive Southwesterners; this is not entirely false and is certainly in keeping with the overall 'truth' of the film. Obliquely the FBI's function is referred to when Clyde tells Bonnie's mother that the law is deliberately building them up in order that their eventual capture will appear that much more impressive.

Indeed the elevation of these essentially minor if deadly criminals to Public Enemy No. 1 status (the term first coined to describe Capone and subsequently attached to a series of other villains as the current title holder bit the dust) was part of the process by which J. Edgar Hoover's federal agency achieved national renown. In this Hollywood played a role too, along with a sensation-hungry popular press. (The best review of this situation, if somewhat over-critical of the FBI, is to be found in Fred Cook's *The FBI Nobody Knows*.)

The Hollywood Production Code, first adopted in 1930, proved during the early 1930s as ineffectual as the Midwestern police. Faced with reduced attendances and closing cinemas, the studios turned out increasingly violent and ever sexier movies to lure the public back. As a result threats of governmental and private censorship loomed, most notably from the Catholic Church. The permanent effects of this were the establishment of the Legion of Decency and the instituting of mandatory sanctions for breaches of the Code. Will H. Hays, president of the Motion Pictures Producers and Distributors of America, appointed Joseph I. Breen as enforcer of the Code with power to award or withhold a Seal of Approval.

The commercial importance of crime movies, however, was too strong to be resisted, and the simple, brilliant solution was to focus attention on the police instead of the criminals. So the G-men entered the movie pantheon with a nickname allegedly deriving from 'Machine Gun' Kelly's nervous exclamation at his 1933 arrest: 'Don't shoot, G-men.' (There still exists some doubt whether Kelly was using the underworld slang for Government men or merely stammering – or indeed whether he even used these words at all. Anyway they became an instant part of the FBI's mythology.) The film *G-Men* came in 1935 from Warner Brothers, the studio that had launched the first gangster cycle with *Little Caesar*, and it starred Jimmy Cagney who had been their *Public Enemy*. The same ingredients and the same quantity of violence remained. But where Prohibition and the first gangster films tended to glorify crime and by implication criticise society, the new wave of films and the public outrage at current real-life depredations (especially the string of kidnappings of which the Lindbergh case was the most sensational) glorified investigators and tended to make the audience condone unorthodox methods of law enforcement, canalising discontent into a lust for vengeance.

As I've said, there was little doubt in anyone's mind (including Capone's own) that gangster movies of the early 1930s were about Capone. Both Ben Hecht and Howard Hawks report having received visits from representatives of the incarcerated mobster during the filming of *Scarface*. In his autobiography Hecht claims to have convinced them that the film wasn't about Capone. Hawks, according to Kenneth Allsop in *The Bootleggers*, reacted differently:

> 'The man said that the Big Fellow was opposed to gangster films, particularly those that show underworld characters as rats and not heroes. I told him that the Big Fellow would have to lay down his money at the box office if he wanted to see how I was doing the film. I believe Capone is giving funds to the campaign against this kind of movie.'

Was there any truth in this last statement? It's difficult to say. It is just possible that as a *soi-disant* respectable citizen and generous contributor to Catholic causes, Capone may have made donations to organisations associated with the movement that brought about the Legion of Decency. Not that he need have worried too much about his fictional portraits. That was the problem of Will H. Hays, and in 1934 Hays sent an urgent telegram to Joe Breen that read in part:

No picture of the life or exploits of John Dillinger will be produced, distributed or exhibited by any member ... This decision is based on the belief that the production, distribution or exhibition of such a picture could be detrimental to the best public interest. Advise all studio heads accordingly.

The ruling remained in force until 1945, Hays's last year in office. Meanwhile the gangster/G-man cycle had petered out with a strongly elegiac fizz in Raoul Walsh's *High Sierra*, to be replaced by private eye films and the war movie. The latter offered a new roster of heroes and villains and even greater opportunities for patriotically condoned violence. When shortly before VE-Day Monogram Pictures released *Dillinger*, the Hays Office was unruffled: John Dillinger had been dead 11 years and his scarcely remembered career seemed trivial beside those of the public enemies in Berlin and Tokyo, whose final reel was approaching its end. *Dillinger* anyway did not spark off any imitators. The big studios were shifting gear from war films into peacetime 'now-it-can-be-told' espionage stories like *13 Rue Madeleine* and *House on 92nd Street* (note the specificity of the locales – which anticipates *St Valentine's Day Massacre* but differs markedly from the abstract character of the classic gangster movie). Darryl F. Zanuck, who launched the gangster film when head of production at Warners, had returned to his own 20th Century-Fox lot from wartime service to initiate this new cycle. His executive producer Louis de Rochemont brought to the task his experience with the thudding narrative style of *March of Time* (a form better known now through the parody of it which opens *Citizen Kane*). Within a year this semi-documentary movement had turned to civil crime with *Boomerang, Call Northside 777, Kiss of Death* and *Street with No Name*.

Zanuck described his policy at Warner Brothers as stories 'snatched from today's headlines'. The new style might have been called 'extracting stories from today's files'. And there was no shortage of local or federal agencies willing to cooperate to secure a little publicity for their activities. One result of this was that it was always the official view the public was given, and the commentaries were frequently personalised in the voice of an FBI man, a cop or a treasury agent. Where some possible criticism of authority might be implied, careful disclaimers were made of the kind that accompanies the waving of the Stars and Stripes at the conclusion of *Call Northside 777* or, some years, later hypocritically precedes the action of Elia Kazan's *On the Waterfront*. There is no such cant in either *St Valentine's Day* or *Bonnie and Clyde*, which is both part of their honesty and a cause – in the minds of some observers – for anxiety; by implication and intention they are subversive. Names of course were changed in these 1940s semi-documentaries – as much to further the ends of cinematic convenience as to protect the innocent.

Then in 1947 came a significant amendment to the Production Code, which read:

> No picture shall be approved dealing with the life of a notorious criminal of current or recent times which uses the name, nickname or alias of such notorious criminal in the film, nor shall a picture be approved if based on the life of such notorious criminal unless the character shown in the film be punished for crimes shown in the film committed by him.

There were three reasons for this amendment: the increasing use being made of seemingly authentic material, the precedent created by the award of a Seal of Approval to *Dillinger*, and most important of all, the death on 25 January 1947 of Al Capone, who had died a free man after having served a mere seven years in gaol for income tax evasion. The new Code provision, confirming as it did the lifting of Hays's old restriction, made any honest account of Capone's life virtually impossible and gravely restricted, perhaps even vetoed, any moderately realistic approach to the facts of contemporary organised crime. So the anticipated flood of Capone movies was blocked at the source; only Joseph H. Lewis's *Undercover Man* (1949), which dealt extremely circumspectly with the Treasury investigation of the Capone empire, readily comes to mind. Anyway, with the House Un-American Activities Committee raking over the cold ashes of the pre-war years, no one in Hollywood was feeling in a particularly nostalgic mood, and Will Hays's successor, Eric Johnston, was not exactly encouraging controversial or socially critical movies. In 1948 he told a meeting of screenwriters:

> We'll have no more *Grapes of Wrath*. We'll have no more *Tobacco Roads*. We'll have no more films that show the seamy side of

American life. We'll have no more pictures that deal with labour strikes. We'll have no more pictures that show a banker as a villain.

There were of course a fair number of crime films in the years that followed. Hollywood could scarcely survive without them. In *Key Largo* (1948) Edward G. Robinson's Johnny Rocco was even daringly presented as an anti-communist. There were plenty of flabby attempts at grappling with organised crime and dozens of movies about juvenile delinquency, stressing its environmental origins and usually exploiting its violence. Before and after Huston's *The Asphalt Jungle* (1950) there were frequent pictures concerning elaborately planned robberies, and in that same year there was the only major attempt to recapture the pristine glory of the pre-war Warner Brothers gangster films – Raoul Walsh's *White Heat* with James Cagney.

But it was in the late 1950s that Hollywood was struck by another major gangster cycle, this time entirely devoted to resurrecting famous criminals of the inter-war years. Only one of them was an expensive, big studio production, the synoptic *FBI Story* (1959), a lengthy, right-wing, Technicolor advertisement for the Federal Bureau of Investigation directed by Mervyn LeRoy who a quarter of a century before had made *Little Caesar*. It featured many celebrated hoods, though not the Barrow gang. The other films were all medium or low-budget black-and-white movies, biographical in development and mostly semi-documentary in treatment. And they fell into the two groups that I've already mentioned.

On the one hand were the films dealing with organised crime during the 1920s, centred on New York and Chicago. The main Chicago ones were Phil Karlson's *The Scarface Mob* (1959), deriving from the television programme *The Untouchables* (a peculiarly vicious series based on the 1957 memoirs of federal agent Eliot Ness), and Richard Wilson's *Al Capone* (1959). The principal New York ones were Budd Boetticher's *The Rise and Fall of Legs Diamond* (1959), Joseph M. Newman's *King of the Roaring Twenties* (aka *The Big Bankroll*, 1959) about the underworld financier Arnold Rothstein, and Joseph Pevney's *Portrait of a Mobster* (1961), centring on Dutch Schultz (and scripted by Howard Browne, author of *St Valentine's Day*).

On the other hand there were the pictures concerned with the small-time, lone-wolf criminals of the 1930s. Don Siegel's *Baby Face Nelson* (1957), in which John Dillinger also figures, Roger Corman's *Machine Gun Kelly* (1958) and William Witney's *The Bonnie Parker Story* (1958). Together they pretty well exhausted the field. But despite their documentary claims few of them took serious pains to get the facts straight, and none used this wealth of fascinating material for anything more than conventional action entertainment with fashionable period trimmings. *Baby Face Nelson* and *Legs Diamond* stand out from the rest and have been rightly praised. Their influence can be seen in New Wave movies from France. Yet they were not more markedly influential than the ancient *Dillinger*, which was clearly the kind of Monogram picture Godard had in mind when he dedicated *Breathless* to that defunct studio. Its successor, Allied Artists, was responsible for several of the films mentioned above.

Directed by Max Nosseck, an old UFA hand from the pre-Nazi period of German cinema, *Dillinger* has the elliptical, abstract quality that minuscule budgets and short shooting schedules forced on Poverty Row and which Godard was to adopt from choice. Not merely to adopt but, with Truffaut, to integrate into a self-conscious style, at once new and a homage to the American gangster film. In this way the energy, the economy and the exigency of the traditional gangster film have re-entered the American cinema via *Breathless*, *Shoot the Pianist* and *Pierrot le fou*.

That the French cinema has influenced *Bonnie and Clyde* is conjecture on my part, though I would be surprised to hear that Penn hasn't been affected by that source. It is of course quite possible that he could have made his own extrapolation, just as Herbert Blau, by taking his cue directly from Beckett rather than through Jan Kott, came up with a *King Lear* at the San Francisco Actors' Workshop that closely resembled Peter Brook's 1962 Stratford production. But this would not change my argument in any essential way. In linking *Pierrot le fou* with *Bonnie and Clyde*, I am not making an aesthetic point alone, any more than in tracing the relationship between crime movies and real-life crime I'm seeking to discredit the cinema. There has been a continuous interplay between the reality of crime and mass media images, which has influenced the nature of crime, the function of law enforcement, the attitudes of the public and their ability and willingness to act. 'Nothing finer in the Hollywood movie colony,' the real-life Capone assured an interviewer visiting his Florida mansion. Set this against the opening of *Bonnie and Clyde*, where on their first meeting Clyde Barrow affects to take the Dallas waitress Bonnie Parker for a film star.

The St Valentine's Day Massacre opens with a printed statement that 'every character and event herein is based on real characters and events', and to a greater extent than any semi-documentary crime film it sticks to the brief. Sometimes reasonable conjecture is passed off as fact, which is acceptable. To preserve the cool distancing tone of the commentary we are informed of what the forthcoming victims are thinking on the morning of the massacre, which is debatable. The only totally unsupported fabrication is the personal dispatch by Capone of Joseph Aiello on a westbound train; Aiello in fact died later and in different circumstances. The aim of this scene presumably is to link Capone to ritual revenge murder, though the same point is made, on the basis of sounder evidence, by depicting Capone's execution of Scalisi and Anselmi.

Another thing that sets *St Valentine's Day* apart from the usual gangster movie is the frank admission of the characters' racial origins and antagonisms. Words like 'wop', 'Mick', 'Kraut' and 'greaseball' (terms once proscribed by the Production Code) are thrown around in a casual way without being countered by the traditional liberal rebukes that had previously sanctioned their use. These derogatory epithets in this context serve to establish the forces at work within the American melting pot and define the unaccommodated immigrant aspirations that brought about organised crime. The overall effect is quite different from the usual implication of alien villainy.

Unlike the heavily fictionalised *Al Capone*, no names are changed or distorted for purposes of exposition. The film is not primarily a psychological study; the biographical facts given as each character first appears are footnotes to show his relationship to a general set-up, and the situation is illuminated by focusing upon the massacre which brought to a climax the rivalry between the Capone and Moran gangs. The film is not concerned with a personal vendetta, though it acknowledges this element in the brilliantly contrived flashbacks, shot as a sort of bloodstained newsreel, re-creating the murders of Dion O'Banion and Hymie Weiss, and the October 1926 assault on the Hawthorne Hotel, Capone's headquarters in the suburb of Cicero. Indeed in its attempt to elucidate a state of affairs and to avoid becoming entangled in personal psychology, the recent movie it calls to mind is Francesco Rosi's *Salvatore Giuliano*, a Marxist study of the Italian mafia. The only American film I have seen to equal it these past few years is a television semi-documentary on the mafia kingpin Alberto Anastasia, broadcast a few months after his murder in 1957. Eli Wallach played Anastasia, and the programme was built around the notion of a TV producer (Don Ameche) using Anastasia's career as a way of explaining the nature of organised crime, and finally concluding that the task is beyond him.

The commentary at the beginning of *St Valentine's Day* makes two crucial points. First it situates the massacre as lying between nostalgia and cataclysm, between the exhilarating time in which Mickey Mouse was created and Lindbergh made his solo flight to Paris, and the Wall Street Crash. Secondly it refers to the gangs doing battle 'just as modern nations and corporations do'. The analogy is scarcely new, but the treatment is less perfunctory than before. The elimination of the North Side gang is treated as a perversion of a business takeover (in American parlance, a 'raid') or a military operation, suggesting a parallel with the Cold War or a possible association of North Side and North Vietnam. When the Capone executive committee meets in the boardroom, the camera tracks round the gathering in a strangely wavering way to inculcate a sense of unease. The totality of the image the film creates suggests that crime is a part of the American system, a product rather than a perversion of it. Far from being rebels, Capone and Moran are at one with this corrupt society, and the former is rightly shown as a typical middle-class moralist. At the end the commentary fights shy of drawing any conclusions. Perhaps the makers feel they have gone far enough and thus resort to a few platitudes about the massacre arousing public indignation and a demand for reform, suggesting that the same kind of indignation is necessary today.

In view of what follows, as a sort of coda, more elaborate comment was maybe uncalled for. After a laconic statement that no one was ever convicted for complicity in the massacre, we see the violent (and obscure) deaths of the actual executioners and hear of the post-war demise of Moran (in Leavenworth penitentiary of lung cancer in 1957) and of Al Capone in 1947 of syphilis. The film fades out on Capone's marble headstone in a Chicago cemetery – 'Alphonse Capone – Rest in Peace'. When Richard Wilson made *Al Capone* eight years ago, it was necessary to stage a vicious beating of his hero by fellow Alcatraz inmates to satisfy the demands of the Code and release the anger of the audience.

Where *St Valentine's Day Massacre* operates through a measured, even tone, *Bonnie and Clyde* functions by a rapid alternation between farce and tragedy. It is a more sophisticated film and is obviously less concerned with the true identities of its protagonists. The characters' backgrounds are filled in by odd suggestions and through a montage of photographs that accompany the credits. These recall the Walker Evans pictures in James Agee's *Let Us Now Praise Famous Men* and speak eloquently of the poor farming families that had shared little of the 1920s prosperity and were among the hardest hit victims of the Depression. It is the essence of Bonnie and Clyde's situation on which Penn and his screenwriters (David Newman and Robert Benton) have seized.

Many scenes in the film are presented with an almost documentary fidelity: the fight at Joplin; the escape from the besieged motor court; the death of 'Buck' Barrow and the capture of Blanche at the Iowa picnic grounds in July 1933; the final ambush in Louisiana in May 1934. There are also several significant changes or omissions. The real Bonnie Parker left her husband in 1933 to take off with Clyde; she had a voracious sexual appetite and for a while was accompanied by a lover. Neither she nor Clyde – it almost goes without saying – was as beautiful as Faye Dunaway and Warren Beatty, and Clyde was possibly homosexual. The character named C.W. Moss is an amalgam of two drivers, William Daniel Jones and Henry Methvin. Jones joined the gang in much the way described but remained reluctantly; at one point he had to be chained up at night. Methvin's father betrayed the pair to the police, and interestingly the fusillade of bullets which eventually felled Bonnie and Clyde sent their car careering down a hill to finish up in a stream. This strange, farcical touch has been dropped in favour of the shuddering bodies beside and within a stationary car, a decision that tells us a good deal about the film's conception. Among other omissions are numerous opportunities for further violence, such as a raid on a Texas gaol party and several cold-blooded killings, including two highway patrolmen.

In a certain sense, then, the film can be said to be created partly in terms of Bonnie and Clyde's idea of themselves, and to project a timeless, drifting existence, shifting between dream and nightmare. Their undirected energy and unconsidered violence form the one vital element in a society that has come to a halt. In the background throughout there is inactivity: the stores are shut or without customers; the farms have been taken by the banks and boarded up; no one is working in the fields; the rolling stock is idle in the goods yards; in the quarry used for the family reunion the machinery is standing still; the banks they rob contain little money or have collapsed. On the walls, peeling posters from Franklin Roosevelt's presidential campaign suggest a fading hope.

For help and understanding, the Barrows can only turn to the dispossessed; the expelled farmer who borrows Clyde's pistol to shoot at the bank notice on his former property; the working-class man who's allowed to keep his money during the hold-up and later says: 'They did all right by me and I'll buy some flowers for their funeral'; the itinerant Okies who give the wounded couple food and drink. They know they are doomed and cannot bear to contemplate it – the sudden mention of death ends the show they are putting on for the temporarily abducted undertaker and his fiancée. They create roles for themselves because they cannot face what they are; they move incessantly and act irresponsibly, because they lack the capacity to weigh the alternatives, until eventually there are none left.

The Barrow gang's fascination with violence is shared by Arthur Penn. He has sought to examine its roots previously in a variety of ways – through Billy the Kid trapped by his own myth in *The Left Handed Gun*, as a Kafkaesque allegory in *Mickey One*, and in the anatomy of a hate-filled Texas town in *The Chase*. All three move towards *Bonnie and Clyde*, where he appears to see violence as a legacy of the frontier spirit, a result of the repressed sexuality of puritanism, an expression of an undercurrent of nihilism arising from a deep-rooted national frustration. But he contains this conjecture within a film that is both the ultimate artistic comment on the Dillinger mentality and a remarkable metaphor for a large segment of contemporary American life. Planted firmly in the 1930s, *Bonnie and Clyde* has much to tell us of the current ghetto explosion and the milieu that produced Lee Harvey Oswald.

Of the film's other considerable merits, particularly its technical ones, enough has already been written. Perhaps some word is needed, however, on the dangers inherent in this type of picture, a subject on which I have touched earlier. It is the fate of many works of art to be misunderstood, and Penn cannot be blamed for making a film so subtle in its morality as to lay itself open to misinterpretation.

In a recent *New Yorker*, some new men's and women's clothes were advertised as 'The Speakeasy Look', and no one would be surprised to see 'The Bonnie Parker Look' on current fashion pages. Business is business. A more disturbing indication of the differing responses the film invites can be observed in the advertising for *Bonnie and Clyde* itself. The poster used in London was a photograph of the gang posing self-consciously beside a car with the carefully worded, rightly admired, text:

> Clyde was the leader. Bonnie wrote poetry. CW was a Myrna Loy fan who had a bluebird tattooed on his chest. Buck told corny jokes and carried a Kodak. Blanche was a preacher's daughter who kept her fingers in her ears during the gunfights. They played checkers and photographed each other incessantly. On Sunday nights they listened to Eddie Cantor on the radio. All in all, they killed 18 people. They were the strangest damned gang you ever heard of.

This certainly suggests the mood of the film. Outside Central London another poster was used. It featured a crude drawing of Bonnie and Clyde blazing away with machine guns and the caption: 'They're young! They're in love! And they kill people! The most exciting gangster film ever made.'

This reminds me of a conversation that was recorded for a radio programme of mine some years ago with a Hollywood screenwriter who specialised in low-budget thrillers and crime stories. One of his scripts had been turned into a peculiarly inflammatory movie, and it was suggested to this liberal, high-minded fellow that the picture had become 'an incitement to violence'. 'Yeah,' he agreed, 'that's the way it turned out. And I wrote it as an incitement *against* violence.'

This piece on the crime movie was written within a couple of weeks of the British release of the films under discussion. It was fascinating to discover later on that Bonnie and Clyde *had been conceived by Robert Benton and David Newman after reading John Toland's* The Dillinger Days, *a favourite book of mine that had appeared four years earlier. Also and more significantly, it was exciting to hear, and have my conjectures confirmed, that the film had been intended as a homage to the French New Wave, and that Benton and Newman had initially approached both Truffaut and Godard with a view to them directing their script. The American screenwriter mentioned in the final paragraph who provided the title for my piece is Daniel Mainwaring (1902–77), who also wrote novels and scripts under the pseudonym Geoffrey Homes. He's probably best known for* Out of the Past *(aka* Build My Gallows High*), which he adapted from his own novel, and for writing Don Siegel's original* Invasion of the Body Snatchers. *The movie he's talking about here is Phil Karlson's* The Phenix City Story *(1955).*

LA: City of Dreadful Joy (1971)

BOOK REVIEW
Banham, Reyner: *Los Angeles: The Architecture of Four Ecologies*
(University of California Press)

Los Angeles has been called 'the Nowhere City', 'the City of
Dreadful Joy', 'Iowa with palms', 'forty suburbs in search of a
metropolis'. The latest biographer of the first United States president from the area compares his subject with previous incumbents
and notes rather significantly: 'Nixon alone has no attractive colour
of place.'

One of the reasons that Los Angeles has drawn such a bad press
is that its sense of seemingly anonymous sprawl overwhelms the
visitor and makes it a difficult place not only to like but to understand. Another equally important reason is that no city has ever
attracted so many disgruntled writers. Lured there by Hollywood to
be simultaneously enriched and degraded, these troubled exiles have
found in the city around them a perfect image for the inimical, anarchic confusion of modern life. If the title of one book stands for
them all, it's Horace McCoy's *I Should Have Stayed Home*.

Yet through this rich literature and from 50 years of movies, we
have a more vivid and extensive notion of Los Angeles than of
almost any other city in the world. In a single week not long ago,
one could have seen the old LA in the background of Chaplin,
Keaton and Lloyd comedies in the TV series *Golden Silents*, the sad
underside of the town in the classic 1940s thriller *Criss Cross*, also
on TV, and in the cinema two striking European views of the
modern city in Antonioni's *Zabriskie Point* and Demy's *The Model
Shop*. Taking just recent British artists, the city looms as large and
symbolical as ever in Gavin Lambert's novels, John Boorman's

'LA: City of Dreadful Joy' first appeared in *The Times*, 8 April 1971.

thriller *Point Blank* and David Hockney's California paintings. All three are obsessed with the surface, the architectural quality of Los Angeles.

Reyner Banham does not repudiate the hostile literature; on the contrary, he commends the atrabilious world of Raymond Chandler and the apocalyptic vision of Nathanael West. But his happy mission is to explain and interpret the city from the point of view of a visiting architectural historian who is 'an Angeleno at heart'. Like a benevolent psychiatrist he attempts to expose our nightmares to the warm daylight air, where under his generous gaze even the smog disperses. His characteristically lively and vivid book with its 123 aptly chosen photographs and maps is a major contribution to making sense of this disturbing city and to aiding our understanding of urban life.

In historical terms he shows us how Los Angeles developed from the old Spanish pueblo of the mid-nineteenth century up to its present 70 square miles: the carving up of the old Spanish ranches; the extension of the city boundaries to acquire water for the arid plains; the influence of oil and of the inviting climate; the real estate dealers; Hollywood; the port, and the electric railroad system that established the basic ground plan.

The four ecologies of his subtitle are the cultural, topographic and psychological determinants of the local architecture and way of life. First, there is the euphoric 'Surfurbia' of the coast: 'the beach is what life is all about in Los Angeles', and maybe only Perth in Australia, he suggests, could match this aspect of LA. Second, there's the ecology of the enchanting foothills, stretching round his third ecology, the nicely named 'Plains of Id', that grisly area where eucalyptuses and John Birchers flourish, that we most often think of as typically LA. Lastly, there is 'Autopia', the world of the freeways where so many Angelenos spend so much of their lives. The freeways, to Dr Banham, are 'a special way of being alive' and 'one of the greater works of Man'.

Those ecologies he relates to the striking variety of the local architecture. This ranges from the Spanish Colonial Revival through the fantastic creations in the form of restaurants, Simon Rodia's Watts Towers, Hollywood backlot overspill and so on, to the work of geniuses like Richard Neutra, Frank Lloyd Wright and Charles Eames. Over a period of 60 years they've made LA one of the greatest and insufficiently recognised centres of domestic architecture in the world.

To Dr Banham, Los Angeles is a challenge to the conventional wisdom of planners, architects and urban theorists, and though essentially unique in a way too rarely recognised, the city demands our attention. Not just for the light it throws on the American dream and as 'the most potent current version of the great bourgeois vision of the good life in a tamed countryside', but because 'if Los Angeles is one of the world's leading cities in architecture, then it is because it is a sympathetic ecology for architectural design, and it behoves the world's architects to find out why'.

There is little danger while reading this book of forgetting that, for all the judicious historical and technical observation, it is in part a polemical work written by a passionate enthusiast for Los Angeles and moreover by an author who is altogether more sanguine than most (than myself, for instance) about the future of urban life. This is greatly in its favour, and to read it is a continually stimulating experience. There is a danger, however, that because Dr Banham touches on so many issues that go far beyond architecture – which is his subject and, I'm convinced, a real key to the city's mysteries – the book might be taken as a comprehensive study of Los Angeles. This it is not, and to accept it and judge it as such would be not only misleading for the reader but unfair to the author.

The year after reviewing Reyner Banham's book I revisited Los Angeles and felt truly at home there for the first time. He helped me understand the city and fully appreciate the films made in and about the town. His monograph is to be read alongside Thom Andersen's wonderful Los Angeles Plays Itself *(2003), a 169-minute documentary on the way Hollywood has represented the city and its environs with clips from some 200 movies over a period of nearly a century. Banham, who sadly died in 1988 at the age of 66, had a deep understanding of popular cinema and would have loved Andersen's film.*

Cops (1974)

If one were to suggest the ideal hero for the biggest American box office hit of 1974, he would be a tough, middle-aged plain-clothes policeman possessed by the devil in a Midwestern city at the height of the 1930s Depression. To have predicted this even four years ago, when anarchic, youth-oriented, anti-establishment movies were all the rage, would have been to invite hoots of derision. Yet three highly successful movies of 1967–68 – *Bonnie and Clyde*, *Rosemary's Baby* and *Bullitt* – foreshadowed this 1970s fascination with nostalgia, the occult and the cops. And this triple fascination is closely related to the crises and anxieties of the 1960s. Much has already been written about the nostalgia boom and the cult of the occult; less has been said about the police business, which is as interesting, though less socially pervasive, a phenomenon.

There have of course always been police in movies: lovable Irish flatfoots on the neighbourhood beat, the Keystone Cops, federal agents, and so on. In the mid-1930s there was a wave of police films, William Keighley's *G-Men* (1935) prominent among them, after Hollywood producers were requested to transfer their attention from mobsters to lawmen, and there was another cycle in the late 1940s. In both cases they came – as the present one has come – after widespread public criticism had been directed at the industry's alleged social irresponsibility and excessive violence.

Unlike most other countries, America has never been reluctant to have the shortcomings of its police revealed in the cinema. There have been plenty of overzealous cops (*Boomerang*, 1947), crooked cops (*The Street With No Name*, 1948), brutal cops (*Where the Sidewalk Ends*, 1950), neurotically unbalanced cops (*Detective Story*, 1951) and paranoid cops (*Touch of Evil*, 1958), and in virtually all private-eye movies the hero gets pushed around by the suspicious

'Cops' first appeared in *Sight & Sound*, Spring 1974.

official fuzz. Until recently, however, the general tendency has been to depict such men as exceptional and undesirable, the 'normal' cop being a hardworking, honest, well-adjusted family man. In *The Naked City* (1948), for example, the detectives (Don Taylor and Barry Fitzgerald) are shown as kindly, scrupulous men, the salt of the earth when compared with the idle rich they investigate; this excessively bland portrait of the cops was the work of screenwriter Albert Maltz and director Jules Dassin, both men of the left who were subsequently blacklisted. This benevolent traditional view has been upheld through the 20-odd years of TV police series, from Jack Webb's pioneering *Dragnet* up to *Ironside* and the exotic *Mod Squad*. But it has changed in the cinema in a rather interesting way.

The two outstanding police pictures of 1966–67 – Arthur Penn's *The Chase* and Norman Jewison's *In the Heat of the Night* – were impeccably liberal movies in which incorruptible lawmen stood up against, and morally above, ignorant, prejudiced, violent communities in, respectively, Texas and the Deep South. The liberal tradition continued, though with a greater degree of physical violence, through three significant pictures of 1968 – Don Siegel's *Madigan*, Gordon Douglas's *The Detective* and Peter Yates's *Bullitt*, all of which were able to take advantage of the new permissiveness in language and the depiction of the urban milieu. Henry Fonda's commissioner in *Madigan*, Frank Sinatra's New York homicide investigator in *The Detective* and Steve McQueen's San Francisco plain-clothes man in *Bullitt*, were sensible, sensitive men doing a difficult job with the minimum of force in a context of political interference and public indifference. What the pictures further shared was a concern for the mystique of police work and law enforcement that was soon to become familiar.

Outside of these police pictures, in the youth and counter-culture movies, the cops were most frequently presented as vicious, racist and corrupt, the iron fist of a repressive society. To take three representative films of 1969: *Medium Cool* shows up the cops as proto-fascists, beating up the young demonstrators at the Democratic National Convention in Chicago the year before; *Alice's Restaurant* presents the policeman as a moderately amiable but uncomprehending buffoon and archetypal square; *Easy Rider* gives us the cop as paranoid redneck and hippie-hater.

Naturally, it was only part of the great American audience that didn't like cops in the late 1960s – principally the dissident young, blacks and the underprivileged. The Middle Americans, 'the silent majority' that Nixon and Agnew named and courted in the 1968 presidential election, loved cops. The more demonstrative among them carried on their cars the bumper slogan 'Support Your Local Police', an apparently reasonable and inoffensive suggestion, but in reality a badge proclaiming the car's owner as a rightwing supporter of 'law-and-order', another coded phrase for restoring peace to the cities at any price. At the end of *Bullitt* we are shown a dishonest, rightwing politician sporting this sticker on his expensive car.

The two great issues of the 1968 election had been peace in Vietnam and law-and-order in the cities. Nixon promised both but by 1970 had delivered neither. Hollywood wouldn't finance pictures about the war, because the issues were too complicated, the subject too divisive and the box-office prospects highly dubious. John Wayne alone had the nerve to press on in the face of much discouragement to make *The Green Berets*. Instead Hollywood turned to World War Two and the Korean War with three big 1970 releases that handled the war theme in such a fashion the doves and hawks could read diametrically opposed messages into them – *Patton, Tora! Tora! Tora!* and *M*A*S*H**. The most significant of these for its calculated ambivalence is Franklin J. Schaffner's *Patton*, a model of how to present a character in such a way that he can be either admired or hated, or simultaneously admired *and* hated, and seen as a necessary evil in his particular situation. The opening scene is especially skilful in exploiting different attitudes to the American flag, to uniforms, to patriotic rhetoric, to obscenity, to the charismatic martial leader, the misunderstood hero, the warrior in a civilised society, the inscrutable loner, the martyr in the democratic cause. The picture proved an enormous success with people of all ages and political opinions. Schaffner's film not only opened up the way for a new style police hero but showed the consciously ambivalent fashion in which he should be presented. Shortly afterwards the cinema jumped off the youth bandwagon and on to the police paddy wagon. The pattern for the movie cop was Patton, and most of the characteristics and contradictions ascribed above to the portrait of the World War Two general are shared by the movies' new men in blue.

In the vanguard in 1971 we had Donald Sutherland, leading male

star of the emerging anti-establishment cinema, playing the
uniformed cop in *Klute*, and – more influentially – Gene Hackman
as the foulmouthed racist Jimmy 'Popeye' Doyle in *The French
Connection* and Clint Eastwood as the omni-competent Inspector
Harry Callahan in *Dirty Harry*. The immediate success of the latter
pair led to the wave of police pictures that swept over us in late 1972
and throughout 1973 and shows little sign of abating. We've had
The New Centurions (shown in Britain as *Precinct 45 – Los Angeles
Police*), *Badge 373*, *Walking Tall*, *The Seven-Ups*, *Magnum Force*,
Electra Glide in Blue, *Serpico*, *The Friends of Eddie Coyle*, with (at the
time of writing) *Cops and Robbers*, *Busting*, John Wayne as *McQ*, and
many more to come.

All of them are indebted to *The French Connection* and *Dirty Harry*,
and several show the direct influence of *Patton*. The latter's pre-
credit sequence, for instance, is deliberately echoed in the opening
of both *Electra Glide in Blue* and *Magnum Force*, where the cops are
introduced to us, as Patton is, through items of equipment and
uniform, on which the camera lingers fetishistically; George C.
Scott's playing of the alienated patrolman in *The New Centurions*
frequently recalls his impersonation of Patton. Another picture
many of them evoke is *Psycho* – or at least a single shot in Hitchcock's movie: the huge close-up of the Arizona patrolman wearing
large sunglasses that the fugitive Janet Leigh sees peering down at
her when she awakes in her car on a country roadside. This peculiarly powerful image suggests something menacing and all-seeing,
and it plays on our latent sense of guilt that cops exploit.

One doesn't wish to deny individuality to all of these films.
Certainly they vary in sophistication from the crude, rabble-rousing
B-feature exposé techniques of Phil Karlson's *Walking Tall* (which
is very nearly a reprise of the same director's *Phenix City Story*, made
almost 20 years ago) to the delicately balanced ironies and visual
elegance of James William Guercio's *Electra Glide in Blue*. The
heroes likewise are strung along a spectrum from the hippie cop
Frank Serpico, who nearly paid with his life for exposing the
corruption of the New York force, to the uncouth 'Popeye' Doyle,
though the majority are encountered towards Doyle's end. Nevertheless, because of their shared themes, plots, characters and
locations (mostly San Francisco and New York), they tend to merge
in the memory to form a single extended picture; and a singularly

bloody and brutal one it is.

Several factors intensify this effect. The same professional advisers, writers, producers and cameramen turn up again and again. Philip D'Antoni, for instance, produced *Bullitt* and *The French Connection* and has now directed *The Seven-Ups*, which naturally includes another of his long drawn out, wildly destructive car chases. These crazy police auto Derbys – whose credibility is usually in inverse ratio to their length and virtuosity – are now considered an essential feature of the genre. Casting also lends an air of uniformity – the same actor (Felton Perry) plays Harry Callahan's black assistant in *Magnum Force* and Sheriff Buford Pusser's Tennessee deputy in *Walking Tall*; Mitchell Ryan appears as a mentally disturbed cop in both *Magnum Force* and *Electra Glide in Blue*, and as an apparently sane Boston detective in *The Friends of Eddie Coyle*; Roy Scheider was the hero's sidekick in *The French Connection* before being elevated to the leadership of the special crime squad called *The Seven-Ups*.

They have moreover evolved very rapidly into a semi-enclosed genre in the sense that the films not only refer to or echo each other, but they look into a mirror as it were and take themselves as their own subject matter. In this they resemble a good deal of recent art and popular culture, both good and bad. Thus the problem of crime, its prevention and cure, has moved to the periphery; equally the business of detection is handled in an increasingly perfunctory fashion, the deliberate obfuscation of the plot often concealing this. What the pictures are about is the situation – ethical, aesthetic and existential – of being a cop.

Now all these police heroes are men with if not a social mission, certainly a vocation. Why they have always wanted to be cops is left a mystery or only vaguely explained; sexual maladjustment is hinted at in several instances, as it is in Elio Petri's leftwing Italian police movie, *Investigation of a Citizen Above Suspicion* (this however might result from having such a job), and so is a sense of personal inferiority. Yet oddly, once they are in the force and therefore alienated from the community around them, they experience a second alienation by being constantly at loggerheads with most of their professional colleagues and superiors. This applies as much to crude tough-guys like Doyle, Callahan and Pusser as it does to the naively dedicated John Wintergreen (Robert Blake) of *Electra Glide* and the equally idealistic, equally short Frank Serpico (Al Pacino).

Much time is devoted to talking about what it means to be a police officer, and much energy is expended upon internecine strife, the opponents being according to the circumstances either corrupt, rightwing bigots or lily-livered liberals who insist upon respect for the law, civil rights and such expendable niceties. Indeed these cops despise the fickle public and most of their fellow police officers almost as much as, in some cases more than, the criminals they pursue in the time they have left over from station-house bickering. The comedy of this situation is occasionally perceived, though the paranoia it reveals is scarcely recognised, except in two splendidly humorous moments in *Electra Glide*. The first is when a sergeant prepares a squad of cops for duty at a pop concert by hurling anti-police obscenities at them. (A parallel sequence in *Medium Cool* showed a group of plain-clothes men in a police riot control exercise playing their role as provocative insulting hippies with a little too much enthusiasm.) The other scene is when a deranged detective, in the course of a characteristically self-pitying speech about crime and the high police mortality rate, claims that 'this country is undergoing a carefully formulated policy of police genocide'.

The clearest example of this generic introspection is *Magnum Force*, a poor film admittedly but too easily dismissed as an unworthy, opportunistic sequel to Don Siegel's highly accomplished *Dirty Harry*. *Magnum Force* is not a further adventure for Eastwood's Inspector Callahan but – in John Milius's cunning screenplay – a picture about *Dirty Harry*. Many critics called Callahan a fascist and considered Siegel's picture a reprehensible law-and-order tract that played upon every Middle American prejudice about the young, the Supreme Court, the state of the cities, permissiveness and so forth. *Magnum Force* sets out to challenge this view by making Callahan's opponents not civilian offenders but a team of fanatical young patrolmen. With the approval of a long-service captain, they've banded together to form a secret squad whose mission it is to eliminate criminals (sadistic pimps, labour racketeers, etc.) the law cannot touch.

Such bodies have existed and do exist in fact – the film knowingly refers to the Brazilian police's unofficial 'death squads' and to the citizens' vigilante committees formed in nineteenth-century San Francisco. Groups like these flourish even more in fiction and appeal strongly to the impotent and frustrated on whose fantasies they feed. We saw them in the fiction of Sapper and Edgar Wallace after the Great War, in such post-World War Two entertainments as the British film and play *Noose* (a group of ex-commandos cleaning up Soho), and we're experiencing a revival of them now in the wake of the Vietnam War. *The Seven-Ups* is about an officially approved special squad operating on the very edge of the law. Numerous movies with black heroes – *Slaughter* and *Gordon's War* for example – feature Vietnam veterans using their military training for purposes of rough justice and vengeance back home, there being no thought of calling on the cops to do the job.

Not surprisingly, the blonde, blue-eyed, immaculately turned out leader of the self-appointed executioners in *Magnum Force* has served in Vietnam. He and his friends, the film is saying, are the real fascists, not Harry, who in tracking them down with his customary brutal efficiency establishes himself as the very bulwark of democracy. That the case is crudely and dishonestly put does not take away from the fact that the film's producers found it worthwhile to pursue this political point rather than to pursue ordinary criminals. One scene in the film stands out from the rest for its clarity and wit – a police shooting contest in which hotshot Callahan is outgunned by the secret squad's young leader. Negotiating a surprise target range, Harry loses points by opening fire on a plywood policeman that suddenly appears before him. The spectators gasp with horror and the umpire admonishes him with the words, 'You shot the good guy, Harry.'

Most of these films acknowledge the assistance of the police, are written by cops (Joseph Wambaugh, author of *The New Centurions*, recently returned to duty with the Los Angeles police after becoming bored with the literary life), or are based on the experiences of policemen. (The exploits and personality of the unorthodox Eddie Egan, for instance, inspired both *The French Connection* and *Badge 373*, and he himself has turned to acting, playing both cops and crooks.) Other films purport to follow non-fiction works with some degree of fidelity, as *Serpico* does. Yet for all the claims in the opening and closing titles, for all the apparently unvarnished and unwhitewashed language and deportment, for all the grimy locations and semi-documentary style camerawork, these pictures only intermittently have the feel of reality. They just do not stand up to comparison with such books as John Hershey's *The Algiers Motel Incident* and Morton Hunt's *The Mugging*, which attempt to examine criminal cases and the relationship between the law enforcement agencies and the public in all their many-layered complexity. Indeed the films are ultimately most interesting as exercises in myth making. They're at their best – and not merely as entertainment – when most consciously working as fables.

I have little doubt that these current variations on older figures, myths and attitudes are due quite as much to the disappointments, frustrations and conflicts caused by the Vietnam fiasco – an unwinnable war that betrayed its supporters and rejected its heroes – as they are to the problems of present-day urban life. In the light of this contention it will be interesting to see how the genre develops over the next year or so, and in what direction. The effect of the Watergate affair is cardinal here and could explain the immense and immediate popular response to Sidney Lumet's *Serpico*, which can easily be viewed as a leftwing reformist fable advocating a wholesale cleansing of the system. *The Seven-Ups*, however, is also drawing big crowds and its heroes' behaviour is not greatly different from that of the White House plumbers. So far one minor masterpiece (*Dirty Harry*) and a couple of highly diverting entertainments have emerged from what *could* prove to be less a valuable genre than a repetitive cycle, in which gimmickry is substituted for innovation, thudding overemphasis for depth, pastiche for style.

The cop, we now know, was to continue as a dominant figure in the cinema and on TV and shows no sign of losing his popularity. Clint Eastwood, still thought of as a western star in 1974, was to appear in only three further westerns over the next 36 years, while making numerous cop pictures, including three further episodes in the career of Inspector Harry Callahan. Even John Wayne turned to urban law enforcement as the eponymous cop in McQ *and* Brannigan *before bowing out as an elderly gunslinger in* Rooster Cogburn *and* The Shootist.

Modest Mogul of Ealing:
On Michael Balcon (1969)

BOOK REVIEW
Balcon, Michael: *Michael Balcon Presents ... A Lifetime of Films*
(Hutchinson)

Sir Michael Balcon's short, discreet memoir is an account of a long, happy life and one of the most important single careers in the British film industry. In it he comes over as the generous, fair-minded, commonsensical person that he is, with a dry humour and a shrewd ability to judge character, even if he's not always able to convey the idiosyncracy of his colleagues and employees on the page.

Born into a respectable but impoverished Jewish family in Birmingham in 1896, the year that films switched from peep-holes to the screen, he entered the business as a distributor in the latter part of the Great War after first serving an apprenticeship as a diamond salesman. Aspects of this background are similar to those of the traditional Hollywood movie moguls, though the courteous Sir Michael has little else in common with them. Indeed the only scathing portrait in the book is of the egregious MGM boss Louis B. Mayer, with whom he served an unhappy year in 1937. He never wanted to work outside Britain and, unlike the majority of film people, has retained his native identity and paid his local taxes. As a result a lifetime of films has left him reasonably well-off but not rich.

He started out as a producer in London in the early 1920s, and in the 1930s was head of his own Gainsborough studio in Islington and Gaumont-British productions at Shepherds Bush, where the executive floor was known as the 'Polish Corridor', because 'the Balcons were at the end'. His chief source of pride in this period

---

'Modest Mogul of Ealing' first appeared in the *Observer*, 30 March 1969.

derives from having sponsored Robert Flaherty's *Man of Aran* and given many tyros their first chance, most notably Alfred Hitchcock, whose first film he produced and whose major phase he inaugurated by backing *The Man Who Knew Too Much* in 1934.

The book has two key themes basic to the function of the business. Posed as questions, they are: Why did it take so long for British pictures adequately to reflect our national life and problems? How can a stable native industry be established and maintained?

The central, most rewarding part of Michael Balcon's story concerns his short-lived answer to these questions. When he came to Ealing Studios in 1938, he joined an organisation devoted principally to exploiting the talents of music-hall comedians. Given the sense of national purpose and temporary unity generated by the war, he helped fashion a collaborative style that produced such wartime movies as *The Foreman Went to France* and *San Demetrio, London*, led on to the post-war successes *The Overlanders* and *Dead of Night*, and culminated in the string of classic Ealing comedies and social dramas of the late 1940s and early 1950s. For the first and so far the last time, a British studio achieved a viable style, a shared point of view that still enabled individual artists to realise their personal visions.

As an independent element within the Rank Organisation, Ealing came to an end in 1955. Michael Balcon then entered once more into an unsatisfactory relationship with MGM before starting the ambitious Bryanston group of British producers with which the Osborne-Richardson company, Woodfall, was associated. Finally he headed the celebrated bid to restore British Lion as a significant force in British production. When it became evident that fellow directors were not apparently prepared to help execute his modest plans, he retired.

Balcon's career is exemplary both in the consistent integrity with which he conducted his affairs and the fact that future producers must learn from his mistakes. With the domination of American finance and the continuing two-circuit control of distribution, the industry, for all its seeming affluence, is in as bad a state as ever. For this reason, Michael Balcon regards his life's work as having ended in failure, but he deserves a special place of honour in that important history of the British cinema that still remains to be written.

Some months after this review appeared my first book on the cinema, The Movie Moguls, *was published. I was at the time a member of the British Film Institute's Production Board for experimental film making, chaired by Sir Michael Balcon. He'd liked the book and when I suggested that I was thinking of writing a history of Ealing Studios after completing a study of the western that I was currently engaged on, he greeted the idea with enthusiasm and offered to make his personal papers available to me. However, when* Westerns: Aspects of a Movie Genre, *finally came out at the beginning of 1974, I was still committed to a full-time job at the BBC, and I reluctantly withdrew from the project. As it happens Charles Barr was engaged on an unauthorised book on Ealing, which as the following review indicates, was both different from and better than anything I would have written.*

Clean Fun, Please, We're British
On Ealing Studios (1977)

BOOK REVIEW
Barr, Charles: *Ealing Studios* (Cameron & Tayleur)

Ealing Studios opened in the early 1930s. On its wall it carried the slogan 'The Studio with the Team Spirit', though these words did not take on real meaning until the arrival of Sir Michael Balcon as head of production in 1938, and then not immediately. Four factors, Mr Barr believes, went into forging the corporate identity: the little studio itself (with a minor pre-war tradition of cheap vehicles for music-hall stars such as Will Hay, Gracie Fields and George Formby) facing a village green in a peaceful West London suburb; the 1930s documentary movement, several of whose leading figures (notably Cavalcanti and Harry Watt) were recruited to the Ealing team; the gradual emergence of the notion of a 'people's war' around 1942–43; and the forceful personality of Balcon himself, a mixture of father, uncle, ship's captain, chairman, headmaster and rabbi. Balcon was a man with a mission: to make modestly budgeted entertainment movies of high quality and social purpose. In a memorandum shortly after the outbreak of war he wrote that 'films in wartime are as much a part of the national defence as guns or anything else', and what he had in mind was nearer to the ethos of Army Bureau of Current Affairs than to propaganda.

In 1945 he rethought this policy for peacetime, expressing his vision for the British cinema thus:

> Every shade of opinion should be represented, and the scope of
> the films should go far beyond the purview of the government

---

'Clean Fun, Please, We're British' first appeared in the *Times Literary Supplement*, 22 April 1977.

documentary. Fiction films which portray contemporary life in Britain in different sections of our society, films with an outdoor background of the British scene, screen adaptations of our literary classics, films reflecting the post-war aspirations, not of governments or parties, but of individuals – these are the films that America, Russia and the Continent of Europe should be seeing now and at the first opportunity.

When in 1955 the studio was sold to BBC Television (the company carried on for a further couple of years in a corner at Borehamwood), Balcon devised these characteristic words for a plaque: 'Here during a quarter of a century were made many films projecting Britain and the British character.'

Mr Barr has left to future historians the tasks of examining Balcon's career and complex motivation and the detailed historical development of the studio (Lindsay Anderson's *Making a Film* usefully describes the day-to-day production methods of an Ealing picture), and to other critics the much needed studies of the work of Ealing's two directors of international stature, Robert Hamer and Alexander Mackendrick. What he is concerned with are the progress of the pictures and how the studio, which was so conscious of itself as a microcosm of Britain at its best, reflected the mood of the country in the 1940s and 1950s. Early on he refers to a long forgotten Ealing movie, *Cage of Gold* (1950), in which a young doctor is torn between a lucrative private partnership in Harley Street and a career offering different rewards with his GP father under the National Health. Harley Street is represented by a certain Dr Saville, the NHS by one Dr Mackendrick – a meaningful private joke referring to the fact that Victor Saville deserted Balcon for the bright lights of Hollywood in the 1930s and Alex Mackendrick was the studio's most talented post-war recruit. Only at Ealing could such a joke have been made and a political and professional choice of this kind have its consciously felt counterpart in the movie industry.

Barr sees the first complete expression of the Ealing spirit in *San Demetrio, London* (1943), where the crippled merchant ship limping home becomes an image of Britain and of the people actually making the movie. Ealing became dedicated to the idea of national unity, to the notion of a group drawing cohesively together, ready to absorb those prepared to live by its rules and to reject those who threaten its stability. Through the war years and the period of post-war austerity, this vision made sense and had its final flowering in *The Blue Lamp* (1950), which Barr interprets as a sort of dream of a whole community united – police, underworld and public – in pursuit of an outcast.

Barr speaks of two phrases that haunted him when thinking of the orthodox stream of Ealing films, Ernest Bevin's reference to the British public's 'poverty of desire' and E.M. Forster's description of people who are 'afraid to feel'. The first of the trio of 1949 classic comedies, *Passport to Pimlico*, essentially the work of the legendary Ealing screenwriter T.E.B. Clarke, is the typical, orthodox Ealing picture. Barr contrasts it with the superficially similar work of the directors who made the other great Ealing comedies of that year, Hamer (*Kind Hearts and Coronets*) and Mackendrick (*Whisky Galore*). Their pictures, he argues, contain a critique of Ealing values, bringing into question the cult of simple decency, sexual repression, the ethos of self-denial, the value of social stability, though scarcely in a flagrant or rebarbative fashion. They are Ealing directors all right, but they are temperamentally closer to certain filmmakers of that time (Ustinov, for example, or Powell and Pressburger) who were far removed from Dr Balcon's academy for middle-class English gentlemen.

After 1951, the Festival of Britain year in which, to use Michael Frayn's celebrated terminology, the do-gooding herbivores gave way to the hardheaded carnivores, Ealing entered a period of deca-dence. To Barr, *The Titfield Thunderbolt* (1953) and *Barnacle Bill* (1957) are whimsical betrayals of the Ealing spirit, proposing false communities and reeking of bogus nostalgia. They reflected perhaps the somnolent spirit of the times, but in failing to recognise the increasing complexities of the 1950s and the value of conflict in an open society they indicated that the studio would have no part to play in the new British cinema that was to emerge after 1959. Barr sees Mackendrick's *Man in the White Suit* (1951) as the turning point, the 'definitive Ealing film', one that deals directly with the stagnant society that both Britain and Ealing were becoming. More ingen-iously, not to say fancifully, he treats the same director's last Ealing comedy, *The Ladykillers* (1955), as a symbolic account of post-war Britain in which the criminals stand for the 1945 Labour government and the old lady for the Tories repossessing the nation.

In its brief compass, this judicious, intelligently illustrated book, the first serious study of the one unquestionably important studio in Britain, covers a lot of ground and fully supports the case for approaching films as 'an inner history of our times'. Yet Mr Barr is scrupulous in his attention to what actually happens on the screen, to nuances of camera movement and to the art of comedy of which he writes as delicately here as he did in his admirable book on Laurel and Hardy.

Contrary to what I wrote in that last paragraph, two other British studios have claims to be mentioned alongside Ealing as equally significant contributors to our national cinema: Gainsborough and Hammer, both of which have received much serious critical attention from film scholars over the past 30 years.

Gainsborough entered its prime in World War Two. Its romantic melodramas, often with period settings, frequently relating a repressive present to a turbulent past, were openly emotional and reflected the blackout era of illicit, liberating wartime sex. After an uncertain post-war start, Hammer, home of British horror, took up the gothic torch that had blazed at Universal in the 1930s in the hands of expatriates like James Whale, Colin Clive and Boris Karloff. The understated, stiff-upper-lip stoicism and complex ironies of Ealing were not for Gainsborough and Hammer. Of course, their unbuttoned, transgressive sexuality, while popular with the general public, didn't appeal to, indeed often offended, the fastidious tastes of the leading critics of that period, those who helped create the reputation of Ealing. Today, no history of British cinema in the twentieth century, as art or industry, can fail to relate all three to each other. Yet this does not necessarily mean that Ealing's achievement isn't the most enduring of the three.

Film Choice: *The Lady Vanishes* (1980)

To launch this occasional series in which writers make a personal assessment of their favourite film, Philip French, the Observer's *film critic, looks at a Hitchcock classic.*

Now let's talk about *The Lady Vanishes*. They show it very often in Paris; sometimes I see it twice in one week. Since I know it by heart, I tell myself each time that I'm going to ignore the plot, to examine the train and see if it's really moving, or to look at the transparencies, or to study the camera movements inside the compartments. But each time I become so absorbed with the story that I've yet to figure out the mechanics of that film.

(François Truffaut, Le Cinéma selon Hitchcock, 1966)

If Frank Launder and Sidney Gilliat's adaptation of the Ethel Lina White thriller *The Wheel Spins* had been made in 1936, it would probably have been an amiable little thriller called *Lost Lady*, as long forgotten as its American director, the B-feature specialist Roy William Neill. But the second unit director broke a leg while shooting background material in Yugoslavia, and then the Yugoslav authorities deported the film crew after discovering in the script a satirical opening sequence that cut from goose-stepping Nazi storm troopers to waddling geese. The film was thus postponed, and Neill returned to America. That postponement now looks like an act of divine intervention, for it brought about a miraculous combination of actors, writers and director at the critical moment to produce in *The Lady Vanishes* the most perfectly judged comedy-thriller ever made, a film that illuminates its times yet comes up dazzlingly fresh every time one sees it.

The following year, Launder and Gilliat's screenplay was offered to Alfred Hitchcock who was looking for something suitable to

---

complete a contractual obligation before he headed for Hollywood. Hitch was enthusiastic about the project, the budget was increased, and Launder and Gilliat set about tightening the script. The story remained much the same. A wilful young heiress called Iris, travelling home from a holiday in the Balkans, meets a charming old nanny on a train. The woman thereupon disappears. The foreigners in Iris's compartment deny all knowledge of her existence, as do a pair of cricket-obsessed English businessmen travelling together and an adulterous middle-class English couple who don't want to get involved. Iris seeks the assistance of a debonair British folk song collector, Gilbert, and together they discover that the old lady (who is in fact a British agent) has been kidnapped and is going to be removed from the train at the border disguised as the heavily bandaged patient of the suave Dr Hartz, a servant of the authoritarian regime.

Launder and Gilliat's structural alterations were quite small, but as they worked over their original version, they became increasingly interested in the two insular cricket enthusiasts, Charters and Caldicott, who think nothing is more important than getting home to the Test match at Old Trafford, where England has her back to the wall. So their roles were greatly extended, until they became, as played by Basil Radford and Naunton Wayne, not merely the most remarkable comedy duo our cinema has produced but archetypes of British life, whose manner and diction had a considerable influence on the young Harold Pinter.

They were the first magical ingredient that brought a good script to life. Another was the casting of Michael Redgrave in his first major screen role as the freewheeling Gilbert, playing opposite Margaret Lockwood, an established minor star, as Iris. They are the only British team of that time or since to compare favourably with the sophisticated Hollywood couples of the 1930s like Myrna Loy and William Powell, Cary Grant and Katharine Hepburn, Carole Lombard and Clark Gable. And they were supported by peerless performances from Dame May Whitty, Cecil Parker and Linden Travers (the future Miss Blandish), Catherine Lacey and Paul Lukas.

The next ingredient was Hitchcock, making as his intended farewell to the British scene a classic example of the genre he had pioneered and a sharp judgment upon national character. Never before had the Master achieved such an exquisite balance between comedy and suspense. He was to do so only once more, 20 years later, in *North by Northwest*. When *The Lady Vanishes* opened in the autumn of 1938, it was the first time Hitch had seen his name in lights above the film's title, and he drove round Leicester Square relishing the spectacle.

The final contribution was that of the times themselves. The picture was in production during the spring and summer of 1938 during the run-up to the capitulation at Munich in September, and the international tension gave an additional edge to the whole enterprise.

Here we have a ship of British fools, a carriage load of middle-class types adrift in a hostile Europe on the brink of war: a politically naive hero dedicated to noting down folk songs, a rich heroine returning home to marry a penniless aristocratic drip for his title, a pompous lawyer who'll do anything to avoid the scandal that might keep him off the High Court bench, two childlike cricket fans. The only person carrying the torch for Britain (and carrying the essential Hitchcockian 'McGuffin' in the form of a state secret encoded in a piece of music) is a little old lady. And the party is saved at the end by the heroic self-sacrifice of the only lower-class English person present, the woman disguised as a nun who's caught up with the foreign schemers.

The picture has interesting parallels with *La Règle du jeu*, Jean Renoir's savage portrait of the French upper-middle class on the point of collapse, which was being made across the Channel at much the same time. Both films were prophetic, for two years later the French were to collapse utterly, and the British were to pull themselves together at the last minute. Of the film's English passengers only the blustering lawyer perishes: he deserts the besieged train on its branch line clutching a white flag and is instantly shot down by the enemy.

The Lady Vanishes, which I saw in my sixth year, is inextricably bound up with my memories of the decade that shaped me and which still exerts a powerful spell. When I first saw the film in Leicester, the world of Test cricket that Charters and Caldicott speak of was represented by the 1938 series of cigarette cards depicting the great cricketers of the day, several of whom (Hedley Verity and Ken Farnes among them) were to die in the war. I was being prepared for the dangers the film pointed to by another series of cigarette cards on Air Raid Precautions, and we'd just been issued with gas masks at school.

Of all the artists and writers who influenced my view of the decade (Greene, Auden, Orwell et al.), the only one I actually encountered during the 1930s was Hitchcock, which is hardly surprising as I entered the 1940s pretty well illiterate. Images and subversive ideas from *The Thirty-Nine Steps*, *The Lady Vanishes* and *Jamaica Inn* figure among my earliest childhood memories. In all of them casual incidents of everyday life are charged with menace, and in each case an apparently benevolent, paternal representative of the upper-middle classes (the quietly spoken Tory politician in *Thirty-Nine Steps*, the kindly middle-European surgeon in *The Lady Vanishes*, the ebullient Cornish squire in *Jamaica Inn*) turns out to be a duplicitous villain.

Hitchcock always recalled the time when, for some trivial offence, his father sent the five-year-old Alfred to the local police station. There, for a few minutes that seemed like hours, he was locked in a cell by the desk sergeant and then released with the admonition, 'This is what we do to naughty boys.' It left him with paranoid feelings about cops and authority that lasted a lifetime. Seeing his *Lady Vanishes* always brings back one of the most traumatic incidents of my childhood. The year before I first saw the film I was travelling by rail from Leicester to Liverpool with my father to attend my grandmother's funeral. At Crewe station he got off to buy cigarettes, and the train started up without him. I screamed and shouted, demanding that the communications cord be pulled. The adults in the open compartment either ignored me or made sympathetic clucking sounds. So I knew how Margaret Lockwood felt in *The Lady Vanishes*. Of course my father had got on the train further down and made his way along the corridor back to me. But family trust, railway stations, trains and travel were never to be quite the same again.

At a lunch party arranged by the British Film Institute for a Hitchcock season at the National Film Theatre, the Master's daughter, Patricia Hitchcock, recalled her first visit to a film set as a child. He was directing The Lady Vanishes *at the small, now defunct Gainsborough Studio in Islington and she remembered the great fun her father was having with Basil Radford and*

Naunton Wayne. She owns a present they gave him at the wrap party – a cocktail shaker inscribed with the dedication, 'To Hitch from Charters and Caldicott'. What an item to have on your drinks table.

Doris Day: The Girl Next Door (1980)

It is an interesting and to me pleasing sign of the times that BBC2 should be running a modest Doris Day season, and that tomorrow the National Film Theatre launches a month-long retrospective of her films under the slightly chilling aegis of the British Film Institute's feminist wing.

Since I first heard her husky, beautifully phrased versions of 'It's Magic' and 'Put 'Em In a Box' on *Family Favourites* more than 30 years ago, I have loved the voice, the presence and indeed the very idea of Doris Day. I've seen all but a couple of her 39 movies, some several times and under conditions ranging from an open-air Army cinema in the Egyptian desert (*By the Light of the Silvery Moon*) to New York's Radio City Music Hall (*The Pajama Game*, the first movie I saw on American soil).

In those days every Hollywood studio had its resident 'girl next door', and she told you a lot about the studio's style and its boss's taste. There was the prissily prim Jeanne Crain at Fox, the pertly petulant June Allyson at MGM, the vacuously cheerful Mona Freeman at Paramount, and at Warner Brothers, the home of Cagney and Bogart, there was the tantalising tomboy Doris Day. They all contained within them a steely seed, which is what the young Brazilian revolutionary in Christopher Hampton's play *Savages* had in mind when he defined capitalism as 'the process whereby American girls turn into American women'.

I liked them all, but Day especially, and precisely for the variety of her talents and those apparent contradictions that the young feminists Jane Clark, Diana Simmonds and Mandy Merck believe they are delineating for the first time in a stimulating, well-documented BFI dossier which accompanies their NFT season and bears the same Leavisian title, 'Move Over Misconceptions: Doris Day Reap-

'Doris Day: The Girl Next Door' first appeared in the *Observer*, 30 November 1980.

praised'. It might well have appeared on an article in *Scrutiny* had that solemn journal relaxed just a little.

That Day's gifts as singer, comedienne and actress have rarely received their due is undeniable. Though she mostly worked with journeymen and made only two films with directors of the first rank (Hitchcock's underrated *The Man Who Knew Too Much* and Stanley Donen's bracing *Pajama Game*), the range of her films is considerable. As Clark, Simmonds and Merck point out, she was a tough cookie, as often playing an independent bachelor girl, entrepreneurial type or professional woman as a submissive ex-urban mum or professional virgin, and often combined these two sides.

Some of her films were sharp stuff – *Love Me Or Leave Me*, the biopic of Ruth Etting in which she starred with James Cagney for example, or the 1951 melodrama *Storm Warning*, where she plays a vicious Ku Klux Klansman's shabby wife, whose smart city sister (Ginger Rogers) comes to stay. The organisers of the season don't appear to have noticed that this movie (scripted by the liberal novelists Richard Brooks and Daniel Fuchs) is actually *Streetcar Named Desire* turned into an anti-Southland Warner Brothers social conscience movie.

One might glibly characterise Day as the Jean Arthur of Truman's Fair Deal or the Greer Garson of the Eisenhower years. But the times she lived in were not so simple, complacent or hypocritical as Clark, Simmonds and Merck believe, and she was in her life and work, as they rightly insist, not simple, complacent or hypocritical. It is interesting that after the string of sex comedies with which she ended her film career, her last act before retirement from films was to refuse the role of Mrs Robinson in *The Graduate* as exploitative and naive.

Like many battles to raise or restore reputations, the one fought by successive generations of Day admirers has constantly to be re-engaged in, as old clichés and canards about the Divine Doris are revived and accepted as the received wisdom. This little piece of 30 years ago is not the only occasion on which I've found it necessary to ride to her defence.

A French Love Affair
On Henri Langlois (1983)

BOOK REVIEW
Roud, Richard: *A Passion for Films: Henri Langlois and the Ciné-mathèque française* (The Johns Hopkins University Press)

The word 'cinémathèque', meaning simply 'film library', was coined in 1921 by the French critic Léon Moussinac, but it was to become forever identified with Henri Langlois, who helped found the Cinémathèque française in 1935 at the age of 21. For the next 42 years until his death in 1977, he was its secretary general and did more than any other individual or group for the idea of preserving film and creating a tradition of cinema through constantly keeping the movies of the past on show.

Although his special love was for French and American cinema, he welcomed films from everywhere as well as anything to do with pictures. Along with the cans of films he accumulated (which were initially stored in an old folks' home, the indigent pioneer moviemaker George Méliès entrusted with the key), Langlois amassed the astonishing collection of movie memorabilia, ranging from the original Expressionist set for *Dr Caligari* to Vivien Leigh's dress in *Gone With the Wind*, that since 1972 has been on display in the Musée du Cinéma at the Palais de Chaillot.

His 'passion for films' brought him the trust and devotion of moviemakers throughout the world; his screenings at the Ciné-mathèque created that post-war generation of Paris cinéastes from which emerged the key figures of the New Wave. When in February 1968 the Minister of Culture, André Malraux, cavalierly replaced him with more amenable administrators, his loyal

---

'A French Love Affair' first appeared in the *Observer*, 9 October 1983.

supporters rallied with boycotts of the new regime, protest marches and a shower of angry cables as deadly as a barrage of arrows from a regiment of archers. He was reinstated. The *affaire Langlois* revealed the dangerously overweening side of Gaullism, but also that De Gaulle could be confronted and beaten. As François Truffaut observes in his attractive foreword to Richard Roud's biography, 'the demonstrations for Langlois were to the events of May '68 what the trailer is to the feature film coming soon'.

As organiser of both the New York and London film festivals and programme planner at our National Film Theatre, the American critic Richard Roud knew Langlois well. His book is an important contribution to film history and an instructive study in the relationship between bureaucracy and the arts. But above all it is an affectionate portrait, at once comic and moving, of an eccentric genius, whose off-hand, paranoid behaviour estranged many people, played into the hands of detractors and was often the despair of his dedicated admirers.

Nothing about him was ordinary, starting with his birth in Smyrna at the outbreak of the Great War, and his family's flight from the Turks on a French battleship in 1922. He even lost his virginity at 25 to Jean Renoir's ex-wife, the film actress Catherine Hessling. The first brick in the edifice of his legend, however, is the story that he deliberately failed his *baccalauréat* examination (getting a zero in literature by comparing Molière to Chaplin) to avoid studying law. A shadier corner of his career during the Occupation was his allegedly close association with a Nazi officer (the former German movie archivist Frank Hensel) in the interest of preserving film.

In shape and personality he was an outsize figure, His rolling eyes, vast bulk and wild, imperious manner reminded Truffaut of the crazy Belfast painter impersonated by Robert Newton in *Odd Man Out*. And like Newton's Lukey he inhabited a personal world of creative chaos. According to Roud, Langlois consulted the astrology column of *France-Soir* diligently, regularly visited fortune-tellers, rarely answered letters, and never had a bank account or cheque book. When towards the end of his life he taught a film course at Nanterre, he thought it illogical to pay tax on an income that came from the government and so got into hopeless arrears. At the time of his death, a sick, overworked man, he was sitting all night planning ingenious film programmes for Paris and New York by candlelight, because the electricity (and the phone) had been cut off from his flat.

The debt filmmakers and moviegoers alike owe Langlois was expressed by Jack Valenti in presenting him with a special Oscar in 1974. 'The conscience of the cinema', Valenti called him. For the occasion Langlois wore a special midnight-blue dinner jacket run up as a gift by Pierre Cardin. Characteristically he not only refused to visit Cardin's salon for a fitting, but when a Cardin assistant arrived to take measurements, Langlois wouldn't even stand up.

Re-reading this Langlois review 27 years after it was written, the objects in the Cinémathèque collection that now come first to my mind are Norman Bates's mother's skull, wig and dressing gown from Psycho. *One imagines that, had Universal been willing to let it go, Langlois would have happily dismantled the Bates family house and found the money to ship it to Paris. I'm also reminded that my somewhat critical but by no means entirely unfavourable review of a two-volume* Encylopaedia of the Cinema *that my friend and colleague Richard Roud had both edited and contributed to, led to a furious denunciation and a refusal to speak to me or even acknowledge my presence for nearly three years. This piece on his Langlois book renewed our relationship. Sadly, however, while the hostility was replaced by a reserved civility, Richard remained somewhat frosty on the occasions we met, up to his untimely death in 1989 at the age of 59.*

Alfred Hitchcock: The Filmmaker as Englishman and Exile (1985)

In the history of the cinema there have been only two directors whom popular audiences throughout the world recognise by sight. Great Britain has produced only two directors universally acknowledged as geniuses. They happen to be the same pair – Charlie Chaplin and Alfred Hitchcock. Both came from working-class London backgrounds that they were later to romanticise and lie, or at least deceive, about, and they were shaped by the ethos of the Edwardian world. Both were drawn to America, where they found their fortunes, yet each in his different way remained extremely English.

Strictly speaking, America is not the subject of any movie Chaplin ever made there, only the setting. His last Hollywood picture, *Limelight*, is set in Edwardian England, and he was still a British citizen when he finally left the United States. His first film after returning to Europe was very specifically set in America – the vituperative, sentimental satire, *A King in New York* (1957). His voice never had the slightest hint of an American accent, though he'd long since shed any trace of cockney before he made his first recorded speech. Hollywood supplied the conditions for the fulfilment of Chaplin's art, but the English music hall was what shaped it. The two are inextricable, and one cannot conceive what his career would have been like had he not gone to America.

Chaplin's life was in and of show business. Hitchcock came from a family with no theatrical connections: Catholic, working class and, as his most recent biographer, Donald Spoto, has revealed, more humble and ordinary than Hitch made out. They were not old

'Alfred Hitchcock: The Filmmaker as Englishman and Exile' first appeared in *Sight & Sound*, Spring 1985. This piece was originally delivered in a somewhat different form as a lecture to the American Studies Seminar at Edinburgh University.

English Catholics fallen on hard times, but Irish Catholics of fairly recent immigration. His paternal grandmother was illiterate, his maternal grandfather a police sergeant. The Catholicism and the cop put him in a special, somewhat excluded, section of the metropolitan working class. So he carried a double social strain as he made his way in the world.

As a child Hitchcock was a great theatregoer, quite a reader and a movie fan. But he had no obvious creative gifts or burning desire to express himself that marked him out for an artistic career. A technical apprenticeship enabled him to escape the family's modest greengrocery business, and he was 22 when in 1921 he offered his services as a part-time title designer to the London studio of Famous Players-Lasky. By the time of *The Lodger* (1926) he was established in our rickety native industry, and while in retrospect we can see a clear line in his work that marked him out as a director of thrillers, his oeuvre as it was building remained problematic. Only from *The Man Who Knew Too Much* in 1934 was he 'The Master of Suspense' (a term he probably coined himself), after which he produced only a single picture (the curious sport *Mr and Mrs Smith*, in 1941) that cannot be subsumed under the suspense-thriller genre.

In 1938 Hitchcock was the most admired director in Britain. Proud but insecure, he is said to have driven around Leicester Square again and again to see his name in the neon lights advertising *The Lady Vanishes*. Yet he'd never directed a big-budget movie, he hadn't worked with major stars, most of his pictures lasted under 90 minutes, and none lasted over a hundred. From America offers beckoned, and in 1939 he eventually left under contract to David O. Selznick, who thought of him as a director of European subjects. His first Hollywood picture, *Rebecca*, was set in Europe with an almost entirely British cast, and it was three years before he made a thriller with an American setting. From the start he was a success, and he and his wife and collaborator, Alma Reville, remained in America for the rest of their lives.

While Chaplin was politically engaged and became an outspoken social critic, he remained aloof from the main currents of American life. The politically circumspect Hitchcock's position is much more complicated, and his relationship to America as Englishman and exile is more central to an understanding of his work than has generally been appreciated. It is connected with his background, character, religion, sexuality and the way in which, consciously and unconsciously, he addressed himself to the world.

When interviewers asked him about why he went to the States, Hitchcock invariably spoke of larger budgets, the world audience commanded by Hollywood, the chance to work with major stars. He also said that he didn't make a decision, at least not initially, to settle there, and indeed for some years the Hitchcocks hung on to their London apartment. But he always spoke rather more frankly to Continental interviewers about the shortcomings of British life and culture and suggested to François Truffaut that America had been part of his thinking about the cinema from the very start:

> It never occurred to me to go and offer my services to a British company, yet, as soon as I read that an American company was going to open a studio in London, I said to myself, 'I want to do their titles' … You might say I had an American training. This doesn't mean that I'm a devotee of everything American. But I did regard their movie-making as truly professional … Later on I often wondered about the fact that I made no attempt to visit America until 1937 … I was completely familiar with the map of New York. Years before I came here, I could describe New York, tell you where the theatres and stores were located. When I had a conversation with Americans they would ask, 'When were you there last?' and I'd answer, 'I've never been there at all.' Strange, isn't it?

Truffaut missed, or only half got, the point: 'You didn't want to come here as a tourist, but only as a film director – it was Hollywood or bust.' I would argue that America was a place of reality and dream for Hitchcock. That it held imaginative and social opportunities which Britain could not offer him. To put it rather grandly, he saw in the freer, larger, more dangerous, more socially mobile American society the possibility of discovering the objective correlatives for his powerful feelings about violence and sexuality. Control over the cinema, and over the world, became his way of confronting the insecure core of his being.

Back in 1930, John Grierson, reviewing *Murder*, observed cuttingly:

> Hitchcock is the best director, the slickest craftsman, the sharpest

observer and finest master of detail in all England. There is no doubt about this ... Yet for all these virtues Hitchcock is no more than the world's best director of unimportant pictures. No one he has made has outlasted a couple of twelvemonths, or will – unless something radical happens to change his standard of satisfaction and give his talents something solid to bring about.

This may have spurred Hitchcock's attempt to anatomise a middle-class marriage under stress in *Rich and Strange*, an interesting and evidently very personal film that failed artistically, critically and commercially. Five years later, when established on the road of suspense moviemaking, he essayed a picture of Joseph Conrad's *Secret Agent*, but in a modernised and emasculated version it became merely a superior thriller. This film, *Sabotage*, is however of great interest for several reasons and contains much that is emblematic.

The *agent provocateur* Verloc, on whom the novel and film centre, has been turned from a backstreet purveyor of dubious literature into the proprietor of a fleapit cinema in a working-class area, behind the screen of which he lives and entertains his fellow conspirators. This throws an ironic light on Hitchcock's idea of the movies. Verloc's employer, a scheming diplomat in the London embassy of an unnamed European power, orders him to stage an act of sabotage that will lead the British government to expel political refugees. The effect of Verloc's temporary shutting down of Battersea Power Station is not the expected panic but a good-humoured acceptance of a brief inconvenience – a display, that is, of British tolerance, phlegm, or complaisance. The furious foreigners tell Verloc that his income will be cut off unless he stages something more frightening. Their message concludes with the chilling words 'London must not laugh'. Is one being fanciful in identifying Verloc, played by the ugly, pudgy Oscar Homolka, with Hitchcock? Verloc, the outsider tolerated by the upper classes, living within a cinema that people despise, wanting to frighten them but only inducing laughter, and spied upon by a suave middle-class Special Branch detective disguised (in imitation of Hitchcock's father) as a cockney greengrocer? I don't think so.

Another thing about *Sabotage* is the response it produced from W.H. Auden. Among the brickbats and bouquets that Auden and Louis MacNeice threw at various friends and celebrities in their comic poem 'Last Will and Testament' in *Letters from Iceland* (1937) was a garland for Hitchcock:

> We hope one honest conviction may
> at last be found
> For Alexander Korda and the
> Balcon Boys
> And the Stavisky Scandal in picture
> and sound
> We leave to Alfred Hitchcock with
> sincerest praise
> of *Sabotage*.

The Stavisky Scandal was left for Resnais to pursue 40 years later. But Hitchcock crossed the Atlantic in Auden's wake to embark upon the second half of his career, and as with Auden's pre- and post-1939 work, a similar controversy has raged ever since, with British critics generally preferring the 1930s English works of both. But there is a weight, a gravitas, about Hitchcock's and Auden's American output, and a religious aspect as well, that was new; and a sense too that in exile and loneliness they discovered their mature selves.

Some of the European exiles of that time returned little changed after the war – Brecht, for instance, and the major French trio of Clair, Duvivier and Renoir. Fritz Lang stayed, and so did most of the Germans, and their movies became, as they became, Americanised. British directors like Edmund Goulding, who went to the States in the 1920s, and the early Ealing hand Robert Stevenson, who left for Hollywood at much the same time as Hitchcock, showed little or no sign of their origins in either their style or choice of subjects. This was not the case with Hitchcock. Though he became the supreme Hollywood professional, he couldn't escape, in some ways didn't wish to escape, from his Englishness.

In *The Art of Alfred Hitchcock* (the study Donald Spoto published in 1978 while Hitchcock was still alive, not the somewhat less adulatory biography he wrote in 1983), Hitchcock is compared in the chapter on *Shadow of a Doubt* with Dante, Dostoevsky and Henry James. Spoto then comments:

But the clearest parallel lies with that authentically American

Puritan view of man and his world as flawed, weak and suscep-
tible to corruption and madness. This view found in our earliest
writers – Jonathan Edwards, Edward Taylor, Cotton Mather –
reached its more dramatic development in the hands of Herman
Melville, Nathaniel Hawthorne and Edgar Allan Poe. It stands
opposed to the heady idealism and to the cheery healthy-mind-
edness offered by the Transcendentalists and the Radical Liberals.
To put the case briefly, Hitchcock seems to me the quintessen-
tially *American* film-maker, far more closely in touch with the
country's literary and philosophical roots than Howard Hawks,
Raoul Walsh or John Huston. Hitchcock rejects Emerson's
idealism and simplicity. His dark view of man more closely
resembles the New England Puritan view – as well, I think, as
Graham Greene's view of an elemental struggle between Gnos-
ticism and the Christian ethic.

The New England puritans of the seventeenth century, with whose
immediate descendants Spoto identifies Hitchcock, brought their
theological and social baggage with them from the old country. To
consider them therefore more authentically American than those
rooted in later, native traditions is misleading. However, the relationship he notes does, if true, illuminate the way some earlier
English immigrants, who also thought of themselves as outsiders,
anticipated the complex demands Hitchcock made upon America.

In his personal life, especially from the 1950s onwards when he
was established beyond any possibility of failure, Hitchcock developed an exaggerated Englishness some found tiresome. He became
an English character, Dickensian with a touch of Wodehouse. His
comic persona was most prominently paraded in his deadpan,
pawkily humorous, self-mocking appearances topping and tailing
the 117 editions of his popular TV series *Alfred Hitchcock Presents* in
the 1950s and 1960s. In his personal publicity much was made of
The Times being delivered daily, of the gourmet dinner parties with
oysters flown in from Colchester, and no Americans invited because
he considered they didn't appreciate proper food. He didn't,
however, associate himself with the English cricket club set, a snobbish, upper-class crowd. He employed them from time to time, but
it wasn't their approval he sought. He wanted to be admired by
Americans – and also by the folks back home.

As already noted, three of his first four Hollywood movies were set wholly or partly in Britain. For the later pictures, even where this was not the case, he chose almost invariably to transpose to America plays, novels and stories set in Britain or Europe. It is as if he had to imagine the work, to seize its essence, in a European context before he could realise it in an American one. Ironically the weakest films dramatically are those he did not transpose (*The Paradine Case* and *Dial M for Murder*, set in London but filmed on Hollywood sound stages), and those he returned to England to make (*Under Capricorn*, *Stage Fright* and *Frenzy*). His view of England remained arrested in the pre-war world, as did more generally his ideas about politics and the espionage business.

But by working within his version of American society – partly mythologised, but powerfully, palpably caught on the screen – he was able to turn his stories into resonant fables. An instructive exception is *The Trouble With Harry*, a comedy transposed from the English countryside to Vermont and consciously thought of as an exercise in British black humour, with a closer resemblance to certain of his television films than to anything he had made before the war. It is an uneasy affair, appearing to take place, for all the insistence upon 'fall in Vermont', in some limbo, and is the only movie in the American corpus after *Mr and Mrs Smith* that is principally comic in intention.

In Hitchcock's British movies, figures of authority and menace are usually middle class or foreign – Godfrey Tearle, Paul Lukas, Peter Lorre. Their minions are rarely fully characterised and usually quite anonymous. This continues to be the case throughout the American movies from *Foreign Correspondent* (where his first American suspense hero, Joel McCrea, confronts the British traitor Herbert Marshall) and *Saboteur* (the first Hollywood thriller with a US setting) up to his last picture, *Family Plot* (1976). In *Saboteur*, the head of the German espionage ring is played by Otto Kruger, an American-born but very Europeanised actor, great-nephew of the South African president and a specialist in English roles. For *Family Plot* Hitchcock brought over the British octogenarian character actress and one-time mistress of Rupert Brooke, Cathleen Nesbitt, to take the brief role of the imperious matriarch of a rich, patrician California family whose obsessions launch the film's intrigue.

In-between we have Sir Cedric Hardwicke as the American

murder victim's father in *Rope*, Tom Helmore (who had appeared in *Secret Agent* in 1935) as the scheming San Francisco shipping magnate in *Vertigo*, Anthony Quayle as the defence lawyer in *The Wrong Man*, Brian Aherne as the prosecuting counsel in *I Confess*, Claude Rains as the Nazi ringleader in *Notorious*, Sean Connery as the Philadelphia publisher in *Marnie*, and another octogenarian actress, Ethel Griffies, as the voice of the apocalypse, the ornithologist in *The Birds*. Most importantly, there is Leo G. Carroll who, imperturbably British throughout, appears as the insane head of the mental institution in *Spellbound*, the senator in *Strangers on a Train* (here given the director's daughter, Patricia, as *his* movie daughter), and the duplicitous chief of the CIA in *North by Northwest*. In this last movie, Carroll's suave super-spy quarry is played by James Mason. In none of these films is there the slightest attempt to explain or justify a British person's presence on the American scene.

There are two significant exceptions to this pattern of casting, and they are arguably Hitchcock's most perfectly achieved movies. The first is *Shadow of a Doubt*. The only British actor here is the Dublin-born veteran of the London stage Henry Travers, probably best remembered as the rose-growing station master in *Mrs Miniver* and the apprentice angel in *It's a Wonderful Life*. In *Shadow of a Doubt* he plays the gentle father of a California small-town family disrupted by the appearance of his handsome homicidal brother-in-law, Charlie (Joseph Cotten). The director set out to create for the first time a plausible, authentically American community and cannily engaged as co-author the playwright Thornton Wilder, creator of the archetypal All-American place called *Our Town*. Consciously or unconsciously Hitchcock sought to place himself in it in a double way. As the father, the Henry Travers figure, he's a quiet, law-abiding paterfamilias, obsessed with the art and craft of murder. This is the chief topic of conversation between the father and his equally retiring chum, played by Hitchcock's longtime friend and collaborator, Hume Cronyn. The murderous Uncle Charlie, who is conjured up, willed into the plot by Travers' frustrated, romantic, deeply bored daughter, also called Charlie (Teresa Wright), is the dangerous side of Hitchcock.

So we have an American community devised and endorsed by Thornton Wilder (a special credit thanks him for his contribution) that provides a forum for an encounter between Hitchcock's tame social persona and his threatening, concealed identity, between one might say his comic, comfortable bourgeois superego and his uninhibited, romantic, murderous id, for the possession of ... a daughter. Some strange, very complicated feelings lurk here, and they throw a revealing light on the picture that came three years later, *Spellbound*, the thriller which launched Hollywood's post-war obsession with Freudian psychology through a movie ostensibly aimed at explaining and justifying the therapeutic value of psychoanalysis. Hitchcock never underwent analysis, but spent some years in the early 1940s reading secondary, interpretative texts.

The other movie that falls outside the pattern I've been describing is *Psycho*, made 17 years later and the occasion of some bitterness on Hitchcock's part. 'British humour,' he told Truffaut, 'is quite superficial and it's also very limited. The British press raised violent objections to *Psycho*, there was hardly a critic who had any sense of humour about this picture.' More than that, in fact. His old friend C.A. Lejeune, critic of the *Observer*, hated the picture and left before the end. She saw in it the writing on the wall and put in her resignation after 30 years service. Whether she told Hitchcock this I don't know. Probably not. But in one respect she was right. *Psycho* can be seen as a turning point in cinematic history. It cut off one generation from another, providing a shibboleth for admission into the new cinematic sensibility.

For the Spielberg generation of movie brats and their successors, the graduates of the film schools that sprang up in America during the 1960s, *Psycho* represented manipulative, autonomous cinema at its purest, the director as puppet master, playing with actors and audiences, a movie of pure, near-totalitarian will. Of course it's much more than that, and this is what makes the picture not merely superior to its endless imitations but a classic of satirical social commentary. Donald Spoto has pointed out that there is a specific visual link uniting *Shadow of a Doubt* and *Psycho* (the Master's last black-and-white film). A scene between Joseph Cotten and his would-be victim Teresa Wright in the earlier film, staged at night in profile on a house porch, is exactly reproduced in *Psycho*, when Anthony Perkins stands beside, and sizes up, his victim, Janet Leigh. But *Psycho* is the dark mirror image of *Shadow of a Doubt*. This is the later Hitchcock disillusioned with America and with money (money being from first to last the film's motif for social contamination and moral corruption). Here we have another instance of America as moral geography for Hitchcock. Janet Leigh flees from a settled community to thrust herself upon a reluctant killer who has withdrawn from the mainstream of American life. In *Shadow of a Doubt*, the killer is drawn across the continent by the mystical power of his victim.

Another, some might think more important, aspect of the casting of the American movies is the assignment of roles over some 20 years to Cary Grant and James Stewart. Four parts apiece – Grant in *Suspicion*, *Notorious*, *To Catch a Thief* and *North by Northwest*; Stewart in *Rope*, *Rear Window*, *The Man Who Knew Too Much* and *Vertigo*. The rationale of this casting, perceptively dealt with by Spoto in his biography, is now the subject of fairly general agreement, and it broadly reflects the roles played by the pair in their only co-starring picture, *The Philadelphia Story*, made in the same year as *Rebecca*.

Grant is the debonair international sophisticate Hitchcock would ideally like to have been. He is reprieved, dramatically and symbolically, from the gallows in *Suspicion*, and thereafter was frequently on Hitchcock's mind as an actor he needed but usually couldn't get. From being the working-class Bristol lad Archie Leach, he had transformed himself into the classless, happily *déraciné* international movie idol Cary Grant. He was the screen lover of Ingrid Bergman and Grace Kelly, of Joan Fontaine and Eva Marie Saint, that Hitchcock could never be. But Hitch could stand by and direct him in this role.

James Stewart on the other hand, the middle-class Ivy League graduate who'd become a Middle American Capraesque hero, was the insecure, lovable man from Main Street that Hitchcock would think of as his Americanised self. Hitch's awkward bulk became Stewart's gangling, awkward height. In *Rope* he is (like Henry Travers in *Shadow of a Doubt*) a man obsessed with the *mise-en-scène* of murder, shocked to find his former pupils transforming his innocent, hypothetical disquisitions on Orwellian 'Cosy English Murders' into Nietzschean atrocities of a Leopold-Loeb kind. In *Rear Window*, Stewart is the photographer as voyeur, fearful of true intimacy with his blonde fiancée (Grace Kelly), projecting his lusts and murderous fantasies on to the neighbours in his New York courtyard. His impotence is symbolised by a broken leg resulting from his physical daring while taking pictures; he only emerges from his protective shell when his fiancée comes to share his voyeuristic obsession. In *Vertigo*, possibly the supreme masterpiece of the Hollywood oeuvre, Stewart is incapable of touching his living idol; he must wait until he feels responsible for her death and then attempt to reshape another woman in her image.

The weakest picture of the Stewart quartet is the 1956 remake of *The Man Who Knew Too Much*. But it is far more interesting than the one feeble picture of the Grant four, *To Catch a Thief* (made immediately after *Rear Window* and allowing Grant to make love to Grace Kelly in the most sexually explicit scene in the oeuvre, a sequence that prevented a whole generation from ever again innocently participating in a firework display). It is customary nowadays to prefer the 1956 *The Man Who Knew Too Much* to the original 1934 British version. I cannot accept this. The earlier movie is crisp, unpretentious, consistently gripping, the later one overblown, slack, gross. But if viewed as a key allegorical work in the context of Hitchcock's career, then the remake is a major film.

In 1948 Hitchcock came back to England accompanied by the world's most alluring female star, Ingrid Bergman, to take his native city by storm. Press photographers followed them around London. 'A Cockney Shows His Star the Town', was how *Picture Post* headed its five-page story. But the movie they made together, their third collaboration, *Under Capricorn*, was badly received. A deeply disturbed Hitchcock then rushed out the contrived, light-hearted English piece *Stage Fright*, which did better financially but didn't much help his reputation except in the eyes of his London critics, who thought it a proper homecoming.

With these two films in the background, we can see his remake of *The Man Who Knew Too Much* (made on British and North African locations, but with the studio work done in Hollywood) as a commentary on his relations with his native country. In the British film, the parents of the kidnapped child return home from Switzerland to face their crisis. In the remake they are visitors to London, a Midwestern doctor (James Stewart) and his wife (Doris Day), a big-band vocalist who has given up her career to be a subservient homemaker of the Eisenhower era. As a show-biz celebrity she is surrounded by boozy, uncomprehending British friends, one of them named as the Palladium impresario Val Parnell. This situation can be interpreted at one level as an allegory about Hitchcock and Bergman's traumatic post-war visit to London, and at another as about Hitchcock the American and Hitchcock the Englishman returning to a city he's lost touch with, where he's treated as a celebrity but not acknowledged as an artist. In this reading the contentious Hollywood oeuvre is represented by the kidnapped child, no longer a sweet English girl but a brash American boy designed to put up the backs of British audiences.

In both movies the international conspirators planning the assassination of a foreign ambassador at the Albert Hall use a chapel as their front and indulge in bogus, comic rites. The co-scenarist of the original film was the rightwing Catholic satirist D.B. Wyndham-Lewis, and it is unlikely that, then or later, Hitchcock would have treated the Catholic Church in a similar way. For example, in his first characteristic Hollywood thriller, *Foreign Correspondent* (1940), the journalist hero Joel McCrea is lured to the top of Westminster Cathedral by an assassin, Edmund Gwenn. The clumsy, diminutive English killer attempts to push his rangy American victim over the bars but instead propels himself to a precipitous death. This is recorded in long shot, filmed by a second unit in Britain with great care and at some expense during the London Blitz. The location must have been important to Hitchcock for him to have gone to so much trouble. Evidently he thought the scene a combination of sacrilege and miracle – the hero delivered, the villain punished for his sins. Few Americans would have recognised the building or known of its significance for the director. Oddly enough, Eric Rohmer and Claude Chabrol in their pioneering 1957 study of Hitchcock, while placing great emphasis for the first time on Hitchcock the Catholic, merely refer to the scene as taking place 'on the top of a tower'.

The Man Who Knew Too Much is a series of interruptions and violations – a holiday ruined, meals and parties cut short, a supposedly important concert at the Albert Hall stopped at its climax, a religious service curtailed and so on. This is much more so in the case of the remake than the original, and it is this that makes it a peculiarly modernist work, that relates it to *Waiting for Godot* or *The Discreet Charm of the Bourgeoisie*. The heavy-handed, ponderous quality that I dislike in it is part of the agonised scrupulousness others admire. No one could think the 1956 *Man Who Knew Too Much* a lightly considered undertaking.

The fact that Hitchcock should have chosen this particular film to remake is significant, because along with *The Lady Vanishes* (the least personal, most felicitous of his later British assignments) it was a major turning point and a financial peak in his pre-war career. There is a famous comment by Hitchcock to Truffaut, comparing the 1934 and 1956 films: 'Let's say the first version was the work of a talented amateur and the second was made by a professional.' He may have believed this, and thought it a sufficient reason to remake the picture. This wasn't, however, what he told British interviewers in 1956. His explanation then was that the 1934 version hadn't been shown in America, whereas in fact it had met with considerable success for a modestly budgeted British movie, something no London journalist bothered to check on.

Hitchcock's first straight American thriller after the new *Man Who Knew Too Much* was *North by Northwest*, shot in 1958. It isn't precisely a remake of anything he'd done before, but it does have a symmetrical place in his work, as well as being his last Cary Grant movie after his final two with James Stewart. His first thriller set in America, *Saboteur* (1942), centred on a journey from California to New York by a Los Angeles factory worker framed for a murder caused by an act of wartime sabotage and bent on clearing his name. His quest ends famously on the top of the Statue of Liberty. An identical transcontinental journey would have taken the expatriate Hitchcock, guilt-ridden over letters from home accusing him of dodging the wartime column (many written by his old producer Michael Balcon), back to the European battlefield. *Lifeboat*, the following year, took him out into the North Atlantic. In fact he did return, at great risk and at some financial loss (and without the protection of his wife, Alma Reville), to make a couple of movies with a group of émigré French actors for exhibition in France after the Liberation. Hitchcock was unhappy about *Saboteur*, despite good reviews and satisfactory box office returns, probably because of the tepid performances by Robert Cummings and Priscilla Lane, minor stars both, though as American and as 1940s Hollywood as he could have asked for.

With *North by Northwest* he recapitulated the journey of *Saboteur*, going in the other direction. His hero is also wrongly accused of murder, but this time he's a smooth, successful advertising agent played by Cary Grant. His name, 'Roger Thornhill', is so well known to movie fans that in the 1984 occult political thriller *Dreamscape* the centre of activity was called Thornhill College (with a crucial subsection dubbed the Bates Building in memory of the motel Anthony Perkins managed in *Psycho*). The jobs were well chosen – *Saboteur*'s leather-jacketed war worker in the 1940s has been replaced by a Madison Avenue executive in the second Eisenhower term. The Cold War was the context and Mount Rushmore the ultimate destination, where Hitchcock knew the climactic shoot out should take place when he hired Ernest Lehman as screenwriter. As Lehman has told us, Hitch arranged a mini-retrospective to show the kind of synoptic entertainment he intended this to be. We now see that it brought a wonderful decade of filmmaking to a triumphant conclusion.

The most celebrated scene in *North by Northwest* is the pursuit of Cary Grant in the Midwestern cornfield by a crop-dusting plane equipped with machine guns. After the hapless Roger Thornhill has been encouraged to get off the Greyhound bus in the Indiana countryside, he is kept hanging around for an unconscionable time, then starts running for his life. Indiana is the crossroads of America, the state that has produced more national archetypes than any other in the union. This is the home of Wendell Wilkie, Cole Porter, James Dean, Jimmy Hoffa, Kenneth Rexroth, John Dillinger, Howard Hawks, Theodore Dreiser, Alfred Kinsey; the state Robert and Helen Lynd chose for their classic sociological study *Middletown* (based on the town of Muncie); the flat terrain where the extraterrestrials visited the yearning, unfulfilled electrician in *Close Encounters of the Third Kind*.

I seize on the isolation of the urban sophisticate Cary Grant in rural Indiana because there is endless emphasis upon Indianapolis, the state capital to which the film's deserted road leads, as the hometown of the couple played by James Stewart and Doris Day in *The Man Who Knew Too Much*. Cary Grant, the Manhattan sophisticate at bay in the countryside – probably Hitchcock's greatest sequence of terror in the open air, and one of the cinema's most disturbing exploitations of agoraphobia – is thus taken to the terrain of Hitchcock's American alter ego, James Stewart. Hitch's classless, stateless ideal is at a loss in the world of his awkward, graceless, confidently rooted persona.

We might also note something more sombre. Hitchcock was notoriously obsessed by blondes, from Madeleine Carroll in his British pictures, through a succession of American actresses – Joan Fontaine, Grace Kelly, Eva Marie Saint, Vera Miles, Tippi Hedren. The first blonde star of the first rank he encountered and worked with on American soil was Carole Lombard, and *Mr and Mrs Smith* was supposedly undertaken out of friendship for her and at her request. She was a peculiarly spirited person, and aware that Hitchcock's most famous saying was that 'Actors are cattle', she set up three stalls on the set of *Mr and Mrs Smith* for the first day of shooting, each occupied by a cow, and each cow bearing around her neck one of the names of the film's stars, Robert Montgomery, Gene Raymond and herself. Less than a year after making *Mr and Mrs Smith*, Carole Lombard was killed in a plane crash on her way back to Hollywood from Indianapolis during a war-bond selling tour. Fort Wayne, Indiana, was Lombard's birthplace, and the cornfields sequence concludes with Grant driving away unscathed after an aircrash.

After *The Birds* in 1963, there was a steep decline in the quality of Hitchcock's movies, and at the beginning of the 1970s he returned to work in Britain for the last time with *Frenzy*. It was based on a low-life novel called *Goodbye Piccadilly, Farewell Leicester Square*, a title with elegiac qualities suggesting the music hall of Hitchcock's youth and the world that ended in the horrors of the Western Front. But he didn't hire its author, Arthur La Bern, to write the script. Instead he engaged Anthony Shaffer, a student of detective fiction and a master of pastiche, and the film, although set in the Britain of the 1970s, belongs to the inter-war years. A serious dislocation is announced at the start by casting Jon Finch, an actor still obviously in his twenties, as the brutal hero, a former Battle of Britain pilot.

The film's killer, who frames Finch, is a smooth psychopath played by Barry Foster, who brutally murders women, raping them as they are dying. His trade is that of greengrocer – and his chosen weapon is the necktie, symbol of the public school world, the clubby exclusivity that denied Hitchcock his proper place in English life. Older viewers of *Frenzy*, like Hitchcock himself, would remember those old advertisements offering a course in self-confidence and social advancement that carried the slogan 'Are You

Gagged By the Old School Tie?' accompanied by a picture of a man with a striped tie around his mouth. Let that tie slip a little, and an inhibiting cravat becomes a vengeful garrotte.

The relationship between the sweaty, guiltily innocent Jon Finch and the self-possessed, innocently guilty Barry Foster in *Frenzy* closely parallels that between the edgy, guiltily innocent lower-middle-class tennis star (Farley Granger)* and the smooth, innocently guilty society playboy (Robert Walker) in *Strangers on a Train*. Foster and Walker both murder the estranged wives of the men for whom they have an implicit homosexual love, simultaneously freeing the husbands while making them objects of suspicion, who can only clear themselves by naming the killers. It is perhaps not by mere chance that when Finch books into a hotel while on the run with his mistress, he should use the pseudonym 'Mr and Mrs Oscar Wilde'. Also that Hitchcock should have brought out of retirement to appear as the hotel's landlady Elsie Randolph, who 40 years before played a fashionable socialite on the cruise ship where the couple's marriage breaks down in *Rich and Strange*.

Only one film followed *Frenzy* – *Family Plot*, a British novel transposed to California, with Hitchcock making his personal appearance as a silhouette behind the door of a coroner's office. But whereas a cast of youngish British stage actors had responded uneasily to his direction in *Frenzy*, a youngish cast of American film actors served him outstandingly well in *Family Plot*.

We know that Hitchcock was unwell while directing this picture, and in the four years between then and his death he was by all accounts a depressed, heavy-drinking, leering, discontented man, taking care of a demanding wife (half-paralysed and deeply suspicious) upon whom he had depended for over 50 years. Despite the praise that had been heaped on him by the film industry, critics and the moviegoing public, he was divided against himself, rancorous, frustrated. The end recalls that of Evelyn Waugh, another Catholic identifying with an earlier England who retreated into himself,

---

* In *Rope*, Granger played the agonised half of the duo of clearly homosexual killers. In 1978 he took over the role of the gay murderer in the Broadway production of Ira Levin's *Deathtrap*, a comedy thriller much indebted to Anthony Shaffer's *Sleuth* that takes a less censorious view of homosexuality and homicide than Hitchcock's contemporaries did.

becoming an internal exile rather than seeking a place abroad. Both put their tensions, contradictions and fears into their art, transmuting pain and trauma through the alchemy of anguished creativity. In day-to-day life maturity and serenity eluded them. They adopted masks to conceal this, and for most of the time this social act was surprisingly successful. We now know the price both had to pay.

British Cinema and the Post Office (1985)

I don't know much about philately, but I know what I lick, and the first movie stamps ever issued by our Post Office have left an odd taste in my mind.

Four years ago, in a column of discursive commentary on cinematic matters I was writing for *Sight & Sound*, I remarked favourably on a striking set of five stamps issued by the Swedish post office based on famous stills from Sjöström's *The Phantom Carriage* (1920), Stiller's *The Atonement of Gösta Berling* (1924, featuring Garbo in her first major role), Molander's *Intermezzo* (1936, Ingrid Bergman in the film she subsequently remade in Hollywood with Leslie Howard), Sjöberg's *Frenzy* (1944) and Bergman's *Cries and Whispers* (1972). Cinephiles the world over would recognise all or most of these movies and could acquire the set for less than a pound.

'What iconic scenes from 60 years of British moviemaking could match this Swedish quintet?' I wondered aloud. The editor of *Sight & Sound*, Penelope Houston, and I were pleasantly surprised by the interest this off-hand remark aroused, and she printed the designs for five stamps submitted by a Woodford reader, Mr M.F. Pride. They depicted stationmaster Will Hay on the phone in *Oh Mr Porter!* (11½p), a fireman in action from Humphrey Jennings's *Fires Were Started* (14p), Olivier and Terence Morgan duelling in *Hamlet* (25p), Orson Welles as Harry Lime illuminated in the doorway in *The Third Man* (50p), and Trevor Howard and Celia Johnson back-lit at night in a cobbled street beside the railway station in *Brief Encounter* (£1). A very good if slightly conservative choice, and the Post Office could have taken them up as they stood.

Indeed, as we now know, the Post Office's contribution to British Film Year is a series of five, admittedly most elegant stamps, which celebrate not the art of the cinema but that of the portrait

'British Cinema and the Post Office' first appeared in the *Observer*, 20 October 1985.

photographer. Far more prominent than the subjects' golden autographs at bottom right are the cameramen's credits on the left. These stamps depict Bill Brandt's Peter Sellers (17p), Cornell Lucas's David Niven (22p), Snowdon's Chaplin (29p), Angus McBean's Vivien Leigh (31p) and Howard Coster's Hitchcock (34p). Hitchcock and Chaplin will be virtually unrecognisable to most moviegoers in these portraits; the former died an American citizen, the latter made his whole career in the States. Sellers is impersonating a Frenchman in a film directed by an American. Vivien Leigh is here posing, I believe, for a portfolio designed to secure her the part of Scarlett O'Hara. David Niven is a creation of Hollywood, though I don't resent his inclusion.

Why wasn't Sir Michael Balcon, head of Ealing Studios, there? Or Leslie Howard, George Formby and Gracie Fields? I would like to have seen Basil Radford and Naunton Wayne honoured. The fact that there is a rule prohibiting living people other than royalty appearing on British stamps shouldn't extend to stills from movies produced by an industry not a century old. There is a simple philosophical distinction to be made between actors and the characters they impersonate on the screen.

The Post Office could make up for this unimaginative performance over the next few years. It is 30 years too late to mark the centenary of the birth of William Friese-Greene. But how about centenary stamps for Alexander Korda (1993) and Michael Balcon (1996) as neatly designed as the 1975 American issue for the D.W. Griffith centenary, a sepia CinemaScope-shaped ten-cent stamp with the great man on the right and a movie camera to the left?

This piece has a particular place in my affections. First, it brought more money than I got for the whole piece to an anonymous contributor to Reader's Digest *who submitted the opening line to one of that magazine's sections that fill out the spaces at the end of articles. My parents, lifelong subscribers to the* Digest, *would have been proud. Second, and even more significant, this line – 'I don't know much about philately, but I know what I lick' – was included in* The Penguin Dictionary of Twentieth-Century Quotations *(1993). I was preceded by Marilyn and Percy French and followed by Sir Clement and Sigmund Freud.*

Sadly on the philatelic front, nothing has come about in Britain along the lines of the excellent 'Legends of Hollywood' series that the US Post Office has been issuing these last 20 years, blocks of which I have framed to hang on my staircase. Children have always had rather brutal jokes about stamps, but the first subtle one I recall is from Frank Muir and Dennis Norden's BBC Radio comedy show Take It From Here c.1951 when the Labour government's majority was being eroded in a series of by-elections. One of the show's stars, Jimmy Edwards, inquired of the supporting actor Wallas Eaton (who was later become a cherished figure in the Australian cinema's New Wave) if he knew anything about philately. 'No Jim. But his brother Clem had a narrow run last Thursday.'

The Drive-In Critic (1989)

BOOK REVIEW
Briggs, Joe Bob: *Joe Bob Goes to the Drive-In* (Penguin)

Joe Bob Briggs is a 19-year old, thrice-married Texas redneck, veteran of 6,800 drive-in movies, living a beer-swilling, junkfood-guzzling existence in a trailer park in Dallas. He scorns hard-top cinemas ('indoors', he sneeringly calls them), and in January 1982, as connoisseur of downmarket al fresco cinematic fare (Texas boasts 223 drive-ins), he began writing a raunchy Friday column for the *Dallas Times Herald* that rapidly developed a local and, through syndication, national following.

Joe Bob writes with an appalling candour about the exploitation movies most fastidious critics loathe – low-budget horror, kung-fu, soft-core skinflicks. And after totting up the score sheet of exposed breasts ('garbonzas'), mutilations, rolling heads, gross-outs, auto-collisions, he awards a number of stars and puts his seal of approval on a film with the sign-off slogan 'Joe Bob says check it out'. He loves Bruce Lee, Charles Bronson and Chuck Norris. In 1982 he invited Roger Corman, 'The King of the Drive-Ins', to Dallas to receive the first JBB Life Achievement Award (an engraved Chevy hubcap). His *bête noire* is the 'indoor wimp' Steven Spielberg, because he corrupted local hero Tobe Hooper, director of the *Texas Chainsaw Massacre*, by luring him to Hollywood to direct the genteel horror flick *Poltergeist*.

Because drive-in moviegoing and his daily life are inextricable, Joe Bob also tells us about his problems with a string of bimbos with names like Wanda Bodine, Cherry Dilday and Mary Ellen Masters, and the imbroglios they get him into in motels, shopping malls and drive-ins, including a few days in 'Crossbar Hotel' (i.e. jail). We

---

'The Drive-In Critic' first appeared in the *Observer*, 9 April 1989.

learn too about his political opinions. He despises East Coast liberals and commies (there are no drive-ins in Russia), and in 1984 he writes an open letter to Ronald Reagan on the occasion of the Republican Party's presidential convention in Dallas, inviting him to a festival of vintage Reagan films. 'You're a drive-in kind of guy,' he assures Ron. 'You were making drive-in movies before there were hardly drive-ins.'

In April 1985, however, Joe Bob wrote a column satirising the American pop industry's fund-raising 'We are the World' charity effort, in which the stars of horror flicks sang a number called 'We are the weird'. It was obscure and none too funny, yet got into print. This proved the last straw for a local coalition of feminists, Baptists, blacks and other right-thinking people. Their combined pressure led to the *Times Herald*'s editor making a front-page apology. From that moment Joe Bob was dead in Dallas.

Joe Bob is in fact, though the British reader will have trouble inferring this from a coyly presented collection, the creation of John Bloom, the *Times Herald*'s serious, intellectual, mild-mannered movie critic. Bloom dreamt up Joe Bob in discussion with the paper's features editor as a way of looking at a whole area of movies that were either patronised or ignored, and the columns skilfully combine satire, parody and social comment. This British edition would have been more valuable had it contained as an afterword Calvin Trillin's thorough and thoughtful essay on the Joe Bob Briggs affair that appeared in the 22 December 1986 issue of the *New Yorker*.

Trillin's article suggests that in the comic persona of Joe Bob, the decent liberal John Bloom was letting his id off the leash, and that his creation took possession of him the way the dummy in *Dead of Night* gained the upper hand on ventriloquist Michael Redgrave. Bloom quit the newspaper and, while writing serious journalism in his own name, derives most of his income appearing in cabaret as the vulgar, male-chauvinist, xenophobic Joe Bob.

But in those often hilarious, frequently inspired *Times Herald* columns, Bloom contributed a colourful character to the rich American tradition of comic vernacular literature that includes Twain's Huck Finn, Peter Finaly Dunne's Mr Dooley, Ring Lardner's baseball players, John O'Hara's Pal Joey and, in case the list should appear wholly dominated by overbearing males, Anita Loos's Lorelei Lee. Check it out.

Joe Bob left his fans with another phrase in addition to 'Check it out.' After a characteristic bit of leering innuendo, he'd invariable say, 'If you know what I mean? And I think you do.' I don't know what has become of Joe Bob since the drive-ins were driven out and joined the American trail of ghost towns.

Welles Reinstated (1990)

The week's major event, of course, is this morning's one-off (for contractual reasons) screening at the National Film Theatre of Orson Welles's *The Magnificent Ambersons*, painstakingly restored to its original 131-minute length by Kevin Brownlow, using the footage recently discovered in the RKO archives. The new material crucially changes the tone of the last third of the movie, giving it a political dimension and a tragic aspect only hinted at in the version released in 1942.

Brownlow also came across a fragment of the score Welles commissioned from the then unknown Leonard Bernstein, who was in California at the time, convalescing and writing his Clarinet Sonata. RKO rejected Bernstein's music out of hand as too avant-garde. Those lucky enough to be at the NFT at noon today (all tickets were snapped up within an hour) will be able to judge for themselves, when Carl Davis conducts his augmented arrangement of the Bernstein fragment as a prelude to the restored *Magnificent Ambersons*. For them it should prove a day to remember.

The above piece had people ringing the NFT to inquire about returns and resulted in, among other things, an angry call to Kevin Brownlow from a well-known producer demanding why he hadn't received an invitation. As a consequence I was asked by the then arts editor of the Observer *to include a note in the following Sunday's paper which read: 'Did I provide too much authentic-sounding detail last Sunday about the restored* Magnificent Ambersons? *Do I carry so much conviction that everything I say is believed? Some of my closest friends failed to check the date at the top of the page after reading those two paragraphs.'*

'Welles Reinstated' first appeared in the *Observer*, 1 April 1990.

Satyajit Ray at 70 (1991)

I have above my work desk an autographed photograph of Satyajit Ray and Akira Kurosawa walking pensively three or four feet apart in front of the Taj Mahal. It is a constant reminder of the great heights the cinema can reach and why writing serious criticism can be an honourable activity. Seeing Kurosawa's *Rashomon* in 1952 was, after a childhood exposed to ferocious anti-Japanese propaganda, a healing and enlightening experience. Encountering *Pather Panchali* four years later was an introduction to an India far removed from the literature of the Raj and quite different from anything I had previously come across in the cinema. I recognised, however, a certain affinity with the fiction of R.K. Narayan, whose novels I had read due to the advocacy of Graham Greene.

My admiration for Ray grew year by year. I saw him on stage several times in the 1960s and was struck by his impressive presence and articulacy. I did not meet him, however, until the mid-1970s when I attended a film festival in Delhi and accompanied Ray and Kurosawa on the visit to Agra where that photograph of them was taken. Also on the trip were Michelangelo Antonioni and Elia Kazan, and the quartet took part a couple of days later in a discussion recorded for TV on 'Humanism and the Cinema', all four of them defining themselves as humanists. I hope the tape has been preserved. The odd thing, though you wouldn't notice it as they sat at the TV table, was that the orientals towered over the diminutive occidentals.

At the opening of the festival I had been introduced to Ray by the late Gene Moskowitz of *Variety*, one of his first champions in the West. To my amazement Gene always addressed him as 'Satch'.

'Satyajit Ray at 70' was one of the 66 contributions to *Satyajit Ray at 70*, a tribute with photographs by Nemai Ghosh and foreword by Henri Cartier-Bresson (Brussels, Eiffel Editions, 1991).

Ray seemed most affable but I still felt rather in awe when a few days later, knowing he was staying at the same New Delhi hotel (he was president of the festival jury), I plucked up courage and called his room to see if he could find a moment to see me. (I was officially representing the London *Times* – had I declared that my true employer was the BBC, I would have been denied admission to India as a result of my association with the organisation that had broadcast Louis Malle's *Phantom India* films, a series that had led to the temporary expulsion of all BBC correspondents.) To my surprise Ray said he'd come right down, if that was all right. It was. When he arrived, he explained that he had been stuck for two hours with a Latin American journalist who spoke little English and didn't appear to have seen any of his films. Still, he hadn't felt able to eject her and had seized on my call to make an honest exit. Suddenly I discovered that the phrase 'he doesn't suffer fools gladly' isn't necessarily a compliment. Fools of all kinds are among the chief characters of great art. So why should they not be respected in life too? After all that is what most of us are, whether Brazilian journalists attending Indian film festivals or highbrow British critics writing profiles. Fools abound in Ray's movies and he suffers them gladly.

I recall our conversation in vivid detail (the first of several in India and London), because Ray never seems to say anything either portentous or trivial. I had bought the previous day and read at a sitting his book *Our Films Their Films*, published that month in Calcutta, and we talked about Renoir, Ford and other directors and issues he had raised. His modesty was ridiculous – he hadn't even sought to have the book published in London. I said I'd try to publicise it, and the day I arrived back home the *New Statesman* eagerly accepted a review (the literary editor was a Ray admirer), which resulted in it finding a larger distribution and readership in the West.

We also talked about Dickens. I had recently seen *The Middle Man* and thought its representation of Calcutta rather Dickensian. 'Well, yes,' he said. 'I think you have a point.' He gently pressed me, and I came up with some specific parallels of incident and character. Then he told me that he had been in thrall to Dickens as a teenager (I'm not certain, but he may have said that Dickens meant more to him than Kipling) and that one of his teachers at Calcutta's Presidency College was Humphry House, the great Dickensian scholar who was teaching at Oxford when I was an undergraduate.

He revealed a knowledge of Dickens that not surprisingly far surpassed my own.

Later that week Tom Milne and I talked with Ray about his current project, *The Chess Players*. He had shot the studio material in Calcutta in a relatively cool winter and was about to embark on the location work in Lucknow. Sadly neither Tom nor I was free to accept his invitation to stay in India and watch him in action. But we did become involved in the casting for the remaining third strand of the film. Who was to play General Outram, the Scottish soldier who completed the British imperial project by annexing Oudh on the eve of the Indian Mutiny? Several performers were discussed, Guinness and Olivier among them, but we came down to two – Alec McCowen and Richard Attenborough. Tom and I left Delhi knowing that either would be excellent and believing that the pair, had they known about the role, would be fighting over it.

A few months later at a party for Ray at the Indian High Commission in London, the conversation between Ray, Tom Milne and myself rapidly turned to the casting of Outram. Ray was sad. He had made approaches to Attenborough but had received no response. The project, the money, the shooting schedule (Calcutta in mid-summer) must have seemed overwhelmingly unattractive. Tom and I were amazed. Had he spoken to the man himself? No. Leaning on a slight professional acquaintance with Attenborough, I offered to intervene but suggested that Ray himself should try to contact him directly, say who he was and a few words about his movie.

That was all it took. Attenborough threw himself into the picture. He gave a magnificent performance under atrocious conditions wearing a weighty military uniform in a cramped Calcutta studio with ineffective air conditioning at the height of summer. The appearance was a prelude to his production of *Gandhi*.

Ray is a genius, a great filmmaker rooted in his complex Bengali culture and at the same time a detached, cosmopolitan intellectual. He has made some great films, numerous fine ones and nothing mediocre by lack of ambition. His pictures constitute an oeuvre; they complement and comment on each other. None of his films wants for admirers, but I would like to put in a word for the under-valued *Ganasatru*, his Indian version of Ibsen's *An Enemy of the People*. Though not among his more innovative cinematic achievements, it may well be his most courageous work from a moral and political point of view in the way it challenges orthodox opinion and religious complacency. Jorge Luis Borges once said that the best form of criticism was a work in another form on the same theme or subject as the original. Ray's *Enemy of the People* not only comments upon Ibsen's play and the religious fundamentalist involvement in contemporary American politics but it also anticipated the controversy surrounding Salman Rushdie's *The Satanic Verses*.

In 1978 Ray was in Britain for the London Film Festival premiere of The Chess Players. *His film ironically interweaves the story of two chess-obsessed nabobs with the final moves of General Outram's power game in Oudh that swept the Indian board for the British Raj in 1856, an event that immediately preceded the Mutiny and its suppression. Visiting him to record a radio interview at his hotel, I found he was greatly amused that the festival was putting him up at the Imperial.*

This Is the Special Edition (1991)

Introduction to the festival of 60 newspaper films at the National Film Theatre to celebrate the Observer*'s bicentenary.*

Journalists turn up in movies from all over the world, but the newspaper movie as an informal genre is essentially the creation of Hollywood after the coming of sound, and pictures made elsewhere about the press are in its shadow. There were movies set in newspaper offices in the silent era, and in the 1920s Hollywood lured some gifted journalists to Hollywood, most notably the former *New York Times* writer, Herman Mankiewicz, and the veteran of several Chicago dailies, Ben Hecht. Mankiewicz, who was to be the co-author of the greatest newspaper film, *Citizen Kane*, arrived in Hollywood early in 1926. Later that year he invited Hecht, soon to become the co-author of the greatest of all newspaper comedies, *The Front Page*, to join him. His telegram read: 'Will you accept 300 per week to work for Paramount Pictures? All expenses paid. The three hundred is peanuts. Millions are to be grabbed out here and your only competition is idiots. Don't let it get around.'

With the coming of sound word did get around, and dozens of journalists flocked to a Hollywood in desperate need of people who could produce sharp, speakable dialogue and who knew their way around town. What they knew best was newspapers, and they wrote scripts for hundreds of movies aggrandising, damning or merely exploiting their own profession. In the process they turned journalists and their female counterparts, the so-called sob sisters, into popular heroes and heroines, on a par with cowboys, cops, gangsters, aviators and hoofers. Few of them returned to ill-paid journalism, though one long-forgotten actress went the other way: the B-feature star Elaine Shepard quit Hollywood to become a

'This Is the Special Edition' first appeared in the *Observer*, 9 June 1991.

reporter and even wrote an autobiography called *Forgive Us Our Press Passes*.

The golden age of the Hollywood newspaper film was from the early 1930s to America's entry into World War Two, from the first film version of *The Front Page* (1931), a raucous celebration of cutthroat yellow journalism, to *Citizen Kane* (1941), a complex examination of how a great newspaper proprietor came to betray his early ideals. Not every Hollywood star appeared in westerns, but at some time or another every star has played a journalist. One recalls Edward G. Robinson as the conscientious editor in *Five Star Final* (1931), being forced downmarket by his venal proprietors; James Cagney as the crime reporter framed by the mob in *Each Dawn I Die* (1939); James Stewart as the leftwing reporter reluctantly covering a society wedding in *The Philadelphia Story* (1940); Spencer Tracy as a sports reporter married to political columnist Katharine Hepburn in *Woman of the Year* (1942); Fredric March as the journalist exploiting the imminent death of Carole Lombard in *Nothing Sacred* (1937), the most savage of all satires on unscrupulous newspapermen.

Lee Tracy, who created the role of Hildy Johnson in the 1930 Broadway production of *The Front Page*, was typecast for the next dozen years as a fast-talking reporter in low-budget movies with titles like *Clear All Wires, Behind the Headlines* and *Power of the Press*. And in one of his few pre-war appearances out of the B-western saddle, John Wayne appeared in *I Cover the War* (1937) as a news cameraman reporting from the Spanish Civil War.

The stereotypes of the tough editor chomping a cigar, the brash crime reporter instructing the city desk to 'hold the front page' and the suave foreign correspondent scooping his rivals in distant hot spots shaped the public's attitude towards the press and influenced the way newspaper people thought of themselves. But the filmmakers were really helping to consolidate the legendary, romantic role that journalists had played in American life since the Revolution, when the First Amendment to the Constitution enshrined the freedom of the press. Traditionally, in any frontier town, the first institutions set up after the blacksmith's forge and the saloon were the church, the schoolroom and the newspaper office.

At the same time the journalist had, and has, a special dramatic function as the ideal person to represent the filmmaker and the audience. To a much greater extent than those other inquiring figures – the cop, the federal agent and the private eye – the reporter is licensed to cross social divides, move around the country, go abroad. It is his duty to observe, ask questions, seek out the truth. At best he can be a crusader for justice, a disinterested servant of the public good, taking in some of the functions of the priesthood without being clothed in sanctity.

Unlike the polarisation of good guys and bad guys in westerns or crime movies, the behaviour of the journalist as hero is not very different from that of the journalist as villain. They dress in similar fashion, talk fast and crack wise, resort to identical forms of subterfuge to get their stories, and are gregarious loners. The difference between them is one of motive or social purpose. In *Call Northside 777* (1948), for instance, a Chicago reporter (James Stewart) starts out cynically exploiting the story of an elderly cleaning woman attempting to clear her son, long incarcerated for murder, and ends up putting his career on the line by crusading for the man's acquittal.

Like Stewart in *Call Northside 777*, the movie journalist usually becomes the hero of the story he is engaged on. But in *Citizen Kane*, the reporter Thompson – charged by the editors of *News on the March* with discovering the meaning of 'Rosebud', Kane's dying word – is a pure catalyst, an agent of change wholly unaffected by the changes he brings about. We learn almost everything about Kane and nothing about Thompson. If he sat opposite us in a bar we would not recognise him.

After World War Two, as TV came to eclipse the cinema as a medium of entertainment and to challenge print as a principal source of news, the newspaper movie ceased to be a staple of Hollywood. This didn't bring it to an end, and four major stars had memorable journalistic roles in the post-war decade: Gregory Peck as the reporter posing as a Jew to expose anti-Semitism in *Gentleman's Agreement* (1947); Kirk Douglas as a disgraced journalist exploiting a local tragedy to buy his ticket back into the big time in *Ace in the Hole* (1951); Humphrey Bogart as the editor of a liberal daily vainly keeping up standards in the face of sleazy competitors and exposing corruption in *Deadline USA* (1952); Burt Lancaster as the grotesque rightwing columnist spreading poison across America from his Broadway lair in *Sweet Smell of Success* (1957).

Before Hollywood capitulated to TV and started making series for the small screen and leasing its backlist to the box, the cinema treated television with contempt, mocking those who worked for it and the programmes it transmitted. By the 1970s, however, Tinseltown was in thrall to the glamour of the new medium. Pauline Kael sensed this movement in her classic 1971 essay on *Citizen Kane*, seeing one of its historic aspects as recording the shift from print journalism to visual journalism. In Welles's 1941 film, a newsreel reporter (working for a lightly disguised version of Henry Luce's *Time Marches On*) looks into the life of a press baron.

The progress Kael describes can be seen in the four different film versions of *The Front Page*. In 1931, it was a tough, amoral, wise-cracking newspaper comedy. In 1940, under the direction of Howard Hawks, it became the sleek, sophisticated screwball comedy *His Girl Friday*, the hero transformed into an ace woman correspondent (Rosalind Russell) while the hard-bitten editor (Cary Grant) becomes her ex-husband. In the 1974 remake, Billy Wilder goes back to the original, adding some fashionable bad language, lovingly laying on the late 1920s nostalgic detail (Wilder himself had been a reporter in Europe at that time) and turning the play into an odd-couple, buddy-buddy movie by casting Jack Lemmon and Walter Matthau in the leading roles. Thirteen years later, in Ted Kotcheff's wretched *Switching Channels* (1987), the setting is a 24-hour cable TV news station of no clearly discernible standing, whose manager (Burt Reynolds) conspires to keep his top reporter and ex-wife (Kathleen Turner) working for him.

In moving from newspapers to TV there can be an immense loss of individuality. As *Broadcast News* (1987) demonstrates, the TV reporter is just a member of a team involved in complex technical operations. He is subservient to the producer and the anchorman who, however dim he might be, dominates the TV screen because he unerringly picks up cues, wears his clothes well and exudes the right charisma. But a star like Jane Fonda isn't going to languish behind a typewriter or a word processor when she can be out there in *The China Syndrome* (1978) and *The Electric Horseman* (1979), emoting, microphone in hand, before a camera.

The conjunction in the early 1970s of the Pentagon Papers affair and Watergate gave the newspaper movie a shot in the arm. It led to *The Parallax View* (1974), in which long-haired investigative reporter Warren Beatty courts death while probing a rightwing organisation involved in political assassination; *Three Days of the Condor* (1975), which concludes with disillusioned intelligence employee Robert Redford presenting the *New York Times* with documents relating to a government conspiracy; and pre-eminently *All the President's Men* (1976), starring Robert Redford and Dustin Hoffman as Woodward and Bernstein, the *Washington Post* reporters who became heroic international celebrities. There were several movies reacting to this liberal wave, most significantly *Absence of Malice* (1981), scripted by the Pulitzer Prize-winning journalist Kurt Luedtke, an attack on liberal investigative journalism bent on showing that Woodward and Bernstein were bad precedents men.

For most of the history of British cinema the reporter has been a B-feature figure, as often as not an American visitor. There have been odd attempts to celebrate provincial journalism (Norman Wooland and Sarah Churchill challenging corrupt property developers for their West Country paper in the charming *All Over the Town*, 1949) and to chronicle Fleet Street (Jack Hawkins agonising over the day's news as the caring editor of a national daily in *Front Page Story*, 1954). But the reporter in British movies has usually been a comic, pathetic or dour figure rather than a romantic one. In the best British press film of recent years, *Defence of the Realm* (1985), the twin heroes are an elderly leftwing soak (Denholm Elliott), who can't work a tape recorder, and a dashing, apolitical slob (Gabriel Byrne), both of whom pay with their lives for probing an establishment cover-up.

Graham Greene began his writing career as a provincial newspaper reporter in Nottingham in the 1920s, and as a film critic for the *Spectator* in the 1930s he compared British newspaper movies adversely with their American counterparts (he particularly liked *I Cover the Waterfront*). Later as a novelist he created three fictional journalists of unforgettable seediness. The first is Minty, the expatriate freelance hack in *England Made Me*, impersonated in the 1972 film by Michael Hordern. The second is Hale, the sweaty Fleet Street crime reporter in *Brighton Rock* (played in the 1948 film by Alan Wheatley) who exposed the South Coast racetrack gangs and has been sent back to Brighton on a demeaning circulation-building assignment that leads to his murder. The third and most significant is Fowler, the embittered foreign correspondent covering the last days of France's Indo-China War in *The Quiet American*, published in 1955 and controversially filmed by Joseph L. Mankiewicz in 1958, starring Michael Redgrave. The movie turned the novel's critique of American foreign policy on its head, thus robbing its seedy hero of his one supremely redeeming feature – his political sagacity. But ten years later the film was forgotten, and Greene's novel was in the knapsack of every correspondent covering the Vietnam War.

British filmmakers have usually gone abroad to make real heroes of journalists: to South Africa to record the resistance to the authorities of the liberal editor Donald Woods (*Cry Freedom*, 1987) and the Communist opponent of apartheid, Ruth First (*A World Apart*, 1988); and to Cambodia to observe the *New York Times* reporter Sydney Schanberg forced to desert his local assistant (*The Killing Fields*, 1984). Woods, First and Schanberg were all played by Americans, though marginal roles were found for British actors: in *The Killing Fields*, for instance, Julian Sands impersonated the *Sunday Times* foreign correspondent Jon Swain. Curiously, among the disastrous changes wrought by Hollywood in bringing Tom Wolfe's *The Bonfire of the Vanities* to the screen was turning Peter Fallow, the sleazy, drunken British journalist working for the New York paper *The City Light*, into an American.

On the continent, movie journalists have almost invariably been seen as unprincipled hacks at home and Byronically posturing intruders when working in trouble spots abroad. Among the exceptions have been the Italian journalists exploring the mysterious death of the flamboyant, populist oil tycoon Enrico Mattei in Francesco Rosi's *Kane*-like *The Mattei Affair* (1972); the photo-journalist who makes common cause with the dedicated Greek public prosecutor in Costa-Gavras's *Z*; and François Truffaut as an obituarist on a French provincial paper in the 1920s, keeping alive a disappearing past in *The Green Room* (1978).

It is perhaps to the credit of Soviet filmmakers that they have refrained from turning the craven hacks of *Pravda* and *Izvestia* into movie heroes. The Eastern European cinema's journalistic pantheon is reserved for critics of the system and would-be martyrs. The two most remarkable pictures are Karoly Makk's *Another Way* (1982) and Andrzej Wajda's *Rough Treatment* (1978). In *Another Way*, Livia, the easy-going wife of a Hungarian army officer, and

Eva, a lesbian journalist incapable of compromise, meet as colleagues on the Budapest weekly newspaper *The Truth* in 1957, the year after the revolution. The rejection of their attempt to expose municipal corruption in a provincial town draws them together as lovers, the film thereby linking sexual and political repression. Livia is shot, but not killed, by her outraged husband. Eva is killed in a suicidal attempt to cross the border into Yugoslavia. In *Rough Treatment*, a celebrated Polish foreign correspondent (modelled on Wajda's friend, the legendary Ryszard Kapuscinski) is first lionised on TV, then gradually undermined and destroyed by the authorities, treacherous colleagues and his own family. 'I worked on this film in a blind rage,' Wajda said at the time. 'It has no flourishes, its impact was to come solely from a logically constructed chain of events.'

We still await the great journalism movie of glasnost and perestroika.

Sadly those newspaper movies of the Soviet Union's last days and of the new Russia have yet to reach us, though God knows there have been enough great stories there.

Sniping at the Front Line
Film Critics Collected and Recollected (1991)

BOOK REVIEW

Kael, Pauline: *Movie Love: Complete Reviews 1988–1991* (Abrahams)

Lejeune, C.A.: *The C.A. Lejeune Film Reader*, ed. Anthony Lejeune (Carcanet)

Powell, Dilys: *The Dilys Powell Film Reader*, ed. Christopher Cook (Carcanet)

Grenier, Richard: *Capturing the Culture: Film, Art, Politics* (Ethnics and Public Policy Center)

Film reviewers work at the front line of criticism, and it has been their customary fate to be sniped at from all sides. Rarely have their reports on the fray been made widely available to posterity other than in a form that serves the person quoting them. Thus younger students of the cinema are most likely to know the writings of C.A. Lejeune and Dilys Powell through quotations in academic texts bent on exposing their snobbish, middle-class inability to perceive the subtleties of Gainsborough melodramas in the 1940s, or in sneering articles about the way contemporary British film critics flinched at Hammer horror movies in the 1950s. But despite the exigencies of weekly journalism (and to an extent because of them), some of the best criticism of movies has always been found in the columns of regular reviewers, in their account of what that fine periodical movie critic Robert Warshow called 'the immediate experience'.

It was not until the late 1960s, when cinema became fashionable in the United States and a subject of academic study, that collections of newspaper and periodical criticism began to appear, and

---

'Sniping at the Front Line' first appeared in the *Times Literary Supplement*, 16 November 1991.

then only in America. The immense success of Pauline Kael's *I Lost It at the Movies* in 1965 stirred publishers, and thereafter several volumes a year appeared – from the living (Stanley Kauffmann, John Simon, Andrew Sarris, Renata Adler) and the dead (Otis Ferguson, Harry Alan Potamkin). The most remarkable consequence of this interest in what had only a few years before been thought of as a dying industry and art form has been the publication of everything Pauline Kael has written for the *New Yorker* in the quarter of a century since she became the magazine's movie critic in 1967.

Ill health more than age (she is a mentally vigorous 72) persuaded Kael to announce her retirement early this year – a decision that shocked and saddened her readers – and *Movie Love* contains her last regular reviews. Her passionate nature leads her to blow hot and cold, and, while never directly political, her collections are presented as reports on the state of the national morale. Her enthusiasm for the anarchic work of Pedro Almodóvar continues, but she finds little to praise in current American cinema. Her chief delights lately have been derived from performances rather than writing or direction, especially the screen appearances of the former nightclub and television satire show comics like Robin Williams, Bill Murray and Steve Martin. 'Mostly,' she observes in the introduction, 'what has been sustaining is that there is so much to love in movies beside great moviemaking.'

Kael remains the only American critic to be regularly available here, and British publishers have been reluctant to take on collections of film reviews. There are commercial considerations at work, but also a more general attitude of disdain. The British Film Institute and the burgeoning cinematic academia served by its education department view newspaper and magazine reviewing with contempt. They see it as impressionistic, unbuttressed by theory, lacking in intellectual rigour. The academics and para-academics would rather produce their own cinematic canon and write their own history. But a history of the cinema must entail a study of contemporary press reactions, especially the work of those critics who aspire to something more than playing the role of reviewer as tipster. A start has been made in this direction by the publication of *The C.A. Lejeune Film Reader* and *The Dilys Powell Film Reader*, books in which I must declare a personal interest, though neither a financial nor a hands-on editorial one. Having several times heard such collections described as uncommercial, I had the opportunity of bringing together the editorial director of Carcanet and a Hong Kong-based lawyer passionately interested in the movies. The latter had consulted me over what he might do to help British film culture (not his term, of course), and the first results of his generous subvention are these two books. I hope others will follow.

Born in Manchester in 1897, C.A. Lejeune (the initials stand for Caroline Alice) wanted to be a theatre critic but settled for being the *Manchester Guardian*'s first fulltime movie critic, an appointment facilitated by the fact that the paper's editor, C.P. Scott, was a family friend. In 1928 she moved to the *Observer*, where Ivor Montagu (table tennis champion, friend of Eisenstein and subsequently producer for Hitchcock) had been the paper's first critic. She remained there until her retirement in 1960 and died in 1973.

Dilys Powell was born in Bournemouth in 1901 and read Modern Languages at Oxford. (Had Lejeune not decided to give up her place at Somerville and read English at Manchester, they might well have overlapped at the same college.) She spent ten years in Athens, where her first husband was Director of the British School, and on his death in 1936 she returned to England and rejoined the *Sunday Times* (for which she had worked after graduating from Oxford), becoming the paper's film critic in 1939. 'In the early days,' she recalls, 'editors didn't appoint people as film critics because they knew anything about the cinema or were thinking seriously about it. It was just somebody who hadn't got a post who could put three words together in roughly the right order.' (The situation has not radically changed.) Ms Powell held the job until 1976, when she became the victim of cynical job manoeuvring at the *Sunday Times* and moved to *Punch*, where in her ninety-first year she continues to write with great verve.

So for much of this century, and for 20 years appearing opposite each other in what were then the only two serious Sunday newspapers, these two women dominated the British film-reviewing scene. Their provincial, middle-class backgrounds and literary educations were similar, and their tastes, while far from identical, were much alike. Both were passionately concerned about the creation of an authentic British cinema and celebrated it judiciously. To a degree that might surprise, even alarm, younger readers, they mixed freely with filmmakers and stars, frequently quoting in their reviews information gleaned from these encounters.

Lejeune is the more imaginative when taking the long view: her first piece on seeing and hearing a talking picture in 1928 (a version of Edgar Wallace's *The Terror*, which preceded *The Jazz Singer* to London) and her 1939 essay on the challenge of television are both wise and uncannily accurate. Dilys Powell, on the other hand, is the better critic film by film, though she stumbled in 1941 over *Citizen Kane* (having to see it a second time to register its significance), while Lejeune wrote one of the most perceptive appreciations of Welles's picture to appear that year.

They are witty, urbane ladies (a word neither would find objectionable) and both could have earned their living as humorous columnists. Lejeune's review of the wartime movie *Millions Like Us* consisted of three words, 'And millions don't', and she often wrote her pieces in verse. The star of the 1945 Hollywood picture *Cross My Heart* inspired these lines:

> I always feel that Sonny Tufts
> Is something rather large from Cruft's:
> Which gives his work, in moderation,
> A certain dogged fascination.

Much of the excitement in these two books – and this is one of the great values of such collections – is seeing how movies one knows well struck critics at the time. Sometimes this can produce a curious *frisson*, as in Lejeune's 1941 review of *Pimpernel Smith*. 'The great quality of *Pimpernel Smith*,' she writes, 'is that it makes you feel you could go out and do the same thing tomorrow.' That was precisely Raoul Wallenberg's reaction when he saw the film at the British Embassy in Stockholm, and it led to his heroic work to save Jews from Eichmann in Nazi-occupied Budapest and to his abduction and disappearance when the Soviet army arrived.

Though uniform in appearance, the books are organised on different principles. *The C.A. Lejeune Reader* has been edited by her son Anthony, whose first published work at the age of 18 was the introduction to his mother's small collection *Chestnuts in Her Lap* (1947). The presentation of the reviews is chronological, with lengthy extracts from her autobiographical writings, and some of the choices and omissions are odd. Rather perversely, the notices of *Citizen Kane* and *The Magnificent Ambersons* have not been included.

The linking editorial commentaries are written with a personal warmth that makes the book in part an act of filial piety, and quite clearly Anthony Lejeune shares his mother's distaste for the general course of British life in the post-war years. As a man of the right, he thinks her insufficiently sensitive to leftwing propaganda, though she makes short shrift of *Mission to Moscow*, the Warner Brothers' 1943 apologia for Stalin, a picture much admired by her contemporaries. The last review he includes is of *Psycho*, directed by her longtime friend Alfred Hitchcock. Dilys Powell was charmed by the movie, having discussed it a few weeks before with Hitchcock in his Los Angeles office. Lejeune walked out in disgust before the end and faithfully reported this to her readers. This action precipitated her departure from the *Observer* four months later, though whether it persuaded her to retire or indicated to the paper's editors that she was growing out of touch remains obscure. It was probably a mixture of the two.

The Dilys Powell Reader has been edited by the filmmaker and critic Christopher Cook, and his approach is altogether more scholarly. He is a lifelong admirer of Powell's work, and his aim is to make out a case for its importance for film students as well as for general readers. Three years ago George Perry of the *Sunday Times* edited *The Golden Screen*, a chronological selection of Powell's reviews to mark her 50 years as a critic. Cook has cast his net wider to include magazine articles, broadcasts on BBC Radio 3 and extracts from British Council pamphlets as well as reviews, and he has arranged the pieces thematically. There are sections on the British cinema, genre, stars and actors, the Touchstone movies and so on. Judging from these books, Powell and Cook are more interested in theory and the craft of criticism than are C.A. and Anthony Lejeune. Powell frequently reflects on the role of the critic and comments on new critical tendencies in the smaller magazines, the work of the *Sequence* critics (Karel Reisz and Lindsay Anderson among them) in the late 1940s, and the writers on *Movie* magazine, who brought *auteur*-ism to Britain in the 1960s. In 1962 she encapsulates in a sentence some critical currents over the previous 30 years, 'from the brisk social pamphleteering of the Grierson period to the invective and aesthetics of *Sequence*; from Lindsay Anderson and commitment to anti-commitment and the beauty of wrists bleeding in buckets'.

The central tradition of British criticism, which Powell and Lejeune exemplify, is a liberal, secular-humanist one. When it departs radically from this it is towards the left, which has been until recently the principal source of attacks on liberalism and liberal values. The same is true of American criticism. However, with the rise of neo-conservatism and the politicisation of arts coverage in the United States (and to a lesser extent in Britain), there has been a search for a new style of political critic who has found his or her new home in such New York-based journals as the *New Criterion*, the *American Spectator* and *Commentary*. The only person in this area to have established his reputation through movie criticism is Richard Grenier.

He is the most interesting critic to emerge since Pauline Kael took New York by storm, and like her he was well into his forties when he arrived on the national scene in the late 1970s. Before that he had been a career naval officer and then a foreign correspondent and a movie scenarist based in Paris. Kael made her name with articles that examined audiences and fellow critics with a ferocity similar to that which she brought to bear on the movies themselves. Grenier's approach is much the same, though he is less concerned with the sensibilities and insensitivities of critics and audiences than with their ignorance and gullibility. He originally categorised himself as a Cold War liberal but would no doubt accept the neo-conservative label, and it is characteristically provocative that he should have invited the rightwing jurist Robert H. Bork to write an admiring introduction to *Capturing the Culture*. Inevitably Bork praises him for 'exposing and skewering the political left'.

Grenier is at his best in the long essays he contributed to *Commentary* between 1979 and 1986, and it was good to see him appearing there again this year with a couple of pungent polemical pieces on the reception of *Dances with Wolves* and the current wave of movies by black directors. Put crudely, his position is that Hollywood of late has been largely dominated by fashionable upholders of radical chic like Jane Fonda, Warren Beatty and Meryl Streep, that the majority of critics are blinkered, bleeding-heart liberals with little knowledge of either art or politics, and that middle-class audiences are suckers for any kind of anti-American propaganda. They are united in their lack of civic and patriotic virtue, and Grenier has taken his title from Antonio Gramsci's battle cry 'capture the culture'. The left has been able to control the mass media and cultural discourse, Grenier argues, because of 'the spiritual estrangement of the artistic and intellectual classes'. It is his project to lead a counter-attack. His allies are the average Middle American hard-hat moviegoers and the actors they have turned into mega-stars: Clint Eastwood, Sylvester Stallone, Burt Reynolds and Eddie Murphy, who stand for sturdy patriotism and (the first three at least) campaign for the Republican Party.

These robust political notions and the aggressive, forensic manner with which they are displayed are accompanied by considerable literary gifts, an analytic intelligence and a formidable knowledge (not always lightly worn) of cinema, history and literature. At his best, Grenier is brilliant, though like those who place their trust in the supposed good sense of the mass public, he is often put in the embarrassing position of having to confront and explain away the immense success of something he dislikes.

There are few positive pieces in *Capturing the Culture*. This is a pity. He should have included his *Commentary* essays on the 'Tory Wit' of Monty Python, his moving defence of *An Officer and a Gentleman* and the different movie treatments of the mutiny on the *Bounty*. But this would have turned *Capturing the Culture* into another collection of film criticism, and this Grenier does not wish his book to be.

More than half of his space is given over to short articles, only some of them on the cinema, written for the rightwing *Washington Times*, for which he has been a regular columnist since the mid-1960s. Here he lowers his sights and descends to cheap liberal-baiting. Often writing in a slick tabloid style, he plays up to his readers' prejudices while at the same time talking down to them. He lays into Martin Scorsese for having accepted money for directing *The Last Temptation of Christ*, accuses Carlos Fuentes of writing for 'the Martha's Vineyard set', dismisses Kennet Branagh's *Henry V* as ahistorical because it appears to take an anti-war stance. His cosmopolitan sophistication deserts him in these columns at the very moment that he flaunts it.

That grand old liberal, the late Dwight Macdonald, himself one of America's most trenchant movie critics, called Grenier 'our best practising movie critic/historian'. To be worthy of that accolade, rather than to seek the good opinions of Judge Bork and Justice

Thomas, Grenier would have been better advised to make a collection drawn entirely from his *Commentary* essays. He should have got his friend Senator Daniel P. Moynihan to write the introduction, chosen a New York trade publisher rather than an allegedly 'non-partisan' Washington think-tank to bring out his book, and left the *Washington Times* columns to moulder in the files.

The Value of Preying Together
Charles Addams and his Family (1993)

There was a time when Adams houses were understood to be neo-classical buildings with light interiors designed by the eighteenth-century Scottish architects Robert and James Adam. Equally, the Adams family meant the distinguished New England clan that provided the United States with its second and fifth presidents. Nowadays, as the result of a frequently revived 1960s television series and two movies of the 1990s (*The Addams Family* and, about to be released, *Addams Family Values*), the Addams family is universally recognised as the collection of Gothic grotesques created by the *New Yorker* cartoonist Charles Addams, and the Addams's house the forbidding Victorian mansion – penumbrous within, topped outside with a steep, spiked mansard roof – where they live.

Charles Addams (as late as 1951, in an adulatory article on the *New Yorker* by W.H. Auden for the *Observer*, he was denied his second 'd') was born in 1912 in a small New Jersey town, the only child of a former naval architect employed by a Manhattan manufacturer of pianos and organs. Both shy and gregarious, he belonged to the Boy Scouts and 'lived in my imagination in the back yard'. He read widely, with *Treasure Island* and Conan Doyle's historical romances among his favourites, books that developed his taste for irony, understatement and British phlegm. The Krazy Kat cartoon trio, John Tenniel's drawings for *Alice* and the Gothic illustrations for fairy tales by Arthur Rackham took his childhood fancy, with the influence of Goya and Gustave Doré added while he was a student at the University of Pennsylvania and New York's Grand Central School of Art.

'The Value of Preying Together' first appeared in the *Observer*, 28 November 1993.

But Addams always wanted to be a comic artist, and from what he calls his 'early puberty' he set his sights on the *New Yorker*. The magazine was launched when he was 13 and published his work for the first time shortly after his twenty-first birthday. At that point he was working for a pulp crime magazine, painting the marks on scene-of-crime pictures to show where the corpses lay.

That first cartoon he later thought 'pretty unfunny', though he viewed it with affection – a hockey player on the ice in stocking feet exclaiming 'I forgot my skates'. A certain taste for the gruesome is there from the start, but there is something brash and uneasy about his early work, as well as a callow eroticism. On these first cartoons the distinctive signature 'Chas Addams' is vertical, open, rather tentative. But the characteristic method is there – that combination of Indian ink and wash, so well suited to the *New Yorker*'s high-quality letterpress reproduction; and by the end of the decade the signature is condensed, horizontal, confidently blocked in.

In *Drawn and Quartered* (1942), the first of the nine macabrely titled collections published in his lifetime, a personal world of ghouls, explorers, witch doctors, witches, giants, monsters, homicidal spouses and crazy inventors is mapped out. The book contains two of his most famous drawings – the woman skier leaving tracks on either side of a tree, and the blasé Manhattanite commenting, 'It doesn't take much to raise a crowd in New York', as he passes a throng of people actually watching a businessman locked in mortal combat with a vast octopus emerging from a manhole.

Boris Karloff wrote an introduction to *Drawn and Quartered*, shrewdly pointing out that the best drawings were the ones without captions and thanking the artist for immortalising him as the family butler. In fact, the butler was initially bearded and didn't resemble Universal Studio's version of Frankenstein's Monster until 1939; and until Addams met and married a beautiful woman (his first wife Barbara Day), the mistress of the house was much less alluring than her final incarnation.

The Gothic house was created in 1937 for a joke about a vacuum-cleaner salesman, and Harold Ross, the *New Yorker*'s founding editor, encouraged Addams to enlarge the family. So he added a husband (his appearance a joke at the expense of the Republican politician Thomas E. Dewey), a grotesque grandmother, sinister children and the cheerful, hairless ghoul (later to be known as Uncle

Fester), with whom Addams was known to identify.

By the early 1940s the Family was happily preparing to pour a cauldron of boiling oil (or, as some think, molten lead) from its mansard roof onto a party of carol singers. This 50-year-old cartoon was reconstructed at the beginning of the first *Addams Family* movie in 1991. An even earlier one – a guest being told 'If you want anything, just scream' – is recreated in *Addams Family Values.*

The Family turns on a single joke – the inversion of the *Saturday Evening Post* covers of cosy middle-American families drawn by Norman Rockwell. It was partly for this reason that Addams's work was thought to be valuably subversive, a contribution to the counter-culture in the bland, conformist Eisenhower years. That was the time when the glossy magazine *McCall's* advertised itself as 'the magazine of togetherness', and notice boards outside churches across America bore the slogan 'The family that prays together stays together'.

For years Addams rejected offers to turn the Family into a television sitcom. But when he learnt that a forthcoming series was setting out to rip him off, he agreed to give a producer the go-ahead, and throughout 1964–65, *The Addams Family* on ABC competed with the rather cruder *The Munsters* on CBS. As soon as this network battle began, William Shawn, Harold Ross's successor, decreed puritanically that Addams Family cartoons would be banished from the *New Yorker.* Addams of course continued to be the magazine's most prolific and popular artist, and it may well be that Shawn's decision forced him to new heights of inspiration. Certainly much of his finest work was done in the 1970s and 1980s. Not until after Shawn's enforced retirement in 1987 (it preceded Addams's death by a year) did the magazine relent and the Family return to its pages.

Shawn had incidentally refused back in 1969 to accept advertising for *Dear Dead Days*, a collection of pictures and drawings of freaks, burial practices, mortician advertisements and so on that purported to be Addams's source book.

Brendan Gill, the *New Yorker*'s longest-serving staff member and the magazine's historian, once wrote that the first question *New Yorker* readers always put to the paper's writers was 'What's Charles Addams really like?' I got the opportunity to find out in the 1970s, after I had written an article for the *Times Literary Supplement* which apparently pleased Addams. Because it treated him as a serious comic

artist and not as a suitable case for treatment, he agreed to break the
habit of a lifetime and record a conversation for the BBC Third
Programme.

His Manhattan base was a penthouse flat in an apartment block
across the road from the Museum of Modern Art, and visitors had
to leave the lift at the twelfth floor and climb a dark staircase past a
door ominously marked '13'. My eyes popped like a character in an
Addams cartoon. The flat into which I emerged was like a little
museum, with rows of ornately carved crossbows and suits of mediaeval armour.

Addams himself was a large jovial man with a bulbous nose, his
once-black hair now grey. Whereas in photographs from the past
he always wore a dark blue suit, he was now casually dressed in
open-necked shirt, pullover and slacks. He served me tea in a mug
decorated with a memorably gruesome detail from a cartoon (a man
being swallowed by a snake) and we proceeded to record a long,
relaxed, informative conversation. He rejected psychological expla-
nations, but he did reveal that he had had a great fear of snakes,
something he had worked out through drawing them.

He assured me he had never drawn or submitted the infamous
cartoon of a ghoulish father telling a nurse in a maternity ward,
'Don't bother to wrap it, I'll eat it on the way home', and he empha-
sised how gratified he was that children got so much pleasure from
his work. 'It's almost my sole contact with children,' he said. 'I've
never had any of my own, and I like to think I have not been
completely out of touch.'

Apart from drawings, Addams's great passion was owning and
driving fast European cars. He had a 1926 Bugatti, a 1928 Mercedes-
Benz, a 1933 Aston Martin and various Alfa Romeos, and it was
generally expected that he would meet his death speeding towards
his Long Island country house. In fact he had a massive heart attack
in 1988, as he was turning on the ignition outside his New York
home. He died within an hour. His third wife, Tee Miller, whom
he married in a Long Island cemetery, arranged a memorial service
in the New York Public Library, where large quantities of drink
were consumed to the strains of a Dixieland jazz band.

So productive was Addams that in the five years since his death
his cartoons have continued to be a regular feature of the *New Yorker*
– until, that is, last February when what was labelled as 'The Last

Cartoon' appeared, a full-page drawing of a mediaeval king (looking like Uncle Fester with a crown) standing on the battlements of his castle and addressing the assembled populace thus: 'And now, as an experiment in democracy, I'm decreeing free elections to choose the national bird.'

Also this year, his second wife, Lady Colyton, endowed the Charles Addams Memorial Prize for the outstanding graduate art student at the University of Pennsylvania, in honour of the man who 'left a graphic style and a comic genre that will always bear his name'.

A Streak of Malice
Graham Greene and the Movies (1994)

BOOK REVIEW
Parkinson, David, (ed.): *Mornings in the Dark: The Graham Greene Film Reader*

Graham Greene was born in 1904, the year after *The Great Train Robbery* was made, and he grew up with the movies, first influenced by them, then influencing them himself. As novelist, screenwriter, critic, producer and provider of cinematic material, no author of comparable stature has been so closely involved with the cinema. Only two works in the Greene canon remain unfilmed, *It's a Battlefield* and *A Burnt-Out Case*, and both were optioned, the first by Simone Signoret, the second by Otto Preminger.

Greene had what we used to call a love-hate relationship with the movies as art and industry. It reflected his passionate and contradictory attitude to the social currents of the century he chronicled. Twice – in 1949 and 1958 – he publicly announced that he would never again become involved in movie production, but his interest never flagged, though his once obsessive moviegoing became infrequent after 1960. Though living close by, he refused numerous invitations to become a juror at the Cannes Film Festival, and in 1979 he turned down an invitation from his former lover, the Swedish actress Anita Björk, to attend the Cannes screening of a Norwegian movie that gave her a rare major part. Appropriately enough, on the more significant of the two occasions that he allowed himself to be filmed, Greene posed as Henry Graham, a retired English businessman, to secure the brief role of a London insurance broker in François Truffaut's *La Nuit américaine* at Nice's

---

'A Streak of Malice' first appeared in the *Times Literary Supplement*, 25 February 1994.

Victorine Studio. This tragi-comic account of the agonies and ecstasies of filmmaking starred Truffaut himself as the embattled artist caught up, Laocoon-like, in the commercial movie business.

In 1970, the year Greene began editing his definitive *Collected Edition*, he was interviewed on stage at the National Film Theatre by Philip Oakes. One of the first questioners from the audience asked if he planned to reprint his film criticism. 'No,' Greene replied. 'If somebody would publish it, I would. No, it's a little bit *vieux jeu* now.' The answer was astonishing. After all, except for the five months when he travelled Mexico's lawless roads in 1938, Greene had written on the cinema nearly every week between 1935 and 1940, mostly for the *Spectator*, but also briefly for the short-lived *Night and Day*, which he co-edited with John Marks, the film critic of the *New Statesman* and first English translator of Céline's *Voyage au bout de la nuit*. This was the crucial period between his most self-consciously cinematic novel, *It's a Battlefield* and *The Power and the Glory*, which saw the evolution of the mature style, the charting of Greeneland (a term coined by Arthur Calder-Marshall, that Greene affected to detest), and Greene taking his place among the pre-eminent authors of his generation.

Two years later, *The Pleasure Dome*, subtitled 'Collected film criticism 1935–1940', appeared, but not under Greene's auspices or from his publisher, the Bodley Head. It was edited by John Russell Taylor, then the film critic of *The Times* and published in an opulent illustrated edition by Secker and Warburg, with an introduction by Greene, which had appeared a dozen years before in an obscure film annual. It struck me at the time as the best collection of film criticism by any British writer, a superb book comparable with the not dissimilar *Agee on Film*. I hold to that view, and the recurrent issues Greene dealt with in the 1930s are uncannily like those of today: the Hollywood juggernaut crushing all before it, the perpetual crisis of the British film industry, the idiocy of the British Board of Film Censors, the English failure to take the cinema as seriously as the other arts, the major exhibitors' lack of nerve, and even the proliferation of remakes.

The Pleasure Dome, however, was an unsatisfactory book for two reasons. First, it wasn't 'the collected criticism'. More was missing from the week-by-week reviews than merely the necessarily omitted libellous 1937 notice of *Wee Willie Winkie* from *Night and*

Day. Secondly, it did not include any of Greene's general, reflec-
tive essays on the cinema. Now David Parkinson has gone far
beyond meeting the demands made by dissatisfied readers back in
1972. His magnificent *Mornings in the Dark* is well over twice the
length of *The Pleasure Dome* and includes all the criticism, going back
to pieces for *Oxford Outlook* and *The Times* in the 1920s, as well as
discursive essays, reviews of movie books, some film scripts and
treatments, interviews (including transcripts of Greene's two NFT
appearances), letters relating to film, a couple of short stories, a
substantial filmography, and his 1956 poem for Malcolm
Muggeridge's *Punch*, satirising the wedding of Grace Kelly and
Prince Rainier.

The reviews form the core of the book, and they stand up well
for their judgment, wit and readability, and for the light they throw
on Greene's mind and development. There is relish in his praise and
punishment, in his hopes and in his despair, and in his love of the
technical language of the movies. Duvivier and Lang he rated most
highly among international directors. He admired Capra, Ford and
Hawks. He noted the promise of both Carol Reed and Thorold
Dickinson on the occasion of their modest débuts. He loved thrillers
(but thought Hitchcock's films, other than *Sabotage*, mere bags of
tricks) and personal documentaries (though he had nothing but
contempt for Flaherty). He rightly preferred the simple early Marx
Brothers films at Paramount to their over-produced MGM pictures,
and in a characteristically felicitous phrase speaks of the Paramount
movies having 'titles as meaningless and undifferentiated as
Kipling's'. On the debit side, he writes of *Top Hat* that 'it doesn't
matter that the music and lyrics are bad' (it does, and they aren't),
and in reviewing *Anything Goes* he states that 'a really dreadful
woman singer murders the Audenesque charm of "Anything
Goes"'. He's talking about Ethel Merman. A statement by Chekhov
about 'life as it is and life as it ought to be' is reiterated, as he argues
with himself about what popular cinema should aspire to.

Greene blasts away at his fellow reviewers for their ignorance,
fatuity and venality. Year after year, he uses the *Observer*'s C.A.
Lejeune as the butt of his jokes about middle-class gentility, just as
in the 1960s he relentlessly pursued his social and literary *bête noire*,
C.P. Snow. There is a consistent streak of malice in this lifelong
practical joker, and one form it takes in the film criticism is the

constant assault upon the sexuality and physical presences of actresses. Madeleine Carroll 'has the less endearing traits of a young elephant'; Garbo is several times called a filly; 'I must confess to a perverse passion for Miss Maureen O'Sullivan, she satisfies a primeval instinct for a really nice girl.' In part this can be seen as expressing the frustrations of a young, unhappily married middle-class Catholic in the 1930s, but the preoccupation emerges with the earliest piece in the book, a 1925 *Oxford Outlook* essay that begins: 'We are most of us nowadays considerably over-sexed.' This article, through its incorrect reference to worshipping the Virgin Mary rather than venerating her, led to a correspondence with Vivien Dayrell-Browning, his conversion to Catholicism, and their marriage.

The sexual criticism took its most notorious form in the *Wee Willie Winkie* review that accused the producers at 20th Century-Fox of manipulating the eight-year-old Shirley Temple's 'dimpled depravity' to appeal to 'middle-aged men and clergy'. It is not without interest that Greene was the first person to acclaim Nabokov's *Lolita* on its initial publication in Paris, and that Shirley Temple in her autobiography confirmed everything that Greene had inferred and implied about her producers and older admirers. The *Wee Willie Winkie* review was not hostile to John Ford, though some think he got his own back on Greene through *The Fugitive*, a terrible movie version of *The Power and the Glory*.

Christopher Hawtree's facsimile anthology of highlights from *Night and Day* in 1985 was the first time the *Wee Willie Winkie* review was reprinted, and it is good to see it restored to the context of the film criticism in Parkinson's *Reader*. Naturally this is the major addition, but there are others of interest, including items as charming as this curt dismissal at the end of a 1939 *Spectator* column:

As for *Man About Town*, it is just one of those doggish American films of sexual and social ambition which sadly recalls Davenant's definition: 'Humour is the drunkenness of a Nation that no sleep can cure.'

Among the general essays, perhaps the most interesting is one called 'Is It Criticism?', published in the Autumn 1936 *Sight & Sound*, which concludes by suggesting that satire is the best weapon for critics in the present situation. But he goes on to add that

I am not sure whether our fellow critics are not more important subjects for our satire than the cinema itself, for they are doing as much as any Korda or Sam Goldwyn to maintain the popular middle-class Book Society *status quo*.

The Critics' Circle did not, I believe, rally to Greene's defence when Sir Patrick Hastings KC was briefed by 20th Century-Fox's solicitors to take him apart in the Strand.

Parkinson has done a remarkable job of tracking down fugitive material, compiling this book and introducing it with an admirable essay. The errors that have inevitably slipped into so grand a project can easily be corrected in later editions. There is, however, one odd aspect. Parkinson concludes the main body of the book with two short stories, one the familiar 'Blue Movie' of 1954 (which I think inspired an episode of *Steptoe and Son*), the other an unknown tale called 'All But Empty', which appeared in the *Strand* magazine in 1947 and was reprinted in *Ellery Queen's Mystery Magazine* two years later. 'All But Empty' is in fact a brief, coarse version of Greene's 1939 Grand Guignol yarn, 'A Little Place Off the Edgware Road', about a macabre encounter with a murder victim in a London cinema. It would be interesting to know under what circumstances Greene wrote 'All But Empty'. I suggest that it preceded the more developed 1939 tale.

Mention of 'A Little Place Off the Edgware Road' raises important issues about the editing of Greene and about Britain in the 1930s. In the post-war years, Greene's quixotic, often naive left-wing views, influenced by a lifelong Americanophobia, took him in odd directions. Orwell remarked in 1949 that 'I have even thought that he might become our first Catholic fellow-traveller', an observation that 30 years later Greene thought most perceptive. But before the Second World War, Greene's robust liberal stance rejected the totalitarianism of left and right, and he wittily exposed its cinematic expression. Those pre-war writings, however, are more than a little tinged with a conventional anti-Semitism of the kind too easily excused as 'gentlemanly'.

In the 1960s, he began quietly editing this out of his fiction as the new editions appeared. The two pejorative uses of 'Jew' to signify libidinousness in the version of 'A Little Place Off the Edgware Road' in *Nineteen Stories* (1947) were omitted from an otherwise unrevised text of the tale included in the *Collected Stories* (1972). In 'Film Lunch', his famous satirical account of a 1937 reception to launch MGM's programme of British films, Greene wrote of Louis B. Mayer's 'little level Jewish voice'. The adjective 'Jewish' disappeared between the 1962 Penguin edition of *The Lost Childhood* and the publication of 'Film Lunch' in *Collected Essays* (1969), and it is the revised version that is included in *Mornings in the Dark*.

Greene was not, however, consulted over *The Pleasure Dome*, nor of course over this new book. There are therefore lines that are painful to read, and which he would almost certainly have suppressed. Remaining, they either explain the animus Greene had towards the Jewish producers who dominated the film industry, or (more likely) demonstrate the prejudices his dislike of their role inflamed. In 1936, he noted that 'we have saved the English film industry from American competition only to surrender it to a far more alien control'. 'Alien' is a code word for Jewish immigrant, as it is later in the same article, where Greene speaks of 'watching the dark alien executive tipping his cigar ash behind the glass partition in Wardour Street'. This is T.S. Eliot's 'Bleistein with a Cigar' moving into pictures. What are we to understand by 'the awful un-Aristotelean waste of this Semitic and commercial craft' (1937)? Most offensively, in the spring of 1939 Greene can remark: 'How the financial crisis has improved British films! They have lost their Semitic opulence and are becoming – English.' The punctuation speaks for itself.

One must add, of course, that Alexander Korda, the Jewish immigrant mogul Greene most frequently lambasted in the 1930s, responded to the critical barbs with kindness. They became close friends, and Korda produced the two movies of which Greene was most proud, *The Fallen Idol* and *The Third Man*.

The best account of how Greene came to appear in Truffaut's La Nuit américaine *is to be found in* Not Prince Hamlet *(published in the United States as* Words Through a Window*), the 1988 autobiography of his friend, the British translator and biographer Michael Meyer.*

The Miner in the Arts (1994)

On the occasion of the opening of Claude Berri's film of Émile Zola's Germinal.

As a child I spent school holidays with my godmother's family in the West Riding. Her father was a miner, and every afternoon I would take Peter, their Yorkshire collie, to meet him as he emerged, covered in grime, from the small nearby pit. In my mind's eye it now seems like a scene from *Lassie Come Home*. Back at the family cottage I'd help his wife fill the zinc tub for the bath he took, screened in front of the fire. I idolised him for the manly work he did, so different from the dull, clean office jobs of my father's lower-middle-class world.

Influenced by this experience and by movies that romanticised the mining community, I wanted to be a collier, and the real possibility arose when Ernest Bevin, Minister of Labour in Churchill's War Cabinet, announced that instead of doing conventional military service, some lads would be randomly chosen by ballot to work in the mines. *Boys' Own Paper*, no doubt under pressure from the Ministry of Information, ran a rousing serial called *Black Diamonds*, the name of a rugby team formed by some public-school Bevin Boys. They took on the local working-class lads to prove they could cut it above and below ground when drafted to work in the Welsh coalfields. Some notable people became Bevin Boys, Eric Morecambe and the playwrights Peter Shaffer and Alun Owen among them. Shaffer's *Black Comedy* (1965), which takes place entirely in the dark, may have been influenced as much by life at the pit face as by the Peking Opera. And when Richard Hughes was invited by the BBC in 1924 to write the first 'listening play', he produced

'The Miner in the Arts' first appeared in the *Observer*, 1 May 1994.

Danger, set down a coal mine where the lights are extinguished by an explosion.

Fortunately, when I came to do my National Service in the 1950s, Bevin Boys were history. By then I had acquired a proper knowledge of the hazards to lung and limb and the backbreaking work involved in mining. Yet a certain romantic attachment remained, and still does for me, an idealisation of the collier as the aristocrat of the working class. Unlike gold-miners he produces something essential and works without any prospect of striking it rich. This explains the popular emotions aroused by pit closures, culminating last week in the end of Tower Colliery, the last deep mine in South Wales.

The ambivalence about coal-mining – an admiration for the heroes who go down the mines, the belief that it is an intolerable way for men to earn their daily bread – is captured in *Germinal*, Emile Zola's seminal novel about the French coal industry, published in 1885. Dismissed by a leading British critic early this century as 'a chronicle of wasted grime', *Germinal* features the incidents and themes that inform all subsequent treatments of mining life in literature and the arts: the harsh work, the constant danger from fire, gas, collapsing tunnels; the miner as a potential agent of political change through mutual dependency in the pit being translated into solidarity above ground; the exploitation, degradation, class conflict and strikes; the sense of a world that is neither rural nor urban; a community of brutalised men cut off from their sensitive womenfolk. From *Germinal* two principal traditions stem, and sometimes intertwine. The first is identified with the greatest writer to deal with coal-miners, D.H. Lawrence, himself the son of a collier. A pit strike is the background to his play *The Daughter-in-Law* (1912) and a death underground is central to another of his plays, *The Widowing of Mrs Holroyd* (1914), but in general Lawrence avoids melodramatic scenes as well as politics. Over a period of 20 years, from his first play, *A Collier's Friday Night* (1906), which anticipates his first major novel, *Sons and Lovers* (1913), up to *Lady Chatterley's Lover* (1928), his view of mining gets bleaker and bleaker. An initial belief in community gives way to seeing mining as the destruction of an older order, the desolation of the land, the disruption of human bonds.

In *Women in Love* (1915), which Lawrence thought his best

novel, Gerald Crich, the colliery owner whose soul has been destroyed by the pursuit of power, leaves the coal-blackened English Midlands to seek a redemptive death in the snow-covered Alps. In *Aaron's Rod* (1922) a collier quits his family to live abroad playing his flute. In *Lady Chatterley's Lover*, Mellors the gamekeeper is a miner's son getting in touch with nature; his employer, the impotent Clifford Chatterley, whose family raped the land it inherited, went straight from studying mining engineering in Germany to the trenches of the Western Front; Clifford's wife, Constance, is an outsider from the Home Counties appalled by what she sees in Nottinghamshire. 'Incarnate ugliness, and yet alive!' she reflects on the miners. 'What would become of them all? Perhaps with the passing of the coal they would disappear again off the face of the earth.'

Lawrence, whom F.R. Leavis called 'the great writer of our phase of civilisation', had a major influence on the generation of working-class authors that sprang up in the 1960s, several of whom (Stan Barstow, David Storey and Dennis Potter among them) were the sons of miners. The toughest on the mining community, though a more compassionate writer than Lawrence, is David Storey. His masterly first novel *This Sporting Life* (1960), filmed by Lindsay Anderson in 1963 and starring Richard Harris, has as its coarse, brawny hero a Yorkshireman who escapes from the mines by becoming a professional rugby league footballer. From his second novel, *Flight into Camden* (1960) to the Booker Prize-winning *Saville* (1976), the sons and daughters of Yorkshire miners are breaking away from home in the manner of Lawrence's alter ego, Paul Morel, to become middle-class professionals.

The other tradition takes a more benign (often sentimental) view of the mining world than is to be found in Zola or Lawrence. This is the tradition of the best-selling authors A.J. Cronin, who drew on his experiences as a medical inspector of mines in South Wales, and Richard Llewellyn, a Welsh miner's son who left the pits to study hotel management.

Cronin's *The Citadel* (1937) and *The Stars Look Down* (1935) became popular British movies of the late 1930s; Llewellyn's *How Green Was My Valley* was turned into an affecting, sentimental Hollywood picture in 1940. During the Depression of the 1930s and in World War Two, the miner was celebrated first as exemplary working-class victim and then as provider of fuel for the fight against fascism. Among the first great European sound movies was G.W. Pabst's *Kameradschaft* (1931), set immediately after World War One and centring on the healing collaboration between former enemies during a mining disaster on the Franco-German border.

Numerous documentaries were made at this time, most memorably Cavalcanti's *Coal Face* (1935), with a verse refrain by W.H. Auden. Humphrey Jennings's documentaries discovered the visual poetry of the industrial landscape, and mining communities also attracted photographers like Humphrey Spender, Bill Brandt, Robert Capa and Edwin Smith. Henry Moore, the son of a colliery employee, made wartime drawings of Yorkshire miners that stand alongside his London shelter drawings. Josef Herman, the Polish émigré painter, lived in Wales and transformed the local miners into heroic figures. Most critics today, however, find Moore's and Herman's work less powerful and authentic than the artists of the Ashington Group, all of them Northumberland miners.

In a thoughtful 1966 Third Programme talk on the collier in fiction (the *Listener*, 28 April 1966), Laurence Kitchin observed: 'Lately the miner has emerged as a folk hero, embodying an epic past ... he was the mediator between fuel and power.' Kitchin's tone was elegiac, coming after a succession of pit closures and the departure of the last steam train from Paddington and shortly before the disaster at Aberfan. How right he was. Except for the remarkable work of Ken Loach – *Kes* (1969) in the cinema, *The Price of Coal* (1977) on television – our filmmakers have turned to the past. They no doubt find political struggles of earlier eras easier to handle, and they prefer pipe-puffing, chapel-going workers dressed in caps and mufflers, their hearts full of socialist hope, a choral song on their lips, to the miners of today. Whatever, since Jack Cardiff's fine Edwardian version of *Sons and Lovers* (1960), most mining pictures have been period pieces.

Martin Ritt's *The Molly Maguires* (1970) takes the side of rebellious miners in the Pennsylvania coalfields of the 1870s. In the Disney production *Escape from the Dark* (1976), a colliery manager's little daughter in 1909 Yorkshire joins some miners' children in rescuing pit ponies, and Ron Goodwin's incidental music is played by the Grimethorpe Colliery Brass Band. The Communist hero of the Australian movie *Strikebound* (1983) leads a 'stay-down' strike in the Victoria coalfields in the 1930s, and John Sayles's politically committed *Matewan* (1987), also based on a true story, re-creates a strike at a West Virginia mine in the 1920s. Now we are back to the beginning with Gérard Depardieu and most of the French acting profession in Claude Berri's epic version of *Germinal*, an assertion of the French cinema's abiding grandeur.

Two significant mining movies followed in the next six years, both elegiac in tone. In the first, Mark Herman's Brassed Off *(1996), Pete Postlethwaite played the leader of a colliery brass band, the only thing left to be proud of in a decaying Yorkshire town. In a crude, corny, irresistible film that packed an Old Labour punch, Postlethwaite delivers a powerful leftwing speech during a miners' visit to London that was cut from the version released in the States. He also played an angelic taxi driver in a brilliant Labour Party political broadcast during the 1997 General Election, directed by Stephen Frears.*

The second film was Stephen Daldry's directorial debut, Billy Elliot *(2000), which contained a heartbreaking performance by Jamie Bell as an 11-year-old Durham lad who falls in love with dancing, much to the disgust of his miner father. The background is the 1984 miners' strike, perceived in the film as a defining moment when the values created by industrial society lost their validity. It's a graceful, lyrical movie, a trifle sentimental, but genuinely felt.*

Hollywood and the Holocaust (1994)

Hitler's concentration camps and the likely fate of the Jews under Nazism were not unknown in the late 1930s nor wholly ignored by the cinema. In 1938 *Professor Mamlock*, a movie about German anti-Semitism and the inevitable movement towards the Final Solution was made by a group of Jewish refugees living in Moscow. Unfortunately their Communist sympathies led to the film being ignored or banned in the West. In Britain the filmmaking twins, John and Roy Boulting, planned a movie about Pastor Martin Niemöller, a Protestant cleric arrested by the Gestapo in 1938 and sent to Sachsenhausen and eventually Dachau for his outspoken anti-Nazism and support for the Jews. However, the project was blocked by the British Board of Film Censors, and it was not until war broke out that they were able to make their picture, *Pastor Hall*, finally released in 1940.

In Leslie Howard's *Pimpernel Smith* (1941), a British liberal rescues scientists and intellectuals from Hitler's grasp just before the outbreak of war. It was seeing this movie at the British Embassy's cinema in Stockholm that inspired the Swedish diplomat Raoul Wallenberg to undertake his heroic mission to save Hungarian Jews from deportation. Meanwhile, in a then neutral America, Charlie Chaplin made *The Great Dictator* (1940), identifying himself through his tramp persona with the persecuted Jews in Germany.

After the occupation of continental Europe and America's entry into the war the cinematic emphasis shifted to upbeat stories of resistance and joint national endeavour. Jews principally appeared as representative figures in ethnically and geographically balanced Hollywood platoons and aircrews. At a 1944 conference to discuss the morale-boosting action movie *Objective Burma!* starring Errol Flynn, studio boss Jack L. Warner remarked: 'I like the idea of

'Hollywood and the Holocaust' first appeared in the *Observer*, 13 February 1994.

having a Jewish officer in Burma. See that you get a good clean-cut American type for Lieutenant Jacobs.'

In 1945 the Allies pushed into Germany, and the extermination camps were liberated, exposing their emaciated survivors, piles of corpses and the dreadful apparatus of destruction. Filmmakers were there in the vanguard of discovery, among them Major George Stevens, head of an American combat camera unit. Having previously specialised in light comedy, Stevens thereafter devoted himself to movies that probed the human condition, *The Diary of Anne Frank* (1959) among them.

In early May 1945, just days before the war ended, the first newsreel films from Belsen and Buchenwald were shown in British cinemas. The effect was immediate. Newsreels were not subject to censorship, nothing like these images had been seen before, and here they were among the cartoons and main features at neighbourhood movie houses. Their impact, as the historian Martin Gilbert says in his magisterial study *The Holocaust* (1986), was 'so great ... that the word "Belsen" was to become synonymous with "inhumanity"'.

In 1945, shortly after the final victory over Japan, newsreels provided evidence of another holocaust, the bombing of Hiroshima and Nagasaki. The Holocaust (the dysphemism chosen by Jewish historians to replace the Nazis' ghastly euphemism, the Final Solution) and the Nuclear Holocaust – the one in the past, the other in the future – were to hang over the next half-century like a mushroom cloud. The phrase 'thinking the unthinkable' entered the language, and both holocausts constituted a peculiar challenge to artists, social thinkers and filmmakers.

Alfred Hitchcock was brought over to Britain in 1945 by his media-mogul friend Sidney Bernstein to compile a full-length documentary from the camp footage. Considered too horrific to be shown in cinemas, the result was deposited in the Imperial War Museum. The euphoria of victory was brief, people's energies were absorbed by the demands of peace: the Nazi hierarchy went on trial at Nuremberg in 1946; the Cold War began at about the same time; and the struggle to create the state of Israel got underway, casting the Jews as dynamic opponents of a prevaricating Britain. Orson Welles's *The Stranger* (1946) launched an endless cycle of thrillers about Nazi war criminals (Welles's villain gives himself away by saying that Karl Marx was a Jew, not a German), and Hollywood embarked on a series of movies attacking anti-Semitism. Ben Hecht, Hollywood's highest-paid screenwriter and leading Zionist, was blacklisted for several years following an anti-British outburst in the late 1940s.

In 1949 the surprise success of William Wellman's downbeat *Battleground* brought the war movie back into favour, and it remained a staple entertainment genre for a quarter of a century. These mainstream pictures touched only occasionally on the Holocaust, as when, for instance, the US army unit in which a GI played by Montgomery Clift is serving liberates a death camp in Richard Brooks's *The Young Lions* (1958).

But in 1955 the French documentarist Alain Resnais made *Night and Fog*, an eloquent meditation on Auschwitz, interweaving black-and-white newsreel material with colour film of the camp as it was in 1955. The commentary was written by the novelist Jean Cayrol, himself a concentration camp survivor. This benchmark movie set the standards for everything that was to follow, though it didn't reach Britain until five years later and was then given an X-certificate. By that time Resnais had established himself as a feature film director with an equally haunting movie, also about guilt, responsibility, memory and the erosions of time, dealing with the other holocaust: *Hiroshima mon amour* (1959).

There was renewed interest in the Holocaust in 1960, when Israeli agents abducted from Argentina the fugitive SS officer Adolf Eichmann, a key figure in the implementation of the Final Solution. His arrest was followed by a much publicised trial and execution in Israel. In the same year as the Stanley Kramer movie *Judgment at Nuremberg* (1961) – a reworking of a 1959 television play now notorious for its sponsors, the American Gas Association, bleeping out references to gas ovens – Erwin Leiser's documentary *Mein Kampf* was widely distributed, and Hannah Arendt's *New Yorker* report on the Eichmann trial introduced us to the concept of 'the banality of evil'.

The finest work from this period is *Passenger*, an oblique, suggestive black-and-white wide-screen film about the relationship between two women, one a German guard, the other a prisoner in Auschwitz who meet, or appear to meet, on a trans-Atlantic liner after the war. Its director, Andrzej Munk, a Jew from Cracow, was killed in a 1961 motor accident while making the film, and his colleagues assembled the material he'd shot. It was released in 1963, and the fragmentary, unfinished quality of this picture invites us to complete it in our minds.

In 1969, the success of Luchino Visconti's *The Damned* confirmed a dubious international taste for glossy psychological dramas about the Third Reich, tales in which '*Sieg Heil*' meets Krafft-Ebing, and was followed by numerous films exploiting the voyeuristic sensationalism of Nazi chic. Two years later, Marcel Ophüls's four-hour documentary, *The Sorrow and the Pity*, looked at the experience of France's Second World War occupation with a hitherto unequalled frankness and was banned from French television for a decade. In its demand for complex arguments and unvarnished truths, Ophüls's movie indicated an alternative to Visconti's: these two streams have since flowed alongside each other and at times intermingled.

This particular period of interest in the Third Reich (called in Germany at that time the *Hitlerwelle*) produced such outstanding French films as Louis Malle's *Lacombe Lucien* (1974) and Joseph Losey's *Mr Klein* (1976), as well as documentaries like Laurence Jarvis's *Who Shall Live and Who Shall Die?* (1981) about America's equivocal response to Jewish refugees before the Second World War. There were also voyeuristic, exploitative, near-pornographic movies, like Liliana Cavani's *The Night Porter* (1974), in which a former SS guard (Dirk Bogarde) and his wartime victim (Charlotte Rampling) meet in 1957 Vienna to re-enact the sadomasochistic games they played in Dachau. One movie from the time, *The Day the Clown Cried*, has, perhaps fortunately, remained sealed in the vaults. Written and directed by Jerry Lewis (*né* Joseph Levitch) and shot in Sweden, it stars Lewis himself as a German clown forced to be a Pied Piper in an extermination camp, leading Jewish children to the gas chambers.

The most widely shown movie of this period, the 1978 television mini-series *Holocaust*, raised the question about whether the American mass media (as opposed to European art-house movies) could properly handle the subject. This sincere, at times powerful film tried to pack too much into its contrived saga of interlocking German families. Its impact, however, was immense, both in America and in West Germany, where it introduced the term 'Holocaust' into popular usage and became a text for schoolroom study.

In 1983, when she published her valuable book *Indelible Shadows:*

Film and the Holocaust, the American scholar Annette Insdorf was able to examine 125 feature films, television movies and full-length documentaries on the subject. In the revised edition six years later she had to consider a further 45 substantial pictures – more than the combined total of westerns and musicals made in the 1980s.

The major films made since her first edition are Louis Malle's autobiographical *Au Revoir les enfants* (1987), in which Malle recalls his friendship with a Jewish boy being hidden from the Gestapo by the priests in his Catholic boarding school in 1944, Marcel Ophüls's *Hotel Terminus: Klaus Barbie, His Life and Times* (1988) and, supremely, Claude Lanzmann's *Shoah* (1985). Lanzmann's nine-and-a-half-hour documentary, among the greatest films ever made, relies entirely on interviews with Jewish survivors, Germans, guilty bystanders, observers and historians, and on visits to the camps as they are today.

It is this complex historical heritage that Steven Spielberg's *Schindler's List* enters. Spielberg and his screenwriter Steven Zaillian, an Armenian-American gentile, have paid special attention to *Night and Fog* and *Shoah*. Two decisions were crucial to its integrity: to shoot in black-and-white, and to eschew the use of existing documentary footage. In sticking to Thomas Keneally's non-fiction novel (published in Britain in 1982 as *Schindler's Ark*) they tell a singular story that illuminates a corner of the experience without claiming to explain the historical catastrophe.

But why do it at all? Should actors play Holocaust victims? Should Auschwitz be rebuilt in a studio? Turning down a request to write a television mini-series on the subject, the American playwright Paddy Chayefsky said: 'The word critics used on *Holocaust* was "trivialise", and, in a sense, that was an unfair criticism, even though accurate. Trivialisation is television.' The 1986 winner of the Nobel Peace Prize and concentration camp survivor Elie Wiesel shares these doubts but wrote an introduction to the second edition of Annette Insdorf's *Indelible Shadows*, praising her critical discriminations, stating:

> Certain productions dazzle with their authenticity; others shock with their vulgarity. *Night and Fog* on the one side, *Holocaust* on the other. Up against Hollywood superproductions, can poetic memory hold its own? Me I prefer it. I prefer restraint to excess,

the murmur of documentary to the script edited by tear-jerk specialists.

Stanley Kauffmann, doyen of American film critics, had high praise for *Schindler's List* in his column in the magazine *New Republic*. He posed this question: 'Is there a need for another film about the Holocaust? Especially after *Shoah*?' And went on to provide a tentative answer: 'Presumably, there are at least some people who have never seen a Holocaust film and may see this one because it's by Spielberg and will have mainstream promotion. Let's hope there are many such.'

The real answer to his question is that for a good many people *Shoah* is too demanding. One wonders how many Channel 4 viewers, to whom it was shown without intrusive commercials, lasted the movie's nine-hour course. The Holocaust was a complex series of events that must never be forgotten. But the way it is remembered and understood is also important. In this respect Spielberg's movie has a valuable role to play.

Lindsay Anderson (1994)
An Obituary

Lindsay Anderson, who died this week at the age of 71, was an ascetic, romantic Scot, a malcontent and an anarchist with a well-deserved reputation as a difficult man. Born in India the son of a future major general, he was back in India during World War Two as an Intelligence Corps officer and helped to raise the Red Flag over the officers' mess to celebrate the Labour victory in the 1945 election. He had three careers – as a critic, a filmmaker and a stage director, and only in the last of these did he let his hair down. I speak figuratively, as Anderson always wore his hair short and brushed forward, which with his beaky nose made him resemble a stern Roman senator, Casca perhaps.

He was a moralist and puritan, the nearest our cinema has come to having an F.R. Leavis, who was in his heyday at Cambridge when Anderson was reading English at Oxford after the war and co-editing *Sequence*, a quarterly much influenced by the combative, denunciatory style of Leavis's *Scrutiny*. In *Sequence* (which ran to 14 issues between 1946 and 1952) and then in *Sight & Sound*, Anderson was the scourge of both the British film industry, which he thought gutless, classbound, smug, insular and unimaginative, and the nation's critics (ditto). He argued for a poetic cinema that was humanist, personal and committed to social change. His idols were John Ford, Jean Vigo and Humphrey Jennings; he heartily disliked Powell, Lean and the American Hitchcock. Like Leavis his influence was immense and his judgments devastating. When in his 1955 *Sight & Sound* essay 'The Last Sequence of *On the Waterfront*' he denounced the end of Kazan's picture as fascistic, we all changed our minds about a movie we loved. His unfavourable review of *The*

My obituary of Lindsay Anderson first appeared in the *Observer*, 4 September 1994.

Searchers (1956) put a generation off one of Ford's finest pictures for a decade. Especially influential was the long 1956 article 'Stand Up! Stand Up!' (the title comes without a trace of irony from George Duffield's hymn) in which he flayed the liberal press for its philistinism and snobbery, attacked the '60 Years of Cinema' exhibition sponsored by the *Observer* for its frivolity, and concluded: 'Our ideals – moral, social and poetic – must be defended with intelligence as well as emotion: and also with intransigence.'

As a documentary filmmaker he was practising what he preached, though it is significant that he felt more warmly towards the working class when viewing them at work in *Every Day Except Christmas* (1957), his portrait of Covent Garden market, than observing them at play in *O Dreamland* (1953), a dispiriting report of a South Coast amusement park. *Every Day Except Christmas*, his finest non-fiction film, was a key work in the Free Cinema programmes at the National Film Theatre to which Tony Richardson and Karel Reisz (also ex-*Sequence* writers) contributed, and Free Cinema was the launching pad for the British New Wave.

But Anderson had established himself as a stage director with *The Long and the Short and the Tall*, *Billy Liar* and *Serjeant Musgrave's Dance*, before he got a chance to make his first feature film, *This Sporting Life* (1963), which began a fruitful association with David Storey. This powerful picture was the last major piece of provincial working-class realism before the British New Wave was replaced by the Swinging London cinema.

Swinging London itself had turned sour when Anderson made his next, possibly best, film, *If ...* (1968), the first of an allegorical trilogy of the State of England, influenced by Brecht, Buñuel and Vigo. This celebration of youthful revolt in an emblematic public school concludes with a homage to Vigo's *Zéro de conduite*, and three years later the fine young Hungarian director Pal Gabor tipped his hat to Anderson by having the rebellious hero of his *Horizon* see the final sequence of *If ...* in a Budapest cinema.

Anderson contributed to *Declaration* (1957), the Angry Young Men's symposium, and co-directed (uncredited) the documentary on the Campaign for Nuclear Disarmament's first Aldermaston march in 1958. Some of the hopefulness and idealism remains in *If ...* Its successors, *O Lucky Man* (1973), a picaresque tour through a hopelessly corrupt Britain, and *Britannia Hospital* (1962), using a rundown hospital as a metaphor for the nation (as Peter Nichols had done rather more subtly in *The National Health*) are atrabilious and bitterly pessimistic.

His work in the theatre was altogether more conventional, with a sympathetic feeling for performers, simple sets and a taste for a heightened realism. He was not particularly successful with the classics (his 1981 *Hamlet* with Frank Grimes, a member of the informal Anderson rep company, was a disaster). But he was sensitive to modern plays, and his Royal Court collaboration with David Storey, that began in 1969 with *In Celebration*, is one of the wonders of our theatre. Fortunately there is a movie record of *In Celebration* made for the American Film Theatre with the original cast; but only cuttings and vivid memories exist for the equally fine *The Contractor* (1969) and *The Changing Room* (1971), both triumphs of naturalistic theatre in a genre that was known at the time as 'the work play'.

Anderson published two books, *Making a Film* (1952), a valuable chronicle of the production at Ealing of Thorold Dickinson's *The Secret People*, and an excellent affectionate monograph on John Ford (1981). He occasionally acted, usually playing unpleasant Establishment types like the anti-Semitic don in *Chariots of Fire*, and was in demand as the narrator of TV documentaries on the cinema, giving a rare authority to Thames Television's 1988 *Ingmar Bergman: The Director* and to last year's three-part *D.W. Griffith: Father of Film* on Channel 4.

I have been on the receiving end of Anderson's waspishness and asperity by mail, face to face and behind my back. I have also been exposed to his charm and enjoyed his good company. He never flattered and he never kowtowed, and he was a keeper and pricker of consciences for two generations.

In conversation he had a method of putting a question that implied an answer and suggested that disagreement would expose your moral inferiority. I recall him leaning across a dinner table to the mild-mannered Bertrand Tavernier and saying: 'Why don't you just come out and say it? – Truffaut was a shit.' And whenever I write about the Oscars I feel guilty, recalling Anderson saying to me: 'You don't really take the Academy Awards seriously, do you?' Of course he had won one himself for his 1953 documentary, *Thursday's Children*.

O Unhappy Man (2000)

BOOK REVIEW
Lambert, Gavin: *Mainly About Lindsay Anderson: A Memoir* (Faber &
Faber)

The French movie critics on *Cahiers du Cinéma* – Chabrol,
Truffaut, Godard, Rivette, Rohmer – who became world famous
as the *nouvelle vague* have received more publicity than their gifted
British contemporaries, Lindsay Anderson, Gavin Lambert, Tony
Richardson and Karel Reisz.

But a case could be made out for the equal importance of this
Oxbridge quartet, who emerged as critics on the influential short-
lived *Sequence*, and the British Film Institute's quarterly *Sight &
Sound*, which they transformed in the early 1950s into a magazine
of world importance before themselves becoming moviemakers.
They wrote with greater lucidity, their best films survive impres-
sively, and they operated in a culture much less sympathetic to the
cinema than that of their French *confrères*.

Richardson was from a Yorkshire working-class background,
Reisz came to England as a pre-war refugee from Czechoslovakia.
Lambert and Anderson were products of the British upper-middle
class who met in 1939 at Cheltenham College, the setting 30 years
later of Anderson's surreal satire *If . . .* They became lifelong friends,
and Lambert's affectionate but sharply unsentimental memoir deals
with a close personal and professional relationship that lasted for
more than half a century until Anderson's death in 1994 at the age
of 71. Two things brought them together – a passion for the cinema
and a rebellious attitude towards the Establishment in all its mani-
festations. Their first joint act of defiance was to perform a Noël
Coward sketch in drag to outrage their headmaster.

'O Unhappy Man' first appeared in the *Observer*, 14 May 2000.

Lambert's title alludes to his friend's 1982 monograph *About John Ford* and is as much about the author as his subject, and this is what makes it so fascinating. The book is in effect about the different responses of two sensitive, intelligent artists to British life and their sexuality during a period of rapid social change, and Lambert brings to it the skills he has honed as screenwriter and novelist.

Both Lambert and Anderson hated the snobbish, blinkered, unimaginative Britain into which they were born. But Lambert turned his back on it in 1956, resigning from the editorship of *Sight & Sound* to settle in America, embark on a successful career as a writer and become a confident cosmopolitan. Anderson remained at home, engaging as a polemicist, theatre director and moviemaker with a society that he wanted to influence and change.

From the age of 11 the precocious Lambert was a guilt-free practising homosexual. At Oxford he became the lover and cinematic collaborator of Peter Brook, was taken to Hollywood as an assistant to another lover, Nicholas Ray, and writes frankly of his cruising days in Los Angeles and the 12-year affair with a working-class Arab in Tangier. He had 'always wanted Lindsay as a best friend'; they never became lovers. But Anderson, by Lambert's account, never came to terms with his gay nature. Born in India, Anderson was the guilt-ridden son of a domineering mother, who left her rigid military husband for another army officer, and his unceasing struggles with a puritanical conscience were recorded in an eloquent journal of which Lambert makes good use.

'It seems then I'm homosexual,' Anderson reluctantly noted at the age of 20, though he never formed a permanent relationship and endlessly complicated his life by falling in love with heterosexual married men, usually actors. Most notable among these inaccessible objects of desire were Serge Reggiani, and three stars from Britain whose careers Anderson helped launch: Albert Finney, Richard Harris and Frank Grimes.

Lambert, we infer, is at peace with himself. Anderson on the other hand was a stranger to serenity, a prickly man whose every activity involved severe moral challenges to himself and others. His refusal to compromise limited the amount of work he accomplished but was central to his important achievements, most notably *This Sporting Life*, *If* ... and *O Lucky Man*.

Capable of being 'totally irrational', according to his long-time collaborator David Storey, Anderson was as complex a mixture of kindness and cruelty as John Ford, one of the triumvirate of cinematic poets he idolised, the others being Jean Vigo and Humphrey Jennings. The last two died young, leaving even smaller bodies of work than Anderson's, but every item a gem. Ford was an idealist whose belief in communities, large and small, became increasingly attenuated, until only the business of making films with friends sustained it. Something of the same happened to Anderson, and his last film, the autobiographical TV essay *Is That All There Is?* concluded with a boat trip down the Thames accompanied by a party of friends to scatter the ashes of Jill Bennett and Rachel Roberts on the waters.

And Here's One They Made Earlier
On Film References (1994)

Dorothy Parker, who subscribed to communism and succumbed to alcoholism, said that the only 'ism' Hollywood believes in is plagiarism. That was in the days when serious people exalted originality and left the lifting of plots to less scrupulous folk. Now Hollywood has discovered a respectable 'ism' – post-modernism, in two of its senses.

First, American movies have become highly self-conscious and self-referential. Second, they practise that aspect of post-modernism identified as 'intertextuality' by the French critic Julia Kristeva. Intertextuality is the process by which authors incorporate into their own films, plays and books – by parody, pastiche or direct quotation – the work of other artists and by implication change our perception of those earlier plays, films and books. An obvious example is the inclusion of whole scenes from *Hamlet* in the 1967 play *Rosencrantz and Guildenstern Are Dead*. Tom Stoppard was, however, only following the example set by Joyce's *Ulysses* and Eliot's *The Waste Land*. Where artistic theft was once covered up, the crooks today positively flaunt their swag.

This sort of rampant post-modernism reaches new heights in the Coen Brothers' *The Hudsucker Proxy*. The movie conflates Frank Capra's *Mr Smith Goes to Washington* (1939), *Meet John Doe* (1941) and *It's a Wonderful Life* (1946), throws in a speech from *Citizen Kane* (1941), features numerous references to Preston Sturges, and has its journalist heroine (Jennifer Jason Leigh) impersonate Katharine Hepburn. This has been the Coens' stock in trade from the start. Their debut was the low-budget *Blood Simple* (1983), which took its title from Dashiell Hammett's *Red Harvest*. They

_____

'And Here's One They Made Earlier' first appeared in the *Observer*, 21 November 1994.

went on in *Miller's Crossing* (1990) to bring together the plot and characters of Hammett's *The Glass Key* with those of *Red Harvest*. A legal discussion between the Coen Brothers and Hammett's estate heard before a literate judge would be an instructive cultural occasion.

There have of course always been self-referential jokes in movies. Alfred Hitchcock began his brief personal appearances in *The Lodger* (1926) before the coming of sound. In *Hellzapoppin'* (1942), the comedians Olsen and Johnson pass a sledge labelled Rosebud. Jean Heather, the juvenile lead in *Going My Way* (1944), appeared later that year in *Double Indemnity* and in seeking a lift from Fred MacMurray asks if he is 'going my way'. Crosby and Hope made comic walk-on appearances in each other's films, and in *Road to Bali* (1952) they come across Humphrey Bogart dragging the *African Queen* through an Indonesian swamp. But these were playful and occasional instances.

It was the *Cahiers du Cinéma* critics-turned-moviemakers of the French New Wave who introduced post-modernist self-consciousness and intertextuality into the movies some years before these terms entered the critical vocabulary. In Claude Chabrol's *Le Beau Serge* (1958), the first real *nouvelle vague* feature, a copy of *Cahiers du Cinéma* is prominently displayed on a kitchen table. The young hero of François Truffaut's *Les Quatre cents coups* (1959) is entranced by a still of Harriet Andersson from Ingmar Bergman's *Summer with Monika*. Jean-Luc Godard's *Breathless* (1960) has an anti-hero modelling himself on Bogart, contains a shot down the barrel of a gun borrowed from Samuel Fuller's *Forty Guns* (1937), and is dedicated to Monogram Pictures, the low-budget Hollywood studio.

Godard introduced what is now a commonplace device, giving roles to his favourite directors – Fritz Lang appears as himself in *Le Mépris* (1963), as does Sam Fuller in *Pierrot le fou* (1965). The American cinema was slow to follow this fashion, though by 1985, when John Landis gave walk-on parts to a dozen directors in *Into the Night* (Jonathan Demme, Don Siegel, Roger Vadim, David Cronenberg, Amy Heckerling among them), it was the scale rather than the practice that attracted attention.

The floodgates opened in America in the 1960s, when Roger Corman's exploitation studio gave the critic Peter Bogdanovich his first opportunity to direct. The result – *Targets* – is now a landmark in professional ingenuity. Corman provided Bogdanovich with $40,000 and two remaining days on a Boris Karloff contract, plus several hundred feet of film left over from *The Terror*, a Karloff movie. From this Bogdanovich shaped a picture about a young director (himself) preparing for the premiere of his first film, a horror flick featuring the final appearance of the great star Byron Orlik (Karloff). A parallel story concerns a middle-class boy killing his family and then shooting motorists at random on the Los Angeles freeway. The two strands come together when the boy, from behind the screen of a drive-in cinema, picks off people sitting in their cars watching Orlik's film.

In perhaps the most significant scene in the film, Bogdanovich and Karloff watch a scene from Howard Hawks's *The Criminal Code* (1930), featuring Karloff in his first starring role. In their book *The Director's Event* (1969), Eric Sherman and Martin Rubin claim that 'this moment marks what is probably the first full-fledged cinematic "quote" in American cinema'. In his next movie, *The Last Picture Show* (1971), Bogdanovich again used a cinema as a central image, in this case for the decline of a small town in post-war Texas. The film opens with a quotation from Vincente Minnelli's *Father of the Bride* (1950) in order to establish the middle-class values to which American girls aspired in the early 1950s. It concludes with a scene from *Red River* (1948), a celebration of the Texas frontier spirit that has died with the cinema's owner. Nowadays almost every movie referred to or watched in a film is significant. Television screens in mainstream features almost always show films that reflect on the characters' lives. In *Sleepless in Seattle* (1993), for instance, Leo McCarey's *An Affair to Remember* (1957) is on the box day and night.

Much of this self-consciousness comes from the growth of film studies and the fact that most young moviemakers are film school graduates. The term 'cine-literate' is used to describe their sophistication, but it also suggests the limitations of their experience. On the other hand, in a society where references to the Bible and classical mythology are no longer widely understood, the mass media provide a new body of shared lore, a crude cultural database for the populace at large. In alluding to, parodying and reworking other people's films, moviemakers are following a practice established by Picasso with his versions of Delacroix and Manet, or Bacon with his variations on Velázquez's *Pope Innocent X*, on to which a frame from the Odessa Steps massacre of Eisenstein's *Battleship Potemkin* (1925) is superimposed. In *Western Bathers*, the most recent painting in R.B. Kitaj's current retrospective at the Tate, the nudes of Cézanne's *Bathers* are transformed into characters from westerns. The painting contains references to the films of John Ford, Sam Peckinpah and Budd Boetticher, and there are stagger-on roles for W.C. Fields and the drunken gunslinger played by Lee Marvin in *Cat Ballou* (1965).

In a seminal 1953 essay, the American critic Robert Warshow rightly called the western 'an art form for connoisseurs'. A sense of connoisseurship, of shared social and cultural experience, is confirmed and consolidated by the referential post-modernist style. Where once spectators were invited to interpret the elaborate iconography of a Renaissance painting, now they can spot references to Billy Wilder's *Double Indemnity* in Lawrence Kasdan's *Body Heat* (1981) and John Dahl's *The Last Seduction* (1994). Or take a special enjoyment in the familiarity of *The Hudsucker Proxy*.

Venice as Backdrop (1994)

The most notable paintings of Venice were done in the eighteenth century for visitors and in the nineteenth century by visitors. In our century, moviemakers have taken over, and the successors to Canaletto, Guardi, Turner and Whistler have created a cinema about visitors made by visitors. Whereas there are sizeable bodies of films about Romans, Neapolitans and Milanese, there is no Venetian *Bicycle Thieves* about the local working class or *La Notte* about the city's rich. Venetians are significant in the cinema only in as much as they impinge on foreigners or visitors from elsewhere in Italy – as shopkeepers, hoteliers, waiters, policemen, gondoliers and assorted exploiters and predators.

The one exception to this rule is that cosmopolitan Venetian, Giacomo Casanova, whose amorous adventures have inspired numerous movies over the past 70 years. Few of them were actually made in Venice, and certainly not the 1946 Hollywood comedy *Casanova's Big Night* starring Bob Hope as a timid tailor induced to impersonate the great lover. This is the movie in which Hope sniffs the air in a Venetian backwater and opines: 'Channel Number Five'. But Alexander Volkov's 1927 silent classic *Casanova*, the work of a team of White Russian émigrés based in Paris, made extensive use of Venetian locations and has a wonderfully graceful performance by the Russian actor Ivan Mozhukhin in the title role. Even today this sumptuous, fast-moving picture packs a considerable erotic charge.

Five years after Volkov's film, Mussolini established, to the greater glory of his fascist state, the world's first film festival with Venice as its setting and the Golden Lion of St Mark's as its major prize. Much later the festival was to be the background of the 1950s West End musical comedy, *Grab Me a Gondola*, which mocked the

'Venice as Backdrop' first appeared in the *Royal Academy Magazine*, Number 44; Autumn 1994.

antics of Diana Dors in Venice, and Henry Jaglom's *Venice/Venice* (1992), in which some denizens of Venice, California, visit the festival. But before the Second World War it hadn't led to any pictures being made there. In those days the big companies largely left the exploration of the world to documentarists and made feature films in the controlled conditions of the studio. The most famous pre-war film set in Venice is *Top Hat* (1935), possibly the best Astaire-Rogers musical. During the last half-hour Fred and Ginger dance 'Cheek to Cheek' and perform 'The Piccolino' in an elegant, black-and-white art deco Venice created in the studio by RKO's legendary designer, Van Nest Polglase. Gondolas glide in the smooth jet-black waters of canals in which the odd happy tourist lethargically swims.

Top Hat established the concept of an ideal, stylised art director's Venice, invariably a nocturnal one, and the most celebrated later examples are to be found in Powell and Pressburger's *The Tales of Hoffmann* (1951) and *Fellini's Casanova* (1976). For the second act of the former, in which Hoffmann vainly pursues a Venetian courtesan, Hein Heckroth created an exotic version of the Grand Canal and an opulent palazzo with the minimum of props, using Venetian red as the dominant colour. For Fellini, Danilo Donato built a fabulous set in Rome's Cinecittà that, in placing the Rialto Bridge, the campanile of St Mark's and S Maria Salute in close proximity, outdoes the most extravagant Canaletto *capriccio*. It is used for the film's opening carnival and for the final scene when a worn-out Casanova dances on the frozen Grand Canal with a female automaton.

By the time *Fellini's Casanova* appeared, it was considered both eccentric and wildly extravagant to create Venice in a studio when Venice was itself a movie set. Steadily over the post-war years, film companies had been going out on location both to achieve greater authenticity and to use up frozen currency. And the British led the way over to Venice with *The Glass Mountain* (1949), in which Tito Gobbi sings the leading role in the premiere of English composer Michael Denison's opera (it's actually written by Nino Rota) at La Fenice. It was followed up by two thrillers that attempted to rework *The Third Man* in Venice – *The Venetian Bird* (1952) starring Richard Todd as a London private eye searching for a former wartime partisan, and *The Stranger's Hand* (1953), a project by Graham

Greene, reuniting Trevor Howard and Alida Valli from *The Third Man*.

Venice was a colourful backdrop for these movies, for chases along dark alleys and beside sinister canals, a tradition kept up over the next four decades of action pictures, most famously in two Bond pictures, *From Russia With Love* (1963) starring Sean Connery and *Moonraker* (1979) with Roger Moore, and in Steven Spielberg's *Indiana Jones and the Last Crusade* (1989). Set in the 1930s, Spielberg's picture took advantage of two of the city's great attractions for producers of period movies. First, you don't have to fill the streets with vintage cars. Second, cover up the TV aerials and much of Venice looks the way it did 200 years ago. Make that 500 years ago, as Orson Welles proved when he used Venice to beguiling effect in *Othello* (1952). Of course you have to dress people in the right costumes, and Welles based the visual style of the film on the paintings of Carpaccio. When Joseph L. Mankiewicz set about filming Ben Jonson's *Volpone*, he got around this costume problem by working from a modernised version of the play called *Mr Fox of Venice*; his picture was released as *The Honey Pot* (1967), a last-minute change from the working title *Anyone for Venice?*

It was predictable that when Rome was chosen for Hollywood's first European CinemaScope production, *Three Coins in the Fountain* (1954), the screenplay would contrive to dispatch two of its American heroines on a trip north so that the widescreen could give its blessing to St Mark's and the Rialto from the air. But the major touristic film came in 1955, when David Lean made his first international production *Summer Madness* (aka *Summertime*), starring Katharine Hepburn as an American spinster who falls first into the canal and then for married Venetian gift shop owner Rossano Brazzi. When Lean went to scout for locations, his producer Alexander Korda gave him an influential piece of advice: 'Don't be afraid of the obvious places, David, go for the big effects, don't be afraid of the Grand Canal and St Mark's.' *Summer Madness* set the tone for future romantic comedies – Venice was the place to go to for holiday adventure, to enjoy the art and spice up your love life. In these times of package holidays and air transport it became the modern alternative to Brighton as the fashionable place for a dirty weekend.

The more sombre side of Venice was explored at this time by

Luchino Visconti in his first movie to be partly financed by Holly-wood, *Senso* (1954), a story of the Risorgimento that begins in 1866 with an anti-Austrian demonstration during a production of *Il Trovatore* at La Fenice. A sense of romantic doom hangs over the city as Visconti traces the blighted affair between an Italian countess (Alida Valli) and an Austrian officer (Farley Granger). Visconti returned to Venice 16 years later to make his biggest international success, his adaptation of Thomas Mann's *Death in Venice* (1971), starring Dirk Bogarde. The popularity of this ambitious movie was perhaps due less to its weighty subject matter than to Pasquale de Santis's stunning photography of the city, the attractive Edwardian costumes and the rich music by Gustav Mahler on the soundtrack.

Though neither the first nor the last Venetian movie, Nicolas Roeg's occult thriller *Don't Look Now* (1973), based on a short story by Daphne du Maurier, looks at the moment like the definitive one. Architect Donald Sutherland is there to restore a decaying church in the sinking city. He and his wife (Julie Christie) are coping with the traumatic experience of their daughter's sudden death, and while their sexual vitality seems to be restored, they are tormented by anxiety and guilt. Their inner state is reflected in a threatening, labyrinthine city where an evil serial killer, who resembles the dead child, stalks the alleyways. In this great film Venice has a Borgesian feel to it and there seems to be an oblique reference to Borges when a blind character refers to the blind Milton's love of La Serenissima.

The architect and his wife are introduced to a new sense of time in which she believes their daughter is trying to contact her, while he, with the greatest reluctance, comes to recognise a gift for precognition. They occasionally touch on the familiar Venice of Lean's *Summer Madness*. More often they stray into backwaters. Waterborne undertakers provided several key images of death in Venice that appear surreal in Roeg's movie, yet are less so to visi-tors who have stumbled across the bars frequented by the city's hard-drinking marine morticians near the ancient moorings of their floating hearses. *Don't Look Now* encompasses the Venice we know before we arrive, the city we are shown, the sinister one we discover hidden inside us. At the end we are left to draw our own conclu-sions about the native Venetians. But the casting of the visiting couple affects the way we look at some key movies of the time.

Julie Christie, who was Dirk Bogarde's destructive, childlike object of desire in John Schlesinger's 'Swinging London' movie, *Darling* (1965), was replaced by Bogarde/Aschenbach's platonic ideal male in Visconti's 1971 *Death in Venice*. In *Don't Look Now*, Donald Sutherland figured with Julie Christie in the most tender, poetic rendering of marital lovemaking in cinematic history. Three years later he was debased, manipulated and humiliated as Fellini's Casanova. One way or another, cine-literate visitors to Venice carry images from Nicolas Roeg's film in their luggage.

Surprisingly, the only movie based on a Henry James story with a Venetian setting is Martin Gabel's *The Lost Moment* (1947), an adaptation of *The Aspern Papers*, whose movie narrator makes nocturnal excursions by gondola through eerie, fog-enshrouded canals without setting foot outside a Hollywood studio. However, an American-financed version of James's *The Wings of the Dove* has long been promised, and with luck it will reach the screen in an adaptation by Claire Tomalin. In a recent article about the shaping of her screenplay, Tomalin observed: 'My bosses were very keen on scenes in cabs and hotels and just about anything in Venice – so much so that I was urged to make Millie's health improve miraculously towards the end in order that she could be taken for a Baedeker tour of the city.'

The Wings of the Dove *reached the screen in 1997, not in Claire Tomalin's version but in one scripted by Hossein Amini and directed by Iain Softley, which made extensive and subtle use of Venice. The cinematographer was the Frenchman, Eduardo Serra, who helped re-create Vermeer's Delft in* Girl with a Pearl Earring *(2003).*

Brothers in the Big House
Prison Movies (1995)

Frank Darabont's striking directorial debut, *The Shawshank Redemption*, is based on a novella by Stephen King. Tim Robbins plays a New England banker serving a double life sentence for murder in Maine's Shawshank State Prison, where he remains from 1947 to 1967. The skill of the movie lies in a narrative that constantly surprises us, while not featuring a single situation or character we haven't encountered several dozen times before.

The Shawshank Redemption belongs to the Cinema of Incarceration, an umbrella title that includes films about prisoner-of-war camps, lunatic asylums, the Gulag, political prisoners, concentration camps, even convents. Its branch of the Cinema of Incarceration is by far the most important. A genre in itself, it became known as the Big House movie from the underworld slang for the large penal institutions in which these films are set. Big House movies are about men, mostly working-class (middle-class characters have a special status in this world), and about male concerns.

Prisons as we know them – places of detention and reformation – are the creation of American idealism. The first such institution was established by Pennsylvanian Quakers in 1790 and the American term 'penitentiary' for a big state or federal prison dates from the early nineteenth century. The jail movie springs from the democratic experience of the United States and is virtually unknown in authoritarian countries.

There had been significant plays about prison life and some campaigning silent films about conditions in jail. But the prison drama really begins with the coming of sound and MGM's *The Big House* (1930), the first talkie to win an Oscar for best screenplay,

'Brothers in the Big House' first appeared in the *Observer*, 29 January 1995.

which was the work of a woman, Frances Marion. The title entered the language, and the movie is as seminal as two more or less contemporary films – *Little Caesar* and *The Front Page* – were for the gangster movie and the newspaper film respectively.

Sound was important for all three genres – the crashing of cell doors, the chatter of machine guns, the clattering of typewriters and, of course, the hard-boiled dialogue. And the timing too was significant. The cinema's archetypal gangster, convict and newspaperman emerged in the last years of Prohibition and the early days of the Great Depression, a time of mass unemployment, organised and disorganised crime, social unrest and the questioning of national values.

The Big House is the story of a weak society playboy (Robert Montgomery) serving ten years for manslaughter following a drink-driving accident. In an overcrowded jail run by a progressive warden he meets a wide range of hardened convicts, becomes wise to prison ways and is finally killed in a mass escape that he has attempted to prevent. The movie's immense success led to endless imitations and the founding of a genre with an iconography as familiar as that of the western.

First, the setting: the galleries of cramped cells; the dark, solitary confinement wing; the concrete exercise yard; the mess hall; the workshop; the laundry; the library; the warden's office; the visiting room; the observation towers and high walls from which search-lights rake the bleak building at night.

Second, the *dramatis personae*. The staff: the warden (fair, remote, weak, out of touch either through liberal idealism or middle-class complacency); the chief guard (rigid, brutal, sadistic, the real master of the Big House); the older guard (sympathetic, well-meaning); the chaplain (naive, spouting platitudes). The convicts: the green newcomer; the institutionalised old-timer; the cowardly bully; the charismatic philosophical leader; the toadying informer; the guy going stir-crazy; the innocent man trying to clear his name.

Third, the daily routine: the opening of cells; marching to meals and work; standing around the yard in groups, smoking; late-night chats; appearances before the warden and parole boards; threats of sexual assaults, visits from relatives, loved ones, lawyers.

Finally, the mandatory but non-routine events: the killing of the informer; the riot; the carefully planned breakout; the release of the convict into an outside world both changed and unwelcoming.

The same themes recur in film after film – injustice and the futility of attempting to reform people in schools for crime; society's lack of concern for the underprivileged; men trying to retain their decency and dignity under difficult circumstances; the battle of wills between armed overseer and defenceless prisoner; the internecine wars; the notion of redemption through physical and spiritual suffering; the meaning of real freedom.

Immediately after *The Big House*, MGM produced *Pardon Us* (1931), the first feature-length Laurel and Hardy film, lampooning the prison movie and released in Britain with the more brutal title of *Jailbirds*. Thereafter the baton (or the night stick) passed into the hands of Warner Brothers, who dominated the genre for the next 20 years. The studio's principal male stars – Edward G. Robinson, James Cagney, Paul Muni, Humphrey Bogart and John Garfield, all men of the city – were far more familiar with the cell bars of the state pen than the saloon bars of the frontier. Indeed, during the 1930s, the heyday of the Big House movie, there were few big-budget westerns.

Ostensibly prison movies are concerned with the treatment of prisoners and the value or otherwise of custodial sentences. A crusading zeal underlies the genre, from the hard-hitting *I Am a Fugitive from a Chain Gang* (1932), through *Riot in Cell Block 11* (1954), an attack on jail conditions inspired by producer Walter Wanger's six months inside (he'd taken a near-lethal pot-shot after finding his wife, Joan Bennett, in flagrante) up to the Robert Redford production *Brubaker* (1980). But *Brubaker* is unusual in having its star play an enlightened warden. Over the past 60-odd years American stars have preferred to play convicts – proletarian heroes or anti-heroes, men of the people – and leave the official good deeds to character actors like Walter Huston (*The Criminal Code*) and Karl Malden (*Birdman of Alcatraz*).

So a tradition started by Muni in *I Am a Fugitive* and Spencer Tracy in *2,000 Years in Sing Sing* (1932) has been carried on in recent years by Paul Newman in *Cool Hand Luke* (1967), Clint Eastwood in *Escape from Alcatraz* (1979) and Kevin Costner in *A Perfect World* (1993). It is not just that the roles are better, or that every actor has a touch of the masochist. It is that the romantic convict of drama is the ultimate rebel outcast, defying the system, standing alone, paying his dues. The prison is an image of society and of life itself, distorted perhaps, but recognisable. There is also the resemblance between prisons and the studios during Hollywood's golden era: the man who had ghosted the memoirs of Warden Duffy of San Quentin was engaged to assist Jack L. Warner, head of Warner Brothers, in the writing of his autobiography.

The existential heroes of this microcosmic world are not unlike Samuel Beckett's isolated protagonists, and it is significant that the actor-director Rick Clutchey became an exponent of Beckett's plays while incarcerated in San Quentin. John Hancock who, as director of the San Francisco Actors' Workshop, introduced Clutchey to the theatre, later made a film based on this experience. Hancock's *Weeds* (1987) stars Nick Nolte as a San Quentin lifer who begins to write plays after seeing *Waiting for Godot*.

American movie prison comedies began with Chaplin in 1915 and have marched alongside the tragedies and melodramas of jail life ever since. The post-war high point is the deadly accurate parody of genre conventions in Woody Allen's *Take the Money and Run* (1971). In Britain, most of our prison films have been comedies – vehicles for the likes of Will Hay (*Convict 99*, 1938), Peter Sellers (*Two-Way Stretch*, 1960) and Noël Coward (*The Italian Job*, 1969). Our censors managed for decades to prevent any serious criticism of the national institutions. The poor are angry? Let them watch *Porridge*.

Serious British prison films have mostly been dull and circumspect. The bold movies have been made by visitors from overseas. The two best pictures on life in our jails were directed by Americans. In his devastating *The Criminal* (1960), Joseph Losey used a British prison as a metaphor for a dubious capitalist society. In Sidney Lumet's ruthless *The Hill* (1965), a warrant officer (Sean Connery), demoted and jailed for protesting against the meaningless slaughter of his men, confronts a martinet chief warder (Harry Andrews) in a Second World War military prison in the North African desert. A more recent picture, *In the Name of the Father* (1993), a very Americanised affair impugning our criminal justice system yet presenting its hero (Daniel Day-Lewis) as redeemed and exulted by his years inside, was the work of an Irishman, Jim Sheridan.

The most impressive prison movie of recent years is a Grande Maison affair, Jacques Audiard's Un Prophète, *which is realistic, contemporary and very French, while honouring all the conventions established in 1930 by* The Big House. *The same is true of Jean-François Richel's* Mesrine: A Film in Two Parts, *about the career of legendary French gangster Jacques Mesrine.*

Losing It to the Movies
Seventy Years of the *New Yorker* (1995)

On 21 February 1925, the *New Yorker* was launched with a cover depicting a Regency dandy, aloofly appraising a butterfly through his monocle. This was the chosen pose – urbane, quizzical, detached – of the scruffy, rough-necked founding editor, Harold Ross. The identical cover depicting this essentially English figure has been reprinted every February for 70 years.

In that first number, Eustace Tilley (as this colophonic dandy came to be known among *New Yorker* staffers) looked at Hollywood with the same amused, patronising disdain with which he observed the butterfly, a gaze he sustained for four decades. The F.W. Murnau–Emil Jannings movie *The Last Laugh*, which opened that week in New York, 'shows up the American photoplay as infantile stuff', the magazine observed. The paper mocked 'the Californian intelligentsia' (i.e. Douglas Fairbanks and Charlie Chaplin) for over-praising Josef von Sternberg's *The Salvation Hunters*, and laughed at Sternberg for his change of name, 'the "von" having blossomed forth under the beneficence of the Californian sun'.

If the *New Yorker* writers could be said to have a love-hate relationship with Hollywood, it was that of loving Tinseltown's money and hating themselves for being seduced by it. Most of the members of that famous Algonquin Hotel Round Table set, celebrated in Alan Rudolph's film *Mrs Parker and the Vicious Circle*, ended up in Hollywood after service on the *New Yorker* under their friend Ross. Gossip columnist Walter Winchell dubbed them 'the gintelligentsia', and the first to 'go Hollywood' was Herman Mankiewicz, the *New Yorker*'s first drama critic and one of Manhattan's greatest wits. Ross fired him in 1926, when he was still out on the West

---

'Losing It to the Movies' first appeared in the *Observer*, 5 March 1995.

Coast for his first screenwriting stint. Mankiewicz cast in his lot with
Hollywood and signalled his decision with a celebrated telegram to
his friend Ben Hecht, offering $300 a week for peanuts, but telling
not to let the word get around. Hecht went on to become Hollywood's most highly paid screenwriter, while Mankiewicz stayed to
enjoy considerable success. By the time the latter won an Oscar for
the screenplay of *Citizen Kane* he was drinking himself into an early
grave.

Of course word did get around, and the Algonquin Round Table
figures led an exodus of New York writers to Hollywood – Robert
Benchley (Mankiewicz's successor as the *New Yorker* drama critic),
Dorothy Parker, George S. Kaufman, Edna Ferber, Marc Connelly,
S.N. Behrman, James M. Cain, Arthur Kober (Lillian Hellman's
husband), John O'Hara, S.J. Perelman. Some stayed to get rich and
become pickled in alcohol and regret. Others made brief, lucrative
forays to the coast. They all mocked Hollywood – in plays
(Kaufman's *Once in a Lifetime* was the first major Broadway satire on
the movie business), comic fictions (Perelman's 1932 *Scenario*, a
Joycean stream-of-consciousness send-up of Hollywood clichés)
and one-liners (Parker's 'The only ism Hollywood believes in is
plagiarism').

Hollywood, however, took the *New Yorker* seriously, plundering
its pages as a source of up-market material for the movies, ranging
from stories like John Cheever's *The Swimmer* to non-fiction pieces
like Truman Capote's *In Cold Blood*. The celluloid results rarely
pleased the denizens of Manhattan's West 43rd Street. James
Thurber, whose relationship with Hollywood got off to a bad start
in 1940 when movie mogul Jack Warner persistently addressed him
as 'Mr Ferber', was incensed by what Sam Goldwyn was doing to
The Secret Life of Walter Mitty. In 1946 this became a *cause célèbre*
when the *New Yorker* writer Frank Sullivan launched 'The Walter
Mitty Association' to protect Thurber's hero from Hollywood.

The magazine's contributor most angered by Hollywood was
J.D. Salinger, whose delicate *New Yorker* tale 'Uncle Wiggily in
Connecticut' was transformed by Goldwyn into the Susan Hayward
weepie *My Foolish Heart* (1949). Salinger resolved never again to sell
a work to the cinema, and two years later he took his artist's revenge.
On the first page of *The Catcher in the Rye*, the narrator, Holden
Caulfield, attacks his gifted older brother, the author of 'this terrific

book of short stories, *The Secret Goldfish*', for becoming a 'prostitute' as a Hollywood screenwriter. 'If there's one thing I hate, it's the movies,' says Holden. 'Don't even mention them.' Goldfish, we're invited to recall, was Sam Goldwyn's original name before he became a Hollywood mogul.

The year that *Catcher in the Rye* appeared, the *New Yorker* published Lillian Ross's classic series of fly-on-the-wall reports about the making and unmaking of John Huston's *The Red Badge of Courage* at MGM. Unremitting in its hostility to the Hollywood system, Ross's *Picture* (the stark, generic, accusatory title of the five-part piece when it appeared in book form) became a journalistic milestone.

For the *New Yorker*, the serious performing art was the theatre, and its centres were New York, London and Paris. The paper had correspondents in both European cities; its only regular American correspondent outside New York wrote on national politics from Washington DC. Great care was taken over the appointment of drama critics. Little attention was given to coverage of the movies. At various times the job was undertaken by the racetrack habitué John McNulty, the short-story writer Robert Coates, the satirist Wolcott Gibbs, and the novelist and theatre critic Brendan Gill, the *New Yorker*'s longest serving writer, who is currently its architectural critic.

A big change came about in 1967 when the British writer Penelope Gilliatt left the *Observer* to become the *New Yorker*'s first truly serious film critic. The following year she was joined by Pauline Kael, who had come to New York from San Francisco after making her name with her first book, *I Lost It at the Movies* (1965). Their appointment was a response by William Shawn, the paper's second editor (he succeeded on Ross's death in 1952), to a major cultural shift towards the cinema. He himself was a moviegoer, and the only piece he signed during his editorship was an introduction to the memoirs of Louise Brooks. In his fiftieth anniversary history of the magazine, *Here at The New Yorker* (1975), Brendan Gill criticised Kael for her garrulity and Gilliatt for her irrelevant scholarship. In 1979 another *New Yorker* writer, Renata Adler, made a savage attack on Kael in the *New York Review of Books* for her vulgar, demotic style.

The Kael–Gilliatt partnership came to a sudden end in 1979. First

Kael went off to work in Hollywood as a production adviser. Then Gilliatt descended into alcoholic madness, plagiarising other critics and writing a crazy profile of Graham Greene. In order to appease Greene and save the paper from publishing an apology (something the *New Yorker* went to great limits to avoid), Shawn agreed to restrict her thereafter to fiction.

Kael was not long absent in Hollywood. As the *New Yorker*'s most popular writer in the American heartland, she was welcomed back to resume her column. Every *New Yorker* word by Kael has been reprinted between hard covers, and one of her few pieces not occasioned by a new release was her influential two-part essay *Raising Kane* (1971), re-valuing *Citizen Kane*. She placed *Kane* in a Hollywood context. Remarkable as *Kane* was, for her it wasn't the iconoclastic intervention into the film business by the New York theatre's *enfant terrible*; it was rather the apogee of the brash Hollywood newspaper comedy that had been launched by *The Front Page*.

It is through this breach in the walls of traditional East Coast taste and received wisdom that the *New Yorker*'s fourth and current editor, Tina Brown, has driven her chariot. Among numerous changes that have disturbed old *New Yorker* readers and attracted young new ones since she moved over from *Vanity Fair*, few have been more significant than the way the magazine has embraced Hollywood and celebrated its studio executives on their own extravagant terms as industrial 'players'. (The current issue offers readers 'angst at the networks – Ken Auletta on global grabs and corporate elbowing among NBC, Fox, CBS and Turner'.) The new relationship established the *New Yorker* as a bi-coastal publication (the now serious adjective 'bi-coastal' was a *New Yorker* joke in 1980) and was sealed through the *entente cordiale* of the journal's first special edition, the 'Movie Number' of 21 March 1994. Launched with a lavish party in Los Angeles, it also confirmed the end of an old tradition – that a *New Yorker* cover should never advertise the matter inside. Eustace Tilley has swapped his monocle for a pair of executive Ray Bans. He's no longer a Regency dandy, he's a Rodeo Drive player.

Dilys Powell (1995)
An Obituary

Critics do not usually get into film encyclopaedias. But Dilys Powell, who died yesterday, did. In Virago's *Women's Companion to International Film*, she appears between feminist director Sally Potter and what Virago's *WCTIF* calls the 'sado-masochistic misogynist' Michael Powell. The editors remark that 'Dilys Powell's role in British film culture cannot be overestimated'. They also give the year of her birth – 1902 (actually it is 1901) – a biographical detail she withdrew from her *Who's Who* entry 40 years ago.

Powell had three great loves – Greece, dogs and the cinema – and she wrote wonderfully about them. But although she published several books about Greece, most notably *An Affair of the Heart* (1957), and *Coco* (1952), a charming 'biography' of her pet poodle, she was nearly 90 before two collections of her film reviews were published. When I asked if she would like a book of her criticism included in a series I was editing, she said, 'Do you really think it is good enough?'

At the age of 24, not long after leaving Oxford (like those other scholarly writer-broadcasters, Marghanita Laski and Janet Adam Smith, she was a Somerville girl), Powell married Humphry Payne and went with him to Athens when he became director of the British School of Archaeology. Widowed in 1936, she returned to London and the *Sunday Times*, where she had worked in the late 1920s. In 1943 she married the paper's literary editor Leonard Russell, and they lived happily at their Regency house near Hyde Park until his death in 1974.

In 1939 Powell, who had first written on the cinema as an undergraduate, became the *Sunday Times*'s film critic, remaining in the post for 37 years, for 21 of them as a weekend double with her friend,

---

My obituary of Dilys Powell first appeared in the *Observer*, 4 June 1995.

C.A. Lejeune of the *Observer*. They were the Scylla and Charybdis of movie criticism, the twin hazards all new films had to confront.

Four years Powell's senior and the *Observer* critic since 1928, Lejeune was appointed as the *Manchester Guardian*'s first movie reviewer in 1922, before anyone quite knew what film criticism was. Powell was 38 when she became a full-time critic, and her model was Graham Greene, then writing a film column for the *Spectator*. From Greene she learnt to look at the cinema as an industry and an art form that affected people's lives, to write about what she saw on the screen, and to aim at brevity, particularity and clear, unpretentious writing. When I included a contribution from Dilys in a radio documentary to mark Greene's seventy-fifth birthday in 1979, he wrote to tell me that her tribute to his criticism was the part of the programme he most appreciated.

In the late 1950s, world cinema underwent a remarkable change with the Kitchen Sink school in Britain, the New Wave in France, and challenging figures emerging in Italy, Scandinavia and Japan. There was also a new excess of violence and explicit sex, and it was at the end of 1960, after being disgusted by *Psycho* and *Peeping Tom*, that Lejeune threw in the towel and never entered a cinema again. Powell, who agreed on most matters with Lejeune (and acknowledged her as the wittier critic), was almost alone in welcoming *Psycho*. Very soon, in her sixties, she found herself sympathising with the young Turks who launched *Movie* magazine and who sought a new appreciation of Hollywood and a proper regard for film-as-film. She was the first major European critic to recognise the gifts as actor and director of Clint Eastwood. In 1972 she wrote an enthusiastic review of Steven Spielberg's *Duel*, his TV film that got a theatrical release in Europe in an extended version. It won his undying gratitude. It was thus with some reluctance that she retired from the *Sunday Times* in 1976 to become movie critic of *Punch*. When *Punch* folded she rejected somewhat indignantly an invitation to write for *The Oldie* – the title offended her.

But she never stopped going to the movies. This year she saw *Natural Born Killers*, *The Madness of King George* and *Heavenly Creatures*. In addition to her writing, Powell was an outstanding broadcaster. Her fluency, unaffected accent, well-modulated voice and calm manner made her a gift to a producer. From its beginnings in 1947, she appeared regularly on the Home Service programme

The Critics (and later on its Radio 3 successor, *Critics' Forum*) and was its most popular contributor. She was also a star of the long-running series *My Word*.

Powell's generosity to younger critics both in public and private was immensely warming; she never saw them as a threat to her pre-eminence, as indeed they were not. Like Lejeune she grew up with the cinema, and together they chronicled its golden years. There will never be anyone like them again.

I'd like to make two further points about Dilys Powell.

First, the London Film Festival was conceived at her dinner table in 1957 in conversation with the witty, acerbic gay actor, translator and broadcaster, Derek Prowse. Derek was Dilys's deputy at the Sunday Times *for some years and widely accepted as her heir apparent. However, one day in the late 1960s his reckless humour got the better of him. Dilys was away on holiday and Derek, as her stand-in, was invited to attend a* Sunday Times *editorial conference. He didn't say much, indeed he seemed to be dozing off when the editor turned to him and said: 'Mr Prowse, you haven't made much of a contribution to our discussion. What did you think of last Sunday's paper?' There was a pause. Then Derek said: 'Well, actually Sir, I just glanced at it. I'm more of an* Observer *man myself.'*

Second, as I've already mentioned, Dilys's early support for Clint Eastwood was noted and much valued by the actor. Pauline Kael on the other hand was his most vociferous critic, denouncing him as rightwing, thick-ear, fascist, sexist. In a BBC TV documentary made in the late 1970s by Iain Johnstone, Powell's warm, reasoned defence of Eastwood was crosscut with Kael's cold, rasping criticque. In 1979 I suspected that the pair featured figuratively in Every Which Way But Loose, *a big popular hit starring Eastwood as Philo Beddoe, a truck-driving, beer-swilling bare-knuckle boxer. Early in the film Philo is accosted in his favourite country music bar by a humourless female academic from the University of California (Kael's alma mater) who's 'doing a paper on the Country and Western mentality'. Her conclusion is that Country and Western fans are a bunch of moronic hardhats, and Philo frightens her away by dropping a set of joke false teeth in her soup. The true heroine of* Every Which Way, *however, is a wonderful old lady called Ma, mother of Philo's sidekick. She's full of guts, tolerance, good humour and resourcefulness. She's radiantly played by Ruth Gordon, though she's not of course as beautiful as Dilys Powell.*

On Film Criticism (1995)

Critics of literature, theatre, music and the visual arts can trace their craft back to roots in ancient Greece. But while it might be claimed that the shadows on the walls of Plato's cave anticipated the cinema, movie criticism is less than a hundred years old. It arose in the first decade of this century when the cinema was recognised as both an art form and as the emerging industry that provided the principal entertainment for the world's urban masses. The sheer novelty of film faded after 1900, and the burgeoning trade press needed to be advised on what would attract the crowds while audiences needed guidance on what was worth seeing. At the same time artists and intellectuals started to write about the aesthetic possibilities of film.

Almost certainly the first was Maxim Gorki, who at the age of 28 reviewed the Lumière Brothers' first programme of films for his local newspaper when it came to Nizhni Novgorod in April 1896. 'Last night I was in the kingdom of shadows,' his piece began. In Britain, George Bernard Shaw and H.G. Wells wrote essays on their hopes for the new medium. In America in 1916, the Harvard professor Hugo Munsterberg and the poet Vachel Lindsay both wrote seminal books on the cinema. In France Louis Delluc (who died in 1924 at the age of 33) pioneered film criticism, launched the film society movement, produced a couple of films, and lives on in the prestigious annual award that bears his name. A milestone event occurred in 1917, when Sweden's leading daily newspaper, *Dagens Nyheter*, sent one of the country's leading poets, Bo Bergman, to review *Terje Vigen*, Victor Sjöström's film version of the epic Ibsen poem.

The 1920s saw the film industry entrenched and the cinema accepted as the century's new art form, what the French call *le septième art*. And it became evident that film criticism was the most

'On Film Criticism' first appeared in the *Observer*, 23 July 1995.

demanding of activities – you had to know about theatre, literature, music, politics, psychology, history, mythology, the visual arts, geography, foreign cultures and folkways. You also had to under-stand a range of new technologies and the professional language they had created, and to comprehend the ideological, political and commercial pressures and constraints under which artists and arti-sans worked. To grapple with the cinema was a way of addressing the twentieth-century experience in all its complexity. This is what attracted writers as different as Graham Greene and Alistair Cooke to film criticism.

Unfortunately, newspaper editors in the English-speaking world over these past 80 years have not quite grasped the significance of the cinema. The tabloid press has usually let loose on the movies any confident ignoramus with a big name and a readiness to feed the readers' prejudices, while the serious press has often employed fashionable literary names to savage and patronise the cinema. Of all critics, those writing about the cinema are the least interrogated by their employers as to their professional credentials. As Pauline Kael once said, every editor's wife is an authority on the cinema, and there is indeed a famous case of a distinguished New York critic losing his job because his review of *Annie Hall* angered the editor's spouse.

There is of course ignorance at different levels – reviewers who know little cinematic history (a recently appointed London critic was praised for a knowledge of the cinema 'that goes back to the Seventies'), reviewers who loathe popular culture, reviewers who despise the arts. Yet while film courses at university might equip you for the general fray, they can never provide the personal body armour for the single combat that writing regular criticism demands.

For a number of years I produced arts programmes for BBC radio, most notably the Home Service Sunday lunchtime series *The Critics* and its Radio 3 successor, *Critics' Forum,* and I employed more critics than anyone else in the business – virtually every writer on the cinema, theatre, literature, the visual arts and broadcasting who could string a succession of sentences together. When they asked what I would ideally like to emerge from any discussion of a play, a film, a broadcast, a book or an exhibition, I somewhat pompously mentioned three things. First, an account of the immediate experi-ence of what you've seen, heard or read. Second, a tentative assessment or judgment, locating it, if appropriate, in an artist's oeuvre. Third, an element of speculation, making larger social and cultural connections. I would usually add the advice of Harold Ross to his *New Yorker* writers: 'Be funny and if you can't be funny, be interesting.'

Every critic must find his own voice, establish his own style, and the *Observer*'s eight movie critics have been a mixed bunch. Our first critic was Ivor Montagu, youngest son of the second Baron Swaythling, the banker Samuel Montagu. An eminent scientist and a lifelong fellow traveller, he was a founder member in 1925 of the London Film Society, a codifier of the rules of table tennis, and a friend of Eisenstein, whom he accompanied to Hollywood in the late 1920s. In the 1930s he produced Hitchcock's *The Man Who Knew Too Much*, *The 39 Steps* and *The Secret Agent*, and made numerous documentaries for the cinema. In 1964 he summed up the thoughts of a lifetime in a Pelican Original paperback, his *Film World*.

This aristocratic leftist was succeeded in 1928 by C.A. Lejeune, who confided in her autobiography that she 'had led a typical middle-class life and been very happy'. She'd been the *Manchester Guardian*'s first film critic, and three years after joining the *Observer* she wrote *Cinema: A Review of Thirty Years' Achievement*, which still reads well. Her witty reviews were sometimes written in verse, but at the end of 1960 in a spirit of disgust, she retired. Her successor, Penelope Gilliatt, had written a famous exposé of gossip writers in *Harpers & Queen* and a dazzling essay on theatre critics that contained the much-quoted crack that 'the characteristic sound of Sunday morning in England is Harold Hobson [then theatre critic at the *Sunday Times*] barking up the wrong tree'. While at the *Observer*, she turned to fiction and playwriting, and in 1971 she received an Oscar nomination for her original screenplay for John Schlesinger's *Sunday, Bloody Sunday*.

For a couple of years in the mid-1960s, Kenneth Tynan, the paper's drama critic, briefly swapped jobs with Gilliatt, because as the National Theatre's literary manager he could no longer review plays. In the 1950s Tynan had been a script adviser at Ealing Studios and worked on Maggie Smith's movie debut, *Nowhere to Go* (1958), and he loved the cinema. But he became frustrated by his inability to influence the fortunes of what he saw, and soon gave up. Gilliatt briefly returned before leaving in 1967 to join the *New Yorker*. The *Observer*, searching around for another sensitive woman, discovered another Penelope – Penelope Mortimer, whose novel *The Pumpkin Eater* had been adapted for the screen by Harold Pinter, and who, in collaboration with her then husband, John Mortimer, had scripted Otto Preminger's *Bunny Lake Is Missing*.

Talked into the job, Mortimer was unhappy with the mediocrity that confronted her each week. Her tenure ended abruptly, and George Melly, the paper's television critic, crossed over to cover movies for three years, bringing to the task a taste for the surreal and the anarchic. After the Second World War, Melly had worked for an avant-garde art gallery while singing with Dixieland bands. When rock'n'roll eclipsed jazz in the early 1960s, his music became a hobby and his writing (including the *Flook* strip in the *Daily Mail*) took over as his major source of income. He'd also scripted a couple of films, the Swinging London comedy *Smashing Time* (1967) and a version of Kingsley Amis's *Take a Girl Like You* (1970). In the early 1970s his kind of music came back into favour, and writing once more became a secondary activity, although some of his best criticism has been done this past decade.

Melly was followed by Russell Davies, a multiple linguist, a jazz musician, a gifted cartoonist and an ingenious parodist. He left the *Observer* in 1978, having had more than his fill of the cinema, and has subsequently edited the diaries and essays of Kenneth Williams. That's when I took over. Back in the early 1960s, when I stood in while the regular critics were away there always appeared at the end of my columns a note stating than the official incumbent was away. A waggish friend suggested that the epitaph on my gravestone should read: 'Philip French 1933–1965. Kenneth Tynan is on holiday.'

Well, I've outlived that one.

The Spanish Civil War (1995)

Ken Loach's outstanding film about the Spanish Civil War, *Land and Freedom*, was the most talked-about movie at Cannes this year. The jury, however, gave the Festival's main prizes to three pictures dealing with the war now raging in the former Yugoslavia. Yet, whatever the outcome of the Bosnian conflict, it is unlikely to loom as large as Spain still does in the consciousness of this century.

The Civil War broke out 59 years ago, in July 1936, when a combination of monarchists, Catholics, fascists and soldiers led by General Franco launched a rightwing revolt against a recently elected Popular Front government formed from a coalition of parties ranging from the centre to the far left. The Germans and Italians came to the aid of Franco. Only France (briefly) and the USSR assisted the embattled Republican government, which had been forced to arm its own citizens.

Volunteers poured in from all over the world. The overwhelming majority were there to fight for the Republican cause in the International Brigades. But a few came to support Franco's Nationalists, the most famous and self-publicising being the South African-born poet Roy Campbell, the wittily bludgeoning scourge of the Auden/Day-Lewis/Spender triumvirate. One group of fascists were recruited in Ireland, and they went into battle with a Nazi tank regiment singing a marching song written by W.B. Yeats. A bloody war with terrible losses on both sides finally ended in total victory for the Nationalists. Spain sank into darkness, living under an authoritarian regime until Franco's death in 1975.

During those years and since, the war has continued to haunt us. Or at least those of a certain age. In 1971, when the critic Diana Trilling was teaching at a leading women's college in New England, she discovered that few students in her class had even heard of it,

'The Spanish Civil War' first appeared in the *Observer*, 1 October 1995.

and the most assertive one told her: 'I don't know much, but I do know enough to know it was our fault!'

While it was in progress, the war was too controversial a matter for the cinema to handle. There were movie documentaries, most famously *Spanish Earth*, directed by the Dutch Communist Joris Ivens with a commentary by Ernest Hemingway, which was used for fundraising in the States. But Hollywood produced only one movie, the muted *Blockade* (1938), starring Henry Fonda and scripted by the Communist John Howard Lawson, later to be black-listed as a member of the 'Hollywood Ten'. The British censors prevented any picture being made here.

With the coming of the Second World War, for which the Civil War was a rehearsal, things changed. In the 1943 Ealing Studios tributes to the army in the Western Desert, *Nine Men*, and to the firefighters of the London Blitz, *The Bells Go Down*, heroic figures are identified as veterans of the International Brigades.

That same year in Hollywood, Paramount filmed Hemingway's *For Whom the Bell Tolls*, the greatest novel about the war, and Warner Brothers allowed Rick Blaine in *Casablanca* to include on his CV his services to the Loyalist cause. There have also been art-house pictures like Alain Resnais's *La Guerre est finie* (1966), starring Yves Montand as a Spanish exile combating the Franco regime in a world grown indifferent to his cause, and a sort of sequel to that film, Joseph Losey's *Les Routes du Sud* (1978) by the same screenwriter, Jorge Semprun, starring Montand as an almost identical writer, a dozen years on. Loach's movie takes us back to the heart of the matter.

There are four principal reasons why this war continues to command our attention. First, the microcosm that Spain became enables us to follow key strands of the twentieth-century experience in compelling isolation – for instance, fascism versus Stalinism, Communism versus democratic socialism, patriotism/nationalism versus internationalism, the vulnerability of anarchism, the role of technology in warfare, and so on.

Second, it involved two generations of writers and produced a vast literature that in relevance and resonance is unmatched by any other war in this or any other century. The possible exception would be the Great War, which certainly produced a more significant body of graphic art, though no single work of the stature of Picasso's *Guernica*.

Wars had been photographed since Roger Fenton set up his tripod in the Crimea, but the modern combat cameraman was really born on the battlefields of Spain, and both *Life* and *Picture Post* were founded in the first year of the Civil War. The gut-wrenching immediacy of Robert Capa's Spanish work created a new kind of photography, and he became a new sort of hero.

Third, we have no better documented way of studying the relationship between intellectuals and politics. Virtually every writer and artist of the time was forced to commit himself or herself to the Republican or the Nationalist cause or to opt for a dangerous neutrality. Bertolt Brecht was introduced to the English-speaking world when London's leftwing Unity Theatre staged *Señora Carrara's Rifles*, his transposition to revolutionary Spain of J.M. Synge's *Riders to the Sea*. Benjamin Britten's *Ballad for Heroes*, written to commemorate the British volunteers, was performed in April 1939 at a concert to honour the International Brigades.

Daily, weekly, writers put themselves on the line through poems, fiction, reportage and essays, the manifestos they were asked to sign and, most famously, the questionnaire sent out by the editors of *Authors Take Sides on the Spanish War* (1937). The book contains 121 responses; 100 pro-government (Samuel Beckett sent the shortest message, 'UP THE REPUBLIC!'), 16 neutral (Ezra Pound among them), and five anti-government (including Evelyn Waugh). Constrained by his recently adopted Catholicism, Graham Greene didn't respond, but the hero of his 1939 thriller *Confidential Agent* was clearly an emissary of the Loyalists (though his country and specific allegiance is not named) in Britain to persuade miners not to assist the fascist cause. The novel became a Hollywood film in 1945 with Charles Boyer, Lauren Bacall and Peter Lorre. It's one of the few adaptations of his work of which Greene approved.

When, 30 years later, a similar book, *Authors Take Sides on Vietnam*, was published, a large number of the invited spokespersons considered themselves unqualified to comment, a situation that provoked a *TLS* editorial: 'It is clearer than ever that there has been a very widespread retreat indeed from the sort of generous and poetical involvement which led some writers to take sides in the Spanish War as well as on it.' But it was precisely the way artists and intellectuals had felt themselves exploited, compromised and betrayed in the 1930s that made so many of them wary during the Second

World War and then in the 1960s.

Fourth, to understand the war in all its complexity is to come to terms with the generation of artists born around the turn of the century. The lure of power, of influence, of fulfilling a social role led many to put their talents at the service of the Spanish Republic. The attraction of becoming Byronic men of action drove many of them to serve with the International Brigades.

But Valentine Cunningham, editor of *The Penguin Book of Spanish Civil War Verse*, rightly points out in his *British Writers of the Thirties*, that '80 per cent of the 2,762 Britons in the International Brigades were working class', adding: 'One of the cruellest injustices to their memory and bravery has been literary people's readiness at losing sight of them in the "poet's war" legend.'

It is true that many people were in Spain as observers and tourists. In Madrid in 1937 you could hardly move in the lobbies of the smart hotels without meeting Pulitzer Prize-winning writers, Goncourt laureates or Stalin Prize-winners. There was a famous encounter in Madrid between those literary men of action, André Malraux and Ernest Hemingway, in which they supposedly divided the battlefield between them, giving the air to the Frenchman (the film and novel *Days of Hope*) and the ground war to the American (*For Whom the Bell Tolls*). Louis MacNeice, far less politically committed than his friends Stephen Spender and W.H. Auden who wrote endlessly of the war, spent his long vacation from teaching classics at London University observing the war in Barcelona; he even developed a manly sweat unloading sacks of powdered milk for an International Brigade unit.

But we must not forget that the poets Julian Bell, John Cornford, Christopher Cauldwell and Charles Donnelly, four of the most gifted poets of their generation, died in the first year of the war. And George Orwell and the sculptor Jason Gurney were badly wounded, the latter never able to sculpt again.

Homage to Catalonia, Orwell's celebration of the classless atmosphere among the Republican militia and his exposé of the brutal Stalinist crushing of democratic socialists, Trotskyists, anarchists and other opponents in the International Brigades, is the greatest non-fiction work written by a combatant. It was reviled at the time by reviewers committed to the Popular Front slogan 'No enemies on Left'; by the time Orwell died it hadn't sold out its slim first edition or found an American publisher.

Gurney's eloquent memoir, *Crusade in Spain*, published post-humously in 1974, is as clear-headed as Orwell's book. Crippled for nearly 40 years, Gurney could still write: 'The fact that others took advantage of our idealism in order to destroy it does not in any way invalidate the decision which we made.'

The Spanish War transformed lives at the time (Orwell's, Spender's, Koestler's), and later Jimmy Porter, the archetypal anti-hero of John Osborne's *Look Back In Anger* (1956), recalls spending a year, around the age of ten, nursing his dying father who had returned fatally wounded from the Spanish Civil War.

Such wounds in our literature are of course symbolic, emblematic. Osborne opens them up in the play when Jimmy observes:

> I suppose people of our generation aren't able to die for good causes any longer. We had all that done for us, in the Thirties and the Forties, when we were still kids. There aren't any good, brave causes left.

Perhaps not. But Angus Calder and Studs Terkel named their classic studies of the Second World War, respectively, *The People's War* and *The Good War*. That's progress of a kind.

This Spanish Civil War piece is somewhat less than exhaustive, though the omitted movies were minor if interesting. In 1937 John Wayne played a newsreel cameraman switched from the Spanish conflict to report on an imminent anti-British uprising in Africa in the Universal B-movie, I Cover the War, *a film I've never seen. I have seen the rather good noir thriller* The Fallen Sparrow *(1953), based on Dorothy B. Hughes's politically committed novel, starring John Garfield as an International Brigade veteran pursued by Nazi agents in the States. On a visit to Moscow in 1981 I saw one reel of a film by Emil Lotyanu,* This Instant *(1969), the story of a Moldavian adventurer discovering himself and dying as a pilot with the International Brigades in Spain. It was rather impressive. For several years, Hugh Hudson, director of* Chariots of Fire, *has been planning a film version of* Homage to Catalonia *to star Colin Firth as Orwell with location shooting in Argentina. A promising project that has yet to be made.*

Sport in Movies
From Johnny Weissmüller to Vinnie Jones (1996)

This month Kevin Costner demonstrates his formidable swing as an ageing golf pro in *Tin Cup*, a movie directed and co-scripted by Ron Shelton, onetime minor league baseball player. Next month in the London Film Festival, the poet, martial artist and Manchester United hero Eric Cantona makes a creditable movie debut as a womanising star three-quarter for Condom Rugby Club in *Le Bonheur est dans le pré*; Vinnie Jones is soon to be seen as a debt collector in *Lock, Stock and Two Smoking Barrels*; and the French tennis star Yannick Noah will make his film debut next year in Hannibal Tartarin's *Le Petit fils*.

There's nothing odd here. For a century there has been a symbiotic relationship between the cinema and professional sport. The first people to be recognised on film and to be paid for their appearance were boxers in the 1890s, and there have been more movies about boxing than any other sport. From Chaplin, Keaton and Harold Lloyd onwards, virtually every screen comedian has entered the ring, and at every major world championship bout movie stars have had ringside seats. Real-life boxers have been courted by the movies. Ex-champions Tami Mauriello and Tony Galento lend authentic muscle to the crooked union organiser Johnny Friendly in *On the Waterfront*; Jake La Motta tends the bar where Paul Newman seeks solace in *The Hustler*; while Cassius Clay pulverises ageing scrapper Anthony Quinn behind the opening credits of *Requiem for a Heavyweight*, before going on as Muhammad Ali to play himself in the fictionalised biopic *The Greatest* and an ex-slave who becomes a US Senator in *Freedom Road*. Our own champ Freddie Mills appeared in several films, most notably as a boxer

'Sport in Movies' first appeared in the *Observer*, 27 October 1996.

sought by the transfusion service because he belongs to a rare blood group in Lewis Gilbert's 1952 thriller *Emergency Call*.

Walk-on appearances usually depend upon the audience recognising the sports personalities concerned or upon them being identified for us. Stirling Moss's half-minute on the screen as James Bond's chauffeur in *Casino Royale* (1967) is funny only if you know who he is. The second-rank golf pros in *Tin Cup* need to be pointed out to the audience by the TV commentators. Of course you can usually recognise the real sportsmen by their bad acting and the actors by the circumspect way the editors and cameramen endow them with sporting prowess. The great popularity of Pro-Am golf, in which top players pair with showbiz personalities, could be said to have started in movies such as *The Arsenal Stadium Mystery* (1939), in which actors Leslie Banks and Brian Worth are supported by the club's real manager, George Allison, and his great, rather shy Arsenal XI of the 1930s. Undoubtedly the worst Pro-Am movie is John Huston's *Escape to Victory* (1981) in which Michael Caine captains a multinational team of POWs in Germany, with Sylvester Stallone in goal, Bobby Moore in midfield and Pelé as striker.

The sportsmen's performances usually remind us of the celebrated John Ford dictum: 'It's easier to teach an actor to ride than a cowboy to act.' There are some notable exceptions, of course, of which the most obvious is C. Aubrey Smith who, six years before the invention of the cinema, captained the English cricket XI in their first Test series against the Springboks. His nickname, 'Round the Corner' Smith, came from his bowling style, though the bewhiskered roué was famous in the 1930s for sidling up to starlets at Tinseltown dances and propositioning them, suggesting that they visit his house after midnight but park their cars 'round the corner'.

It should be said that Smith's roles as straight-batting cricketer and stiff-upper-lip actor were inseparable, and most sports stars who have had acting careers of any duration bring to the screen the skills and grace they demonstrated on the field of play. Jim Thorpe, the Iroquois Indian voted in 1951 'the greatest male athlete of the first half of the twentieth century', had a remarkable career as footballer and athlete. But after winning the pentathlon and the decathlon at the 1912 Stockholm Olympics, he was stripped of his medals because he'd taken money for playing baseball while at college. Thorpe was apparently on his uppers with a drink problem when he moved to Hollywood to act in dozens of B-feature westerns and play one of the natives of Skull Island in *King Kong*.

Other Olympic stars were more fortunate. The multiple gold medallist Johnny Weissmüller used his aquatic skills and physique as the screen's most famous Tarzan, though his acting talents compelled the screenwriter on *Tarzan the Ape Man* (Ivor Novello, who was not unattracted to the star) to fashion the minimal 'Me Tarzan – you Jane' dialogue. After breaking Weissmüller's 400-metre freestyle record at the 1932 Olympics, Larry 'Buster' Crabbe was immediately signed up by Hollywood to play Tarzan, Flash Gordon and Buck Rogers. He never moved out of B-pictures and eventually retired to go into the swimming-pool business.

The sport that in recent years has presented Hollywood with true stars is American football, most notably Jim Brown and O.J. Simpson, who brought to action movies the same elegance, sexuality and menace they displayed on the gridiron.

Top sportsmen and sportswomen, once so poorly rewarded, now receive salaries comparable to movie stars'. They are dealt with in identical terms by the tabloids. As a result they often behave as badly as their opposite numbers on the silver screen.

One of the first famous exchanges between Hollywood and the sporting world occurred in 1953 when Marilyn Monroe, on the threshold of stardom, returned from a triumphant visit to the American forces in Korea, to her husband, the great baseball player Joe DiMaggio. 'Joe, you never heard anything like it,' she said of the applause she received. 'Yes, I have,' he quietly replied.

One of the greatest of all sports movies is George Cukor's Pat and Mike, *teaming Spencer Tracy as a shady gambler and sports promoter who becomes the manager of all-round sportswoman Katharine Hepburn. She not only displays her prowess at golf and tennis, but plays along with the likes of Babe Didrikson Zaharias, Gussie Moran, Donald Budge and Alice Marble. Chuck Connors, former major league baseball player, made his screen debut as a police captain. I have since learnt, incidentally, that the story I relay of Jim Thorpe being a down and out is largely mythical. He was treated extremely badly by the athletic establishment (most especially by the rich adminstrator Avery Brundage), but he actually made a good deal of money.*

Explosive Moments
Bombs in Movies (1997)

Lieutenant Kirpal 'Kip' Singh of the Royal Engineers, one of the leading characters in Michael Ondaatje's *The English Patient*, belongs to that band of intrepid heroes, the disposers of unexploded bombs (UXBs as we've learnt to call them), who began early in World War Two and now practise their hazardous profession everywhere from Ulster to Cambodia. There is enough material in the novel that Anthony Minghella hasn't used in his film version to build a whole bomb picture around Kip.

Kip's literary and cinematic ancestry begins with the troubled World War Two bomb disposal boffin in Nigel Balchin's novel *The Small Back Room* and the 1949 Powell and Pressburger film version featuring the palm-moistening scene of David Farrar dismantling a booby-trapped German device on an English beach. It continues through Robert Aldrich's *Ten Seconds to Hell* (1959), in which a suicide squad of ex-Wehrmacht soldiers led by Jack Palance and Jeff Chandler dismantle bombs in post-war Berlin; *Danger UXB*, the 1978 TV series starring Anthony Andrews as the head of a squadron of World War Two bomb disposal experts; and Otto, the endearing anti-Nazi sapper in Edgar Reitz's *Heimat*, who is blown up as he attempts to demolish a British bomb in 1944.

In these classic existential bomb movies, the heroes pit themselves against unseen, unknown enemies, as if engaging in a murderous game of chess with a malevolent god. A cruder variation on the genre sees the official good-guy expert confront his evil opposite number, the mad bomber, trying to enter into his diabolical mind – Richard Harris v Freddie Jones in *Juggernaut* (1974), Jeff Bridges v Tommy Lee Jones in *Blown Away* (1994), Keanu Reeves v Dennis

'Explosive Moments' first appeared in the *Observer*, 16 March 1997.

Hopper in *Speed* (1994).

All these movies exploit the contrast between the two ends of the cinema's sound spectrum – terrifying silence and eardrum-shattering noise. There is an obvious sexual analogy in the prolonged silence that accompanies the dismantling of a bomb and the quiet relief or appalling explosion that follows.

Alfred Hitchcock, no stranger to sexual innuendo, deeply regretted the scene in his 1936 box-office flop *Sabotage*, in which a lad is blown up on a London bus while innocently carrying an *agent provocateur*'s bomb. 'The boy was involved in a situation that got him too much sympathy with the public,' he told François Truffaut, 'so that when he was killed, the public was resentful.' Despite this, Hitch always drew on the bomb to explain the difference between surprise and suspense. Two men are sitting in a café and suddenly a bomb goes off – that is surprise. But if the audience knows there is a bomb ticking away beneath the table and the men are complacently talking about baseball, that is suspense.

Since this bomb piece was written Britain has become involved in two drawn-out wars, both longer than World War Two, in which UXBs have been replaced by IEDs (improvised explosive devices) of an even more fiendish kind. At the 2010 Oscars, The Hurt Locker, *Kathryn Bigelow's masterly film about a team of US bomb disposal experts in Iraq, won six Oscars, including best film, best direction and best original screenplay.*

Film Endings (1997)

The sections on 'Closing Lines' and 'Opening Lines' in Peter Kemp's *Oxford Dictionary of Literary Quotations* have provoked much comment about how books begin and end. Numerous readers have written letters listing favourite opening lines, and there's been a *Times* leader on the subject. But what about the cinema?

Movie openings need to set the scene, establishing time, place and character, and to intrigue. They rarely risk being as abrupt, epigrammatic or surprising as the sentences that kick off novels. Endings are a different matter. Traditionally pictures go for a dying fall, a conventional image to wind up the action, like a clinch between lovers, a lone cowboy riding into the sunset, the characters heading away from the camera or the camera drawing back from them. But good films have memorable final images or lapidary closing lines, and the best have unforgettable moments that sum up the picture's meaning. Think of Joel McCrea looking up to the mountains as he dies, his lifeless body filling the screen in *Ride the High Country*; the long take of Alida Valli walking down the cemetery road past Joseph Cotten in *The Third Man*; the door in the foreground shutting on the unaccommodated John Wayne in *The Searchers*; the much-imitated freeze and zoom onto Jean-Pierre Léaud as he runs on the beach in *Les Quatre cents coups*. Or remember endings that have entered the language – 'After all, tomorrow is another day', 'Louis, I think this is the beginning of a beautiful friendship', 'Well, nobody's perfect', 'Forget it Jake, it's Chinatown'.

Until the 1970s, movies concluded with a simple 'The End' – or *Fin, Ende, Slut* (moviegoers got to recognise the Japanese, Hungarian or Bengali for 'end') – usually, though not always, followed by a cast list. Nowadays instead of The End, or in addi-

---

'Film Endings' first appeared in the *Observer*, 2 November 1997.

tion to it, there are five minutes or more of credits, listing everyone from stunt persons to caterers. Some moviemakers take up the challenge to keep the audience watching, others just expect them to leave. One strategy is to throw in intriguing pictures or verbal jokes. Halfway through the credits on a comedy from the *Airplane!* team there appears the line, 'If you hadn't sat watching these credits you could be home by now'. Another trick is to string together the outtakes, a device used by Jonathan Demme in *Married to the Mob*, and copied by Jackie Chan, all of whose recent pictures mingle the credits with footage of stunts going wrong, often involving pain and bloodshed for Chan. Music is a good way to hold our attention. Demme keeps us watching at the end of *Something Wild* by having the credits roll down the lefthand side, as on the right the alluring Sister Carol sings the title song straight to camera. Nobody left the cinema during the credits of *Postcards From the Edge* because Meryl Streep reprises her version of 'Checking out of the Heartbreak Hotel' (the best part of the movie). The only time the title song of Woody Allen's *Everyone Says I Love You* (originally written by Bert Kalmar and Hary Ruby for the four Marx Brothers to perform in their 1932 *Horse Feathers*) is sung is over the final credits. Danny Boyle's *A Life Less Ordinary*, ingeniously if desperately, attempts to revive our interest in its characters by recapitulating the story using animated dolls.

Certain people (including myself) always sit through the credits in the expectation of picking up some little nugget of information (e.g. that the Rocky Mountain locations for *Cliffhanger* were actually in the Tyrol). At the end of the French comedy *Les Visiteurs*, we were rewarded by a mediaeval knight saluting us, and the caption, 'The producers greet people who read the credits', but for those who stay to the bitter end of *Bean*, Rowan Atkinson comes on screen to sneer at the wimps still in the cinema.

The Ring Cycle
Boxers in Movies (1998)

Just when you thought it was safe to dismantle the ring, British moviemakers have got their gloves on again and are tapping the old claret.

Next week sees Daniel Day-Lewis as a former IRA gunman running a boxing club in Belfast to bring Catholic and Protestant teenagers together in Jim Sheridan's *The Boxer*, a film on which Barry McGuigan acted as advisor. Shane Meadows, one of the most promising young British directors, moves into the big time with the forthcoming *TwentyFourSeven*, in which Bob Hoskins attempts to revive a Midlands community by forming a boxing team from its aimless youth. Just released on video are Ron Peck's documentary, *Fighters*, a loving essay on the boxing subculture of London's East End, and his feature film, *Real Money*, a story of sport and crime improvised by its cast of real-life pugilists. As these movies suggest, boxing is about the working class and its aspirations to self-respect and success in a world run by the rich: the proletariat spill their blood in the ring but the rules are laid down by the Marquess of Queensberry.

For a variety of reasons (e.g. they don't attract women, European audiences don't understand baseball) sports in the movies have been thought of as dubious box-office if not actual box-office poison – the one exception being boxing. Everyone can follow the progress of a slugfest and, whatever their protestations to the contrary, women are drawn to the spectacle of gleaming male bodies engaged in a Darwinian struggle for supremacy. There is also a strong homo-erotic element. But beyond that, boxing has a special appeal to artists and filmmakers.

'The Ring Cycle' first appeared in the *Observer*, 15 February 1998.

William Hazlitt begins his classic 1822 essay on boxing with an epigraph misquoting Hamlet: 'the fight, the fight's the thing/ Wherein I'll catch the conscience of the king'. Many artists since then have merged 'play' and 'fight', most famously Brecht, who made boxing central to his dramaturgy. He saw parallels between the stage and the boxing ring, encouraged in his audience the 'smoking and observing' atmosphere of the boxing stadium, and viewed the fight game as a paradigm of capitalism.

Like Brecht, boxing is currently unfashionable and politically incorrect, and there is a widespread demand for its abolition. But, also like Brecht, this brutalising, beautiful activity has never been truly respectable, and this has traditionally been part of its appeal. The same is true of the movies, an unrespectable art from the start. Within a year of its invention, the cinema brought to the great American public the gory world of heavyweight championship fights with their black eyes, bleeding noses and cauliflower ears, and thus the movies shared the obloquy attaching to fisticuffs. There have been a few distinguished European boxing pictures: Hitchcock's *The Ring*, Visconti's *Rocco and His Brothers*, Lelouch's *Edith and Marcel*. But they have always been in the shadow of what is essentially an American genre, and never more so than in *My Life as a Dog*, in which a young Swedish boy follows the career abroad of his hero, the heavyweight contender Ingemar Johansson.

At some time in their career, virtually every American male star has gone into the ring. The comedians (Chaplin in *The Champion*, Keaton in *Battling Butler*) show how by guile and good fortune they can escape punishment and skirt the system. The dramatic actors must engage in the struggle – to find a place in society (De Niro in *Raging Bull*), to achieve redemption (Newman in *Somebody Up There Likes Me*), to pay for a sister's operation or a brother's education (Cagney in *City for Conquest*). It is a world where defeat is just a few rounds away. Those who don't box are to be found, like Bogart and Robinson, at the ringside as managers, trainers or gamblers. Meanwhile the actresses, as gold-diggers or agonising partners, watch and wait, though in *The Bells of St Mary's* Sister Ingrid Bergman studies a book on boxing and teaches a bullied pupil the noble art of self-defence.

One unusual feature about boxing movies is that they are often made by artists who either loathe the fight game or are prepared to present it in the ugliest light as an image of a society they dislike. This is the case in such outstanding examples of the genre as Robert Wise's *The Set-Up* (1949) and Mark Robson's *Champion* (1949), both updated from minor literary classics, the first from a novel in verse by Joseph Moncure March, the other from a short story by Ring Lardner. Another interesting aspect is that quite a few of the most notable pictures about pugilists have little or no boxing in them: Burt Lancaster is an ex-fighter waiting for death in *The Killers*; in *The Quiet Man*, John Wayne has been traumatised by having killed an opponent in the ring; Brando has ceased to be a contender when *On the Waterfront* starts; Montgomery Clift establishes his probity by refusing to obey his company commander's order to box in *From Here to Eternity*.

Although black boxers have dominated the ring for decades, there have been few big-budget films focusing on blacks, nothing comparable with the five *Rocky* movies, where most of Stallone's opponents are black. Almost the only one of true distinction is *The Great White Hope*, in which James Earl Jones recreated his stage role as the doomed champion Jack Johnson. The original play was the work of a white author, Howard Sackler. When two years ago, in 1996, the black director Reginald Hudlin got a chance to make a fight film, the result was *The Great White Hype*, a satire on the world of Don King in which promoters conspire to revive public interest in a black-dominated sport by inventing a spurious white heavy-weight contender.

Extra Extra!
Hollywood's Blood Money (1998)

Rupert Murdoch's 20th Century-Fox expressed its gratitude for *Titanic* by giving the film's writer-director James Cameron an *ex gratia* payment of $75m. It followed that gesture last Wednesday by presenting £5,000 and an engraved plaque to the old school of First Officer William Murdoch. This was by way of apologising to his family and community for Cameron's claim in the movie that he had accepted a bribe from a first-class passenger, killed a rebellious third-class passenger, and then blown his own brains out. Is this generosity, parsimony or hypocrisy? Does it represent a new feeling for the truth on the part of William Murdoch's antipodean kinsman?

Rupert Murdoch's attitude to history was cogently expressed during the Hitler Diaries fiasco, when he ordered his *Sunday Times* to go ahead and publish, dismissing the cautionary advice from Britain's most respected historian, Lord Dacre (the former Sir Hugh Trevor-Roper), with the blunt remark, 'Fuck Dacre,' adding, 'After all, we're in the entertainment business.' Not since Henry Ford declared that 'history is bunk' had the votaries of Clio, muse of history, been so roundly dismissed.

But does the fight to clear Murdoch (First Officer William Murdoch of Dalbeattie, that is) suggest that a Truth and Reconciliation Commission should be set up to protect the posthumous reputations of the great and the humble from the callous calumnies of filmmakers? The living have recourse to the laws of libel, as MGM discovered to its cost in 1934 when Prince and Princess Youssoupoff successfully sued for the suggestion in *Rasputin, the Mad Monk* that the Princess had been raped by the libidinous cleric. Since then every film has carried a disclaimer that all characters and

---

'Extra Extra! Hollywood's Blood Money' first appeared in the *Observer*, 26 April 1998.

events in the picture are fictitious and any resemblance to real life is purely coincidental.

Who will protect the dead and the humble? Roman law established the right of families to prevent their ancestors being defamed, but in the modern world calumny can freely begin with the first obituary. However, if some cinematic Archbishop Desmond Tutu were to be let loose, what cases could be argued before him? The representation of Field Marshal Haig as a sanctimonious butcher in *Oh! What a Lovely War*? Dirk Bogarde playing General Browning as an insensitive neurotic in *A Bridge Too Far*? General Montgomery caricatured as a preening dimwit in *Patton*? Charles Laughton for turning that great sailor William Bligh into a byword for sadistic naval incompetence in *Mutiny on the Bounty* and a great king into a buffoon in *The Private Life of Henry VIII*? Who will come to the defence of John Brown, portrayed in *Santa Fe Trail* as a bloodthirsty fanatic, or Joan Crawford, depicted as the self-regarding mother from hell in *Mommie Dearest*? And are there any descendants of Rasputin to demand apologies for 60 years of cinematic abuse culminating in the current cartoon *Anastasia*, which credits him with launching the Bolshevik Revolution and murdering the Romanovs? And what about Marion Davies, whose reputation suffered irreparably from *Citizen Kane*?

The fact is that the movies aggrandise more often than they belittle. They take feet of clay and mould them into heroic statues, making Jesse James, Wyatt Earp and Billy the Kid into legends. Inevitably some people get caught in the crossfire in this process, and occasionally they bear real names, like the Clanton family in movies about the gunfight at the OK Corral. And James Cameron, self-styled 'King of the World', didn't know or care what he was doing to the reputation of William Murdoch when he was creating the moral confusion aboard the Titanic that transformed Kate Winslet and Leonardo DiCaprio into romantic icons for the millennium.

The Designer as Auteur
Ken Adam (1999)

In the new Hollywood comedy *The Out-of-Towners*, a middle-class couple played by Goldie Hawn and Steve Martin enter the gleaming marble lobby of the grand Mark Hotel in New York. Steps lead off the vast concourse to an enticing bar, where polished mahogany surfaces catch the seductive low lighting. This pristine, dream-like place doesn't exist. It's the idea or ideal of an exclusive Manhattan luxury hotel – palatial, intimidating – that the film's central couple might have in their mind's eye, and it was created in a Hollywood studio by the film's production designer, Ken Adam.

Conveying the movie's tone, the set helps dramatise the situation of a naive provincial couple out for an elegant experience and disoriented by the trappings of the big city. Elsewhere in the picture, Adam has selected authentic Manhattan landmarks for key scenes, transformed the Los Angeles Convention Centre into Boston Station, and found a house in Pasadena to stand in for the protagonists' Ohio home. Few members of the audience will be conscious of his work, but the role of production designer is among the most crucial in the filmmaking process, and for 40 years Adam's name on the credits has usually meant something special.

The role of the designer became significant as soon as films began to do something more than simply record the world. The first Oscars in this area were given for 'interior decoration', and the term 'production designer' was coined by David O. Selznick in a celebrated 1937 memo to show the importance he attributed to William Cameron Menzies's contribution to *Gone With the Wind*.

Ideally an art director should combine the skills of an architect, a draughtsman, a quick sketch artist, a quantity surveyor, an art histo-

'The Designer as Auteur' first appeared in the *Observer*, 14 November 1999.

rian and a magician. His job, in collaboration with the costume designer and the cinematographer, is to turn into physical reality the concepts and ideas of others – the producers, the director, the writer – whose notions may be extremely vague or hopelessly expensive.

Born in 1921, Adam grew up in Berlin when some of the legendary sets of movie history were being built at the Universum Film Aktiengesellschaft (UFA) studio for films such as *Siegfried* and *Metropolis*. And like the designers of most of those sets and most of the directors who worked on them, he left Germany with his family when the Nazis came to power. Settling in Britain, he attended a London prep school where he was a friend of the future art critic David Sylvester, one of the finest writers on the arts during the past half-century and curator of the Serpentine Gallery's Adam exhibition. A meeting as a teenager with another exile, Vincent Korda, designer for his brother Alex's London Films and assistant to William Cameron Menzies on *Things to Come*, determined his vocation.

After studying architecture and serving as an RAF pilot in the Second World War, he entered the movies as a draughtsman in 1947, became an assistant art director in the early 1950s and was soon promoted to fully fledged production designer, winning his first Oscar nomination for the European sets of *Around the World in 80 Days* in 1956. To get some idea of his productivity, one might note that two outstanding British directors near his age who also emerged from the forces at the end of the war, Lindsay Anderson and Karel Reisz, directed six and nine feature films respectively in their whole careers. Adam has designed over 50, with more to come.

The range of Adam's work is prodigious: from the distant biblical past of Bruce Beresford's *King David* to the then near future of Stanley Kubrick's *Dr Strangelove*, from the late Victorian charm of *The Seven-Per-Cent Solution*, the Herbert Ross comedy about Sherlock Holmes meeting Sigmund Freud, to the contemporary realism of *Dead Bang*, John Frankenheimer's thriller about American neo-Nazis. The only genre he hasn't worked in has been the cowboy movie, though he made up for this with a magnificently designed version of Puccini's *The Girl of the Golden West* at Covent Garden with sets in the style of a spaghetti western.

Nearly all Adam's films, whether made in Britain, Europe or the

States, have been produced or directed by Americans, starting with Mike Todd's *Around the World in 80 Days*, the Jacques Tourneur horror classic *Night of the Demon* (1958) and Robert Aldrich's *Ten Seconds to Hell* (1959), a brilliant melodrama about a post-war German bomb disposal unit. He came into his own during the 1960s, the era of Swinging London, when there was a boom in British cinema, and the public, under the influence of pop art and an explosion of innovatory graphic design in magazines and TV commercials, was developing a new feeling for matters visual. In 1962, he worked on the first of his seven Bond movies, *Dr No*, and he would have done the second Bond, *From Russia With Love*, had he not been engaged in designing *Dr Strangelove*.

These films made an indelible impression on audiences the world over, and as comedy-thrillers about paranoid megalomaniacs threatening the very existence of the world they sought to control, they were two sides of the same coin. They established a familiar Adam setting that can be found in two of his modest earlier pictures (*Obsession* and *Ten Seconds to Hell*) – the underground shelter, a key locus of power and control as well as of powerlessness and refuge in both the Second World War and the Cold War.

Dr No's subterranean headquarters on Crab Key was the first of many grandiose power centres for Bond villains. But equally fantastic, though near the knuckle of the nuclear button, was the war room of *Dr Strangelove*, the circle of light above the conference table resembling a mushroom cloud. It was so real and so fantastic that the impressionable moviegoer Ronald Reagan expected to preside there after his election. *Dr Strangelove* was very much Stanley Kubrick's picture. But as the Bond series developed, it was clear that the real genius behind it was Adam, and that he was represented on screen by Desmond Llewellyn as Q, the ingenious inventor of the contraptions that made Bond's survival and triumphs possible.

There is immense wit in Adam's work. Who can forget 007's double take as he spots Goya's portrait of Wellington, then recently stolen from the National Gallery, in *Dr No*'s lair? Or the seriously comic design conceit of *The Ipcress File*, Michael Caine's first Harry Palmer film, where the same production team turned Bond on his head? And arguably the funniest aspect of *Addams Family Values* are the sets which bring to life in a marvellous but not unduly extravagant fashion the world of Charles Addams.

Adam has won two Oscars, both for costume pictures, Stanley Kubrick's *Barry Lyndon* and Nicholas Hytner's *The Madness of King George*, each a reconstruction of eighteenth-century Europe using historical buildings and stylistically influenced by contemporary painters. No one would deny him these honours. Yet neither picture has anything quite as exciting or memorable as the set-pieces in less respectable works – his wholly imagined ancient communities in *Sodom and Gomorrah*, his Midas-touched interior of Fort Knox in *Goldfinger*, his black-and-white sweet factory in *Chitty Chitty Bang Bang*, his dream-like evocation of Depression America for *Pennies from Heaven* and the volcanic hideaway he devised for Blofeld in *You Only Live Twice*.

This article on Ken Adam was written on the occasion of the exhibition of his designs at the Serpentine Gallery, London. I wrote an extended essay for the catalogue.

The Critics' Century 1900–2000 (1999)

In 1922, Lenin told his newly appointed cultural commissar, Anatoli Lunacharsky: 'You are considered the protector of the arts. For that reason you must bear firmly in mind that to us, film, of all forms of art, is the most important.' Six years earlier the US Supreme Court had ruled in a censorship appeal from Ohio that movies were 'a business pure and simple', thus not protected by the First Amendment. This judgment remained the law until the 1950s.

But as art or entertainment, in the realms of communism and capitalism all the world's statesmen have embraced the cinema. Hitler staged the Nuremberg Rally for the cameras of Leni Riefenstahl, Mussolini created the world's first film festival at Venice, Stalin watched secretly imported westerns in the Kremlin, and Madame Mao wept over a contraband copy of *The Sound of Music* in Peking.

American presidents, from Woodrow Wilson (who gave the racist *Birth of a Nation* his imprimatur) to Bill Clinton, have welcomed to the White House the leading citizens and products of Hollywood, the catch-all title for what is now the country's second largest industry. Popes have also blessed the new medium, and so has the Dalai Lama who allowed himself to be impersonated in *Seven Years in Tibet* and *Kundun*.

The century began with people believing that 'all the world's a stage'; it ends with most of us convinced that life is a film. The medium has created a new grammar of thought and experience – the flashback, the jump cut, crosscutting, the dream sequence, slow motion, the close-up, the world seen in black-and-white or Technicolor. It has changed the way we dream and is itself a form of dreaming. Through the size of the image on the screen it has transformed our sense of scale, turning actors into stars larger than

'The Critics' Century 1900–2000' first appeared in the *Observer*, 26 December 1999.

anything we see in the sky and making their actions – whether kissing or killing – into gargantuan transactions. It has also changed the nature of fame. In 1914 Charlie Chaplin was a little-known music-hall comedian; four years later he was the most famous man of all time, the first person to be universally recognisable to the educated and illiterate on every continent.

The moving picture camera has become part of our public and private experience, bringing us the horrors of the extermination camps, but also allowing us to record our own lives. It has always run the gamut from the wilfully esoteric to the most calculatedly populist. Movies have both encouraged crime and inspired acts of heroism. It was after seeing Leslie Howard's wartime thriller *Pimpernel Smith* that the Swedish diplomat Raoul Wallenberg set out to save thousands of Jews in Nazi-occupied Hungary.

The anthropologist Hortense Powdermaker dubbed Hollywood 'the dream factory', but Jean-Luc Godard has extolled film as 'the truth 24 times a second'. Initially despised as five-cent entertainment for the poor, cinema is now installed as a proper subject for study in universities. Directing films has become the most desirable and fashionable of professions.

Film records and creates. From the turn of the century, intrepid camera crews have brought the most inaccessible parts of the globe to the cosiest villages of the West, while special effects experts in film studios have conjured up fantasies that bring to life delights and horrors that for centuries remained on the canvases of Hieronymus Bosch. In *King Kong*, fantasy and documentary came together at the height of the Depression in a fable about a filmmaker returning to New York from the back of beyond, not with celluloid dreams but with monstrous reality.

In the 95 years that separate the original version of *The Great Train Robbery* and *The Truman Show*, the cinema has recapitulated the whole history of art from cave painting to post-modernism. It has produced many of this century's greatest artists from D.W. Griffith to Ingmar Bergman, and from the start artists recognised its potency. Maxim Gorki wrote the first serious piece of film criticism in 1896, Rudyard Kipling the first significant fiction about the cinema, *Mrs Bathhurst*, in 1904, Vachel Lindsay the first important treatise on the new art in 1915. The movies have drawn on all the traditional art forms – fiction, painting, theatre, music, dance, architecture, poetry

– and the new Tenth Muse has influenced the development of the other arts and their practitioners. James Joyce opened Dublin's first purpose-built cinema; his protégé Sam Beckett drew on Laurel and Hardy for *Waiting for Godot* and later wrote a scenario for Buster Keaton.

The novel has been profoundly affected, and most leading writers have had their style influenced and their fingers burnt by contact with the movies. Few have failed to record the experience, which for most has been their chief involvement with *laissez-faire* capitalism at its most cruel and seductive. Guardians of public morality saw the cinema as a threat to the social order and sought to shackle it. Entrepreneurs recognised a source of infinite wealth and set about organising the new medium on an industrial basis. Artists, businessmen and moralists have been contending for control of the screen since the earliest days, and the never-ending battle continues.

Twenty-five years ago, when audiences were falling and cinemas closing, my colleagues in the film section of the Critics' Circle believed that by the end of the century we would have gone the way of saddlery salesmen and lamplighters. Such has not proved to be the case. Attendances have revived dramatically, screens have multiplied through TV, cassettes and DVD, and films are available as never before. Movies – their history, their economics, their production, the lives of their makers – are an obsessive interest the world over, the subject of intense discussion and scholarship. What would the claim that 'movies are the new rock'n'roll' have meant 40 years ago, let alone in 1900?

As we enter the twenty-first century, two questions arise. The first is about Hollywood, which first came to global prominence at the end of the First World War. Described in the 1950s by Ben Hecht as 'like Egypt, full of crumbled pyramids, it'll never come back', Hollywood recovered triumphantly from the challenge of TV and foreign competition, as well as from the Supreme Court's attempt to curb its power by decreeing that production and distribution be divorced from exhibition.

Hollywood has become world cinema, a juggernaut crushing every local obstacle in its path, and signing up talent from north, south, east and west. Audiences everywhere stay in their own countries and vote with their feet for Hollywood at the box office. Can Hollywood be checked? Local audiences need a mirror for them-

selves, a cinema of their own, in their native language, articulating
local concerns, expressing shared myths and aspirations. They need
this more than that other institution, a national airline. And the US
independent cinema movement has sprung up because Hollywood
is perceived by many Americans as not truly reflecting their own
lives.

The second question is: have the movies exhausted their possibilities in this hurrying, overheated century? Has the cinema created
a Library of Babel along the lines of Jorge Luis Borges's classic story,
so that every possible plot, scene and character has been defined?
Does nothing remain for future moviemakers but to produce slight
variations on what has already been achieved? If so, only the naive
will see themselves as innovators and only the historically ignorant
will applaud them. But that's the future, and who knows?

'Without Fritz There'd Be No *Star Wars*'
On Fritz Lang (2000)

In 1969 I contributed several thumbnail sketches for a *Sunday Times Magazine* project called 'The 1,000 Makers of the 20th Century', Fritz Lang among them. Lang, aged 79, was living in California, his reputation seemingly unassailable. He was one of the great artists of the twentieth century, a member of that small group of directors – finite because their achievement could never be repeated – who had produced substantial bodies of work both in the silent era and after the coming of sound. He stood, I suggested, among the seminal artists of our time, one of the half-dozen greatest moviemakers.

Twenty years later, and closer to the millennium, the same paper published a revised list. Lang was no longer on it. To find space for post-1970s directors, the editors had decided that some oldsters had to go. It was as if Giotto had been dropped from Gombrich's *Story of Art* to accommodate Damien Hirst. So the year 2000 and the new millennium could not have got off to a better start than with a National Film Theatre Fritz Lang retrospective that, together with its accompanying books and symposiums, should help restore his supremacy.

Lang was born in 1890, five years before the birth of the cinema, the half-Jewish son of a master builder who he claimed was a leading architect. Like those other great Austro-Hungarian cinematic geniuses, Erich von Stroheim and Josef von Sternberg, Lang created himself.

Diligent biographers have exposed their lies, myths and seductive glosses, but nowadays we're inclined to accept the advice of the alcoholic newspaper editor in Ford's *The Man Who Shot Liberty Valance*: 'When the legend becomes fact, print the legend.' In addi-

---

'Without Fritz Lang There'd Be No *Star Wars*' first appeared in the *Observer*, 2 January 2000.

tion to inventing himself, Lang – along with D.W. Griffith and Stro-heim in the United States, Eisenstein and Pudovkin in Russia, Sjöström and Stiller in Sweden – helped create the very idea of the filmmaker as uncompromising visionary. Together they turned the new profession of movie director into one of the grandest, most powerful, most heroic callings, not just of our century but of all time.

The 29-year-old Lang entered the movies in Berlin formidably equipped. He'd studied architecture and law, exhibited paintings, travelled the world, served as an officer in the Austrian army and been wounded four times, published short stories and cartoons. While convalescing at a military hospital in the latter months of the Great War, he sold screenplays to German producers. After less than a year as a script editor, he began directing, and over the next decade he made a succession of extravagant movies on vast sets and with long shooting schedules at the UFA studio.

Gothic met Bauhaus in his morbid Expressionist films, and he established a reputation as an uncompromising, dictatorial perfec-tionist. He was one of the pioneers of the espionage melodrama, the paranoid urban thriller, the historical fantasy epic, the mediaeval allegory, the science fiction picture both in its dystopian mode (*Metropolis*) and its hardware rocketry form (*Woman on the Moon*, the film that invented the countdown).

His megalomaniac super-criminal Dr Mabuse is the predecessor of Dr No and Dr Strangelove. *Destiny* lies behind Bergman's *Seventh Seal*, and Bergman's first German film, *The Serpent's Egg*, is an extended homage to Lang; the tyro Hitchcock watched Lang at work in Berlin; the young Kubrick studied his pictures; *Star Wars* and *Blade Runner* were anticipated by Lang.

His pictures reflected the turbulence of Weimar Germany, a spiralling world of social conflict, unchecked inflation and rapid technological and moral change that led inexorably to the rise of Nazism. The politics of Lang's films were sufficiently confused to make him Hitler's favourite director, and when the Nazis came to power Goebbels offered him the job as head of the Third Reich's new film industry. This, after Lang's brilliantly innovative first talkie, *M* (1931), had commented ironically on the pact between German authority and the criminal underworld.

Lang claims to have fled Berlin the day the Mephistophelean

Goebbels made his offer, joining the greatest exodus of talent the world has ever known. He didn't work in Germany again until the late 1950s, when in the twilight of his career he made three minor works.

Unlike other German exiles – Brecht, Mann, Schoenberg, for example – Lang immersed himself in American culture, driving around the country, reading local newspapers, talking to people and studying comic strips, which he said gave him insights into slang and humour. But the admiration was reciprocal, because the most adventurous New York comic book editor, Jerry Iger, and his two major protégés, Will Eisner and Bob Kane (creator of Batman), were Lang fans. In *The Great Comic Book Heroes*, Jules Feiffer writes: 'Eisner was an early master of the German Expressionist approach in comic books – the Fritz Lang school ... full of dark shadows, creepy angle shots, graphic close-ups of violence and terror.'

The coming of sound and the move to America changed Lang's style. His themes remained the same: the quest for self-fulfilment or revenge turning to ashes, the conflict between free will and destiny, the irreconcilable attractions of the femme fatale and the domestic hearth, the relentlessness of a fate that makes a mockery of our dreams. But the abstract, stylised quality of his European pictures is replaced in the United States by a new solidity and particularity, and fantasy is abandoned.

'American pictures and audiences,' Lang observed, 'are more interested in the fate of the average man, of John Doe, whereas in Europe, especially in Germany, in the days before Hitler, they were more interested in a Nietzschean superman.' Consequently he chose to work with classless, unconventional-looking heroes – Spencer Tracy (in *Fury*, Lang's devastating Hollywood debut, an indictment of vigilantism), and several times each with Edward G. Robinson, Henry Fonda, Glenn Ford and Dana Andrews.

Lang took immediately to the western, seeing it as a democratic development of the Nibelungen sagas, and *Rancho Notorious* (his only movie with Marlene Dietrich) is a bizarre classic of what was coming to be called the adult western. His *Man Hunt* helped create a new genre, the entertainment war flick, and his treatment of the Bonnie and Clyde story in *You Only Live Once* helped launch the Hollywood film noir, to which his fellow German émigrés Otto Preminger, Billy Wilder, Robert Siodmak and Edgar Ulmer contributed. Wilder acknowledges Lang's *M* as the chief stylistic influence on *Double Indemnity*.

Lang also upped the ante on screen violence, staging an almost unendurable fight to the death between Gary Cooper and Marc Lawence as Lilli Palmer looks on in *Cloak and Dagger* (1946), which Hitchcock borrowed 20 years later for *Torn Curtain*. He went beyond this to explore pain and disfigurement in *The Big Heat* (1953), in which Lee Marvin's inner beast emerged to throw a pot of scalding coffee in Gloria Grahame's face. The movie was a turning point in Marvin's career, as *Clash By Night* had been in Marilyn Monroe's the previous year, and *M* for Peter Lorre two decades earlier.

For years it was the received wisdom that the poems Auden wrote before crossing the Atlantic, Hitchcock's British films and the movies Lang directed before his American exile were deeper, richer, more truly serious than anything they produced after they arrived in the States. This is not true. Much of their best work was done there, not despite but because of the liberating, broadening effect of the exposure to America, the size and energy of the country.

The Two Samurai
Kurosawa and Mifune (2002)

BOOK REVIEW
Galbraith, Stuart: *The Emperor and the Wolf* (Faber & Faber)

There have been some notable collaborations between directors and stars over the past 70 years – Josef von Sternberg and Marlene Dietrich, John Ford and John Wayne, Anthony Mann and James Stewart, Martin Scorsese and Robert De Niro, to name four obvious Hollywood examples.

But perhaps the most extraordinary partnership is that between Akira Kurosawa and Toshiro Mifune, the emperor and the wolf of Stuart Galbraith's joint biography. Mifune was in 16 of Kurosawa's 30 films and appeared in a further 130-odd movies, several scripted by Kurosawa. Only two Mifune pictures directed by other filmmakers (Mizoguchi's 1952 *The Life of Oharu* and Kobayashi's 1967 *Rebellion*) are masterworks; the only Kurosawa picture without Mifune universally recognised as great is the 1952 *Ikiru*.

The pair were similar and complementary. Both were heavy-drinking, physically imposing workaholics from middle-class, Westernised families buffeted by the economic and political crises of Japan between the two world wars. Temperamentally the director was a natural aristocrat, the actor a face in the crowd, voted 'the most Japanese man' in a 1960s poll. Kurosawa was nicknamed 'the Emperor' for the imperious, peremptory style in which he dominated the set. Mifune was often compared to a wolf for his fearsome gaze, his menacing walk and the ferocious way he could prance and pounce.

Kurosawa was born in Tokyo in 1910. His father, the head of

'The Two Samurai' first appeared in the *Observer*, 17 February 2002.

athletics at a leading high school, was credited with building Japan's first swimming pool. His initial ambition was to be a painter, but in his mid-twenties he was drawn to the cinema, and in 1937 he became assistant director at the Toho company. He remained there for many years, initially gaining a reputation as a prolific screen-writer before directing his first picture in 1943. Galbraith is fascinating on the exasperating censorship Kurosawa experienced, first in wartime Japan, then under the post-war American occupation.

Mifune was born in Japanese-occupied Manchuria in 1920, grandson of a herbal doctor and son of a portrait photographer. At school he won prizes for karate, archery and swordsmanship. Conscripted in 1940, he used the experience of working with his father to become an airforce cameraman. Fortunately his insolent, menacing manner kept him in the ranks and thus ineligible for dangerous combat photography. Demobbed in 1946, he dressed in a suit cut from the two blankets given him to re-enter civvy street and went for a job as a stills photographer at the Toho studio. Instead he was accepted in Toho's New Face programme for promising young actors.

Established as a versatile director with narrative flair and an eye for detail, Kurosawa scripted Mifune's first film, *Snow Trail* (a thriller inspired by Raoul Walsh's *High Sierra*). He then directed him in four movies – as a gangster, a cop, a doctor and a victim of tabloid jour-nalism – before the sensation of *Rashomon*, which took the world by storm after winning the Golden Lion in Venice in 1951. It changed attitudes to Japan, introduced a hitherto unknown national cinema to global attention, brought the phrase 'Rashomon situa-tion' into the language, and made its director and star famous.

For the following 15 years the pair knew little but critical and financial success and began to live on a grand scale, Mifune driving one of Tokyo's only two black Rolls-Royces (the other belonged to the emperor – the real emperor, that is). A succession of master-pieces flowed from the Toho studios with both period and modern settings and derived from Japanese sources as well as from Shake-speare, Gorki, Dostoevsky, Ed McBain and Dashiell Hammett.

The Idiot, *The Seven Samurai*, *Throne of Blood*, *The Hidden Fortress*, *Yojimbo*, *High and Low* provided Mifune with roles that exhibited an acting range far beyond that of his American contemporaries.

They reworked genres, creating a humanistic cinema that was at once dynamic and contemplative, steeped in Japanese culture yet universal in appeal. They were often about learning from masters (or *sensei*) but never didactic. A new generation of foreign directors was influenced by these seminal works, among them Arthur Penn, Sam Peckinpah and Sergio Leone.

Then, in the mid-1960s, their careers began to unravel as the Japanese film industry fell apart. Kurosawa embarked on two abortive, debilitating Hollywood projects, *The Runaway Train* and *Tora! Tora! Tora!*, the Pearl Harbor epic on which he went clinically insane while directing the Japanese sequences. In 1972 he attempted suicide, recovering to make a series of largely foreign-financed pictures, the best being the Soviet co-production *Dersu Uzala* and the Franco-Japanese *Ran*, his reworking of *King Lear*. His chief supporters were the movie brats who had taken over Hollywood: Coppola, Lucas, Spielberg, Scorsese.

Meanwhile Mifune created his own company and thought to establish an independent identity. But he went from one undistinguished picture to another, working around the world in mostly dismal epics. His production company was in financial trouble, he left his wife for a young actress, and he gave the tabloids a field day when he spray-painted obscenities on the house of his estranged in-laws. He often spoke of working with Kurosawa again, but the emperor never seriously considered him after the mid-1960s. He always felt under the shadow of Kurosawa: of his major 1984 New York retrospective, Mifune remarked ruefully: 'Why not call it a Kurosawa series instead? I haven't done much else worth showing.' The two died within nine months of each other – Mifune in December 1997 of Alzheimer's at the age of 77, Kurosawa in September 1998 at 88, crippled after suffering a damaged spine in a fall, but still writing and even directing his first television commercial from a wheelchair.

Their careers and relationship are fascinating. But in Galbraith's book they have to be pursued through a dense narrative covering 60 years of Japanese cinema and culture, punctuated by accounts of the rise and fall of studios, industrial strikes, thumbnail sketches of every artist, producer and artisan who ever worked with them. There are also details of overseas distribution, endless extracts from American reviews (mostly pretty imperceptive) and an exhaustive filmography which is a book in itself. Astonishingly, this hefty brick of a paperback was written in five years by a 35-year-old American who doesn't appear to have had more than a passing acquaintance with the Japanese language when he began.

The Man Who Shot America
On John Ford (2002)

BOOK REVIEW
McBride, Joseph: *Searching for John Ford: A Life* (Faber & Faber)

The critic and film historian Joseph McBride, believing that John Ford was insuffiently appreciated in his native land, began his search for the curmudgeonly filmmaker in 1970 and was immediately told by Ford himself that 'he had certainly picked a dull subject'.

McBride was a 23-year-old journalist then; Ford was 76 and three years away from his death. One of the two most famous lines from a Ford movie (the other is John Wayne's refrain from *The Searchers*, 'That'll be the day') comes in his mature masterpiece, *The Man Who Shot Liberty Valance*: 'When the legend becomes fact, print the legend.' McBride's determination to discover the facts behind the legend, and to reconcile the myriad of contradictions in Ford's career, accounts for the 32 years he spent on the book, and for its length.

Ford was a notorious romancer and embroiderer. He often claimed to have been born in Ireland rather than in Maine, and to have been christened Sean Aloysius O'Fienne in 1895. McBride establishes that he was born John Martin Feeney in 1894, the youngest of 11 children of Irish immigrants, his father a saloon-keeper, his mother a hotel maid. He took his professional name from an older brother, Francis Ford, who preceded him in Hollywood as an actor-director, yet claimed to have taken it from a car, so that his involvement in films should not disgrace his family.

McBride devotes more than 70 pages to Ford's childhood and youth in New England, establishing how vital to an understanding of the films is his divided nature as a passionate American patriot, fascinated by the country's history, and his awareness, as an Irish-

American Catholic, of belonging to a despised minority who saw themselves as exiles from an emerald utopia.

Thus when it came to the conflict between the US cavalry and the Indians in his great post-war westerns, Ford was on both sides. Moreover, he seemed to regard any persecuted group as honorary Irishmen, whether they were dispossessed Okies heading for California in *The Grapes of Wrath*, Native Americans returning to their tribal hunting grounds in *Cheyenne Autumn* or Welsh miners drawn together by grief in *How Green Was My Valley*. McBride also shows how Ford, who liked to present himself as an untutored roughneck, grew up loving literature, the theatre, the cinema and the visual arts. As a child he watched the elderly Winslow Homer painting on the beach in Maine and this may well have helped shape his famous understanding of composition.

With his brother's encouragement, Ford rapidly learnt every aspect of film craft after arriving in Hollywood in 1914. He soon became a prolific director of two-reel films, most of them westerns. He helped invent the art and language of cinema. By the mid-1920s when he directed *The Iron Horse*, he was a major figure and he took easily to sound. Though he was rarely totally free of the commercial constraints of the studio system, he flourished for more than 50 years. As McBride recognises, he made some indifferent pictures, though only two or three are downright bad.

The largest claim made in this book strikes me as justified. 'Ford is the closest equivalent we have to a homegrown Shakespeare,' McBride writes.

> He chronicled our national history on screen with an epic vision that spanned nearly two centuries, from the Revolutionary War to the Vietnam War. While Ford's vision of America is intensely patriotic, it does not flinch from confronting the country's tragic failures, the times when we did not live up to our ideals. Whatever the events he depicts, Ford's natural allegiance is always with the spirit of the American common people.

Yet Ford was a driven, discontented, often dangerous man. He was an alcoholic who frequently had to be hospitalised after drinking binges. He treated his wife, son and daughter abominably, and days before his death struck his son from his will. But he created a film family from the actors, technicians and assistants who formed his personal stock company and invariably addressed him as 'Pappy'. He was rude, cruel and manipulative in a way beyond anything that can be excused as having a covert artistic purpose. His generosity alternated with a terrible meanness, and he was casually anti-Semitic all his life. He treated John Wayne as if he were his son and turned him into a star, but would frequently humiliate him on the set, making jokes about his wartime draft dodging.

Ford himself took more pride in his remarkable wartime service as head of a special photographic unit than he did in his film work. He covered the Second World War from the Battle of Midway to the D-Day landings, and with the Korean War in 1950 he became a rear admiral. Yet even here he had to embellish a heroic reality, and he lobbied for extra medals and promotion.

In his films, however, ambition and success – as opposed to duty and stoic service – are regarded with suspicion. His politics, in his private life and in his movies, are a mass of contradictions. In the 1930s he was an outspoken supporter of Roosevelt's New Deal, and in a letter to a relative serving with the International Brigades in the Spanish Civil War he claimed to be 'a definite Socialist Democrat, always Left'. But after the war he called himself 'a state of Maine Republican' (a sort of maverick conservative), but told French admirers he was 'a liberal democrat' and gave an interview to the film critic of the communist paper *L'Humanité*. He opposed the blacklist and refused an invitation to meet Joe McCarthy, but was a leading member of the viciously rightwing Motion Picture Alliance for the Protection of American Ideals.

McBride's achievement is that he has brought Ford vividly to life in all his complexity and located him in his times. And this is as good a book as we're likely to get about him. Still, puzzles and paradoxes persist to the end. Shortly before he died Ford bought a family plot at a cemetery in rolling green country, that must have reminded him of Ireland, then moved to a house in the desert that must have recalled his beloved Monument Valley. Of his dying words there are three versions. Did he say 'Holy Mother, Mother of God', 'Now will somebody give me a cigar' or 'Cut!'?

Twenty-one years before the review of the McBride book, I wrote the following piece on Lindsay Anderson's Ford monograph, a work long in gestation and eagerly awaited. As was too often the case then, a last-minute industrial action by the printers resulted in only a small handful of copies of that Sunday's Observer *reaching the streets. Like many people, and not just critics, my relations with the unpredictable Anderson were up and down, though I'm pleased to say that in his last years we were on good terms. After his death I was shown a letter he wrote to my friend and colleague, Alexander Walker, film critic of the* Evening Standard, *saying how pleased he'd been that the* Observer *experienced a strike the weekend this review appeared.*

Barbed Wire Valentine
Anderson on Ford (1981)

BOOK REVIEW
Anderson, Lindsay: *About John Ford* (Plexus)

Lindsay Anderson calls *About John Ford* 'the record of an enthusiasm, an obsession, that has lasted for over 30 years', and it resembles Truffaut's *Le Cinéma selon Hitchcock* in several ways, not least for being as interesting for what we learn of the author as of his subject. Both are works of filial piety by critics-turned-directors, who have made movies reflecting the spirit of their chosen mentors and came to occupy for a time positions of greater intellectual esteem than these ageing masters.

The book is got up like an affectionate tribute with a heroic portrait of John Wayne from *She Wore a Yellow Ribbon* on the front cover, a snapshot on the back of a genially smiling Anderson against the towering buttes and mesas of Monument Valley, the opening bars of Ford's favourite song 'Red River Valley', nostalgic dedications following the title page, and several hundred photographs, many never published before. But on closer inspection the book proves to be a valentine edged with barbed wire.

Anderson came rather late to Ford. In the summer of 1946, aged 23 and between wartime army service and returning to Oxford, he was entranced by *My Darling Clementine*. He saw in this film 'some kind of moral poetry', and now regards Ford as 'a poetic artist' and 'one of the great poets of humanity of our time'. But although he begins by asserting that 'the function of the critic is to make clear, not to obfuscate; to interpret rather than to judge', Anderson rapidly emerges as a stern, unyielding critic in the tradition of F.R. Leavis

---

'Barbed Wire Valentine' first appeared in the *Observer*, 8 July 1981.

and *Scrutiny* than as an enthusiastic celebrant in the manner of Truffaut and *Cahiers du Cinéma*.

Having initially set out in the 1940s to retrieve Ford's reputation from critical neglect, he now returns to the fray to protect him from the over-admiration of the treacherous clerks of academe and the new movie criticism. In this area of the book his methods are not always just and his arguments frequently inconsistent. He is often mean-minded in a way that does little justice to his professed concern for humane values. But although there is much room for disagreement, over his evaluation of individual films and his sense of the shape of Ford's career, Anderson is a shrewd and lucid critic, and the interwoven accounts of his own earnest wrestling with the evolving Ford oeuvre and his personal relationship with the director are fascinating.

Anderson first made contact with Ford through a letter and a copy of the Oxford film magazine *Sequence* expressing his admiration for *Clementine*. Their relations soon foundered on an unanswered letter announcing disappointment at *The Fugitive* (Ford's version of Graham Greene's *The Power and the Glory*), followed by a review in *Sequence* suggesting that *The Three Godfathers* represented 'the tragic decay of a noble talent'. Things were patched up, however, at their first meeting, when Anderson went to Ireland to interview Ford during the shooting of *The Quiet Man* in 1951. Anderson sat in awe as the great director parried his questions, but something about Anderson's own spiky nature appealed to Ford.

On subsequent meetings he tested Anderson's armour with jibes and insults, which was how this difficult and contradictory man confronted the world. In 1957 he was enticed to the National Film Theatre for a private screening of *Every Day Except Christmas*, Anderson's poetic documentary about Covent Garden (this was in its heyday as a vegetable market), and deliberately punctured the mood with prosaic questions. Even in 1964 when Anderson, now the celebrated director of *This Sporting Life*, visited Ford at his Hollywood office, the older man kept introducing him as 'the editor of *Sight & Sound*', a very private piece of jocular abuse. Only at their last meeting in 1973, when Ford was terminally ill, did he speak warmly and express that friendship he had previously only inscribed on photographs.

Socially, politically and temperamentally, these two men were very different. But in certain essential respects they were similar, and clearly noticed this affinity. Indeed Anderson is obviously offering a description of himself when he speaks of Ford as 'an archaic traditionalist in an increasingly conformist climate'.

The Manhattan Projection
New York in the Movies (2002)

BOOK REVIEW
Sanders, James: *Celluloid Skyline: New York and the Movies* (Blooms-bury)

James Sanders's book is about two cities, both called New York: 'one is a real city, an urban agglomeration of millions, the other is a mythic city, a dream city, born of that most pervasive of dream media, the movies'. It is a marvellous account by a practising architect with an encyclopaedic knowledge of the movies, of how the cinema turned Manhattan into an image of metropolitan life, both idealised and nightmarish, that is shared by people the world over. The events of 11 September 2001 have given additional point and poignancy to his book, though it was in such a late stage of production that Sanders was just able to insert a brief prefatory note to acknowledge the fact.

The wise decision not to revise his text saved him from the temptation to give more attention to the World Trade Centre, or to sentimentalise it. In fact it is the building that attracts the greatest opprobrium as an example of soulless anonymity, and Sanders refers to it twice. The first occasion is when he compares the 1933 version of *King Kong* (where the ape scales the Empire State Building) with the wretched 1975 remake (in which Kong slithers up the smooth side of one of the Twin Towers and has nothing to do when he reaches the top). The second comes in a discussion of *Three Days of the Condor* (1975), in which the innocent eccentric Robert Redford goes on the run through the older city while his deadly pursuers, the impersonal CIA, attempt to track him from the World Trade Centre.

Sanders begins at the beginning with the birth of an American

---

'The Manhattan Projection' first appeared in the *Observer*, 1 September 2002.

film industry in New York, and how its immigrant pioneers departed for California, partly because of the climate, partly to escape paying tribute money to those who claimed to own patents to all film equipment. With the coming of sound and the Wall Street Crash, they were followed to Hollywood by the best writers and composers, who, in exile and loathing Los Angeles, created on screen 'a mythic, bigger-than-life movie New York'. They were abetted by the art departments, whose designers – competing with Manhattan's architects – built a magical Manhattan on the sound stages and back lots of the big studios. Their efforts ranged from the art deco nightclubs atop skyscrapers, where Astaire danced with Rogers at RKO, to the grimy tenements at Warner Brothers, where New York gangster Jimmy Cagney battled with Fr Pat O'Brien for the allegiance of the Dead End Kids. As an establishing shot, he says, only Times Square at night announcing a tale of Broadway romance could match the majestic, infinitely varied skyline of New York. In its ultimately magical form this skyline became the Emerald City of Oz. Sanders writes unpatronisingly of such matters, without recourse to architectural jargon and with elegant clarity.

After World War Two, under the influence of combat documentaries and Italian neo-realism, filmmakers returned to the streets of New York. One of the first was Billy Wilder, which caused S.J. Perelman to remark: 'In transferring *The Lost Weekend* to the screen, the producers sought verisimilitude by bringing Ray Milland to Third Avenue (in the past, Third Avenue had been brought to Ray Milland).' The crucial film in this move back east was Jules Dassin's *The Naked City* (1947), which through its TV spin-off made universally famous the concluding tag: 'There are eight million stories in the Naked City. This has been one of them.'

The big Hollywood studios had always been run from head offices in Manhattan, and as production declined in California so an independent or semi-independent cinema grew up around New York, with an annual output that sometimes exceeded 200 pictures. The facilities provided by the Mayor's Office of Film, Theatre and Broadcasting created by John Lindsay in 1966 were a major attraction. With so many movies New York became a barometer of popular attitudes towards urban life. In the 1970s, Pauline Kael called the cinema's New York 'Hell City', and Vincent Canby of the *New York Times* called it 'a metaphor for the last days of American civilisation'. It became exactly that in John Carpenter's *Escape from New York* (1981), in which a future Manhattan is isolated as a maximum security prison. A more optimistic New York was created by Woody Allen, whose *Manhattan* and *Hannah and Her Sisters* paid special, nostalgic attention to the city's architecture.

If Sanders has a special favourite, it's Hitchcock's *Rear Window*, to the production and complex implications of which he devotes a dozen pages, for it brings together many of his chief themes – architecture, community, 'perceived privacy', alienation, isolation, shared and personal space. It was built entirely at Paramount's studio in Hollywood.

From Fear to Modernity
Film Noir (2006)

BOOK REVIEW

Biesen, Sheri Chinen: *Blackout: World War Two and the Origins of Film Noir* (The Johns Hopkins University Press)

Dimendberg, Edward: *Film Noir and the Spaces of Modernity* (Harvard University Press)

The term *film noir* was coined in 1946 by the French critic Nino Frank as a variation on *roman noir*, which is what the French have been calling the British Gothic novel since the eighteenth century. He used it in an essay for *L'Ecran français* while trying to come to terms with the flood of dark, pessimistic Hollywood movies made between 1940 and 1945 that arrived en masse in newly liberated Paris. He and others were surprised to discover that French films produced under the German Occupation were not that different from those being made in Hollywood. Indeed, immediately after the Second World War, RKO remade Marcel Carné's bleak, poetic-realist *Le Jour se lève* (released in 1939, a couple of months before the outbreak of war) as *The Long Night*, with Henry Fonda replacing Jean Gabin, and the original was withdrawn from distribution for a decade. Later, the most controversial French picture of the war years – Henri-Georges Clouzot's *Le Corbeau* (1943), a tale of the corrosive effects of poison-pen letters in a provincial town – was remade as *The 13th Letter* (1951) by Otto Preminger, a key exponent of *film noir*. It is forgotten, however, that Nino Frank preferred *Citizen Kane*, *How Green Was My Valley* and *The Little Foxes* to *Double Indemnity*, *Laura*, *The Maltese Falcon* and *Murder My Sweet* (aka *Farewell My Lovely*), which are now regarded as *noir*

'From Fear to Modernity' first appeared in the *Times Literary Supplement*, May 2006.

masterworks.

A decade after Frank's seminal essay, Raymond Borde and Etienne Chaumeton published their highly influential *Panorama du film noir américain 1941–1953*, though 44 years passed before it was translated into English. In fact, the term 'film noir' didn't become current in the English-speaking world until the late 1960s, a decade that saw a proliferation of film schools across America and a radical revision of Hollywood history, resulting largely from the writings of the French critics-turned-moviemakers, who created the *nouvelle vague*. In 1972, when I was briefly a visiting professor at the University of Texas, a member of the film department dropped into my office to discuss his plans for a course on film noir. He wanted to find out if I knew of any articles on the subject that hadn't come to his attention. There were not many in English at that time (one of them was a surprisingly hostile attack on the genre by Julian Maclaren-Ross, writing anonymously in a 1947 edition of *Penguin New Writing*), and as yet no book in English. Now there's a shelf of them, to which can be added two studies of specialist areas by Sheri Chinen Biesen and Edward Dimendberg.

Biesen and Dimendberg agree that whatever film noir is – a movement, a style, a phase, a genre, a subgenre? – its classical period was roughly from 1941 to the late 1950s, which is to say from Orson Welles's first Hollywood movie, *Citizen Kane*, to the last one he directed there, *A Touch of Evil*. It is an indication of how a certain consensus has grown up that, while Biesen and Dimendberg confirm Borde and Chaumeton's view that the movement really got under way in 1941 with John Huston's *The Maltese Falcon*, both nominate as the first authentic Hollywood film noir *Stranger on the Third Floor*, which the French writers of the 1940s and 1950s had evidently not seen. Directed by the Russian émigré Boris Ingster, this story of a reporter getting an innocent man convicted of murder before himself becoming a murder suspect has most of the essential ingredients. These include a foreign director, high-contrast black-and-white photography, menacing streets, dark, drab interiors with an emphasis on shadows and staircases, a disturbed protagonist who experiences an Expressionist nightmare (one of the cinema's most remarkable dream sequences) and a general sense of urban malaise. It also featured two actors soon to appear in *The Maltese Falcon* and destined to become members of an emerging noir repertory company: Elisha Cook Jr, the genre's favourite fall guy, and Peter Lorre, more or less reprising his role as a psychopathic killer from Fritz Lang's *M*. But *Stranger on the Third Floor* was a box-office failure in 1940 and a little ahead of its time.

Biesen's *Blackout* sees a number of factors coming together to create the noir style, some of them familiar, others less so. First, the rise of Hitler had driven the most gifted German filmmakers into exile, and they brought to Hollywood the legacy of German Expressionism, the roots of which were mostly to be found in German Romanticism. Second, the hardboiled school of writing created in the 1920s by Ernest Hemingway came to Hollywood by way of Dashiell Hammett, James M. Cain, Raymond Chandler and lesser pulp writers. Third, psychology and psychoanalysis in their popular and perverse forms entered American cinema in the late 1930s (Welles called the Rosebud motif in *Citizen Kane* 'dollar-book Freud'). Fourth, the politicised atmosphere of the late Depression merged with the storm clouds of the Second World War in 1941. Fifth, after Pearl Harbor, the major studios were pinched financially with the loss of the continental European market and were affected by the rationing of material for sets, limited power resources, enforced blackouts, and restrictions placed on daytime location shooting for security reasons. In the early 1940s, Californians and their leaders truly believed some sort of Japanese invasion was imminent, and xenophobia directed at aliens of any stripe was widespread.

This combustible brew was accompanied by some relaxation of censorship, around which a generation of suave filmmakers had learnt to manoeuvre. The word 'gunsel', for instance, means catamite, but when used in *The Maltese Falcon* to describe Sidney Greenstreet's sinister young assistant the Production Code administrators thought it meant a gunman or body guard and let it through. Further, when the Roosevelt government's Office of War Information (OWI) set up a Hollywood bureau to see that movies carried positive, patriotic messages, filmmakers reacted with characteristic craftiness. They created or turned to a genre that appeared detached from the war yet provided a provocative form of violent, erotic entertainment that could be a conduit for current anxieties about, for example, the empowerment of women and the shortage or absence of men due to enforced military service. Also, old actors came into their own when younger ones went to war, and some careers were crucially changed. The light comedian Fred MacMurray, movie representative of the decent average Joe, was cast as a weak, easily corrupted insurance man led into murder by femme fatale Barbara Stanwyck in Billy Wilder's *Double Indemnity*. The screen persona of sweet-natured song-and-dance man Dick Powell was changed overnight when he was cast as Chandler's hardboiled private eye Philip Marlowe in *Murder My Sweet* (aka *Farewell My Lovely*).

Biesen uses her research into studio archives, the films' attendant publicity and the contemporary press to bring alive the wartime period of film noir and its transformation into a post-war genre for dealing with troubled veterans returning home, the coming of the Cold War, nuclear angst and the effects of McCarthyism on Hollywood and the nation at large. She tells us of the public demand for 'red meat' entertainment, and the desire of Hollywood to provide it, something amusingly expressed through tag lines thought up by the advertising departments: 'Menace Behind Every Shadow, Suspense in Every Move' (*Ministry of Fear*), 'The kind of woman most men want, BUT SHOULDN'T HAVE! (*Mildred Pierce*).

This was escapist entertainment of an unusual kind, a brief escape into nightmares. Yet it came from serious social critics, European émigrés not exactly happy in America, and leftwing talents discontented with the capitalist system, its exploiters and victims. Edward Dmytryk, Canadian son of Ukrainian immigrants, worked his way up in the cinema business from studio messenger boy to make *Farewell My Lovely*. He followed this with two other crucial noir pictures, *Cornered* (1945) about war crimes and neo-Nazism, and *Crossfire* (1947), centring on returning veterans and post-war anti-Semitism. He was one of the Hollywood Ten, leftwing filmmakers jailed for refusing to cooperate with the House Un-American Activities Committee (HUAC). Unlike the others, he emerged from prison to reappear before HUAC, name former communist associates and go back to work, making large-scale anti-communist and conformist potboilers. But in 1965, some years after the genre's vogue, he directed *Mirage*, an undervalued thriller in the noir style, shot in black-and-white, turning on one of the genre's favourite themes – amnesia. It indicted the military-industrial establishment Dwight D. Eisenhower had warned against in one of his final speeches as president, and it helped open the way for a new kind of political cinema that was to include such post-Watergate movies as *The Parallax View* and *Three Days of the Condor*.

Though somewhat repetitious, Biesen's book is readable, informative and jargon free, and if memory serves aright, the University of Texas professor who supervised her dissertation from which the book derives was the same man who consulted me about the genre back in 1972. The same cannot be said for *Film Noir and the Spaces of Modernity* by Edward Dimendberg, a teacher of film and architectural theory at the University of Michigan. His book is dense, bordering on the opaque. Filmgoers interested in learning about architecture, urban life and the cinema would be better advised to read James Sanders's superb *Celluloid Skyline: New York and the Movies*. Dimendberg's concern is with the way film noir exploits our sense of anomie and alienation through its representation of the city and its varied spaces, the manner in which we are disturbed by the intrusion of the modern and its practitioners, and our nostalgia for a vanishing past and the sense of community it represented. He draws on an immense range of professional and speculative thinkers, from Le Corbusier to Jean-Paul Sartre, and most clearly states his fascination with the genre when he writes:

> As a prominent example of twentieth-century American popular culture set in the metropolis, a feature it shares with the contemporaneous forms of jazz and hardboiled fiction, *film noir* remains unique for its engagement with urban subject matter more often encountered in social and architectural histories than Hollywood narrative film.

Dimendberg is capable of going for 17 pages – talking about architects, designers and theorists such as Lewis Mumford, Frank Lloyd Wright, Le Corbusier, Sigfried Giedion and Norman Bel Geddes – without mentioning a single movie. He even ignores the fact that Bel Geddes's daughter Barbara appeared in such noir classics as Anatole Litvak's *The Long Night*, Max Ophüls's *Caught*, Elia Kazan's *Panic in the Streets* and Hitchcock's *Vertigo*. Still, there is much of value in Dimendberg's book, including nuggets like the suggestive notion that the recurrence of figures falling to their deaths from high-rise buildings is an instance of 'Bernd Jager's assertion that falling entails a loss of lived space'. One such defenestration, though he doesn't mention it, occurs in Dmytryk's *Mirage*. He is at his best when analysing individual films, as in the extended comparison between the sensational New York photographs by the tabloid cameraman Weegee in his book *The Naked City* and the realistic film noir of the same name.

Dimendberg is little interested in films that render New York as one of the world's most desirable and romantic cities. Vincente Minnelli's Judy Garland romance *The Clock* sticks in the mind as persuasively as John Farrow's menacing film *The Big Clock*, both equally authentic depictions of Manhattan. When Woody Allen wanted to make an oppressive picture of urban menace, he didn't attempt to present his beloved New York in a different light. Instead, in *Shadows and Fog* he recreated an Expressionistic 1920s Weimar Germany.

Both Sheri Biesen and Edward Dimendberg recognise the amorphous nature of film noir and note the phenomenon of neo-noir. But clinging to their personal theses, they avoid looking at the noir western (Robert Mitchum in Raoul Walsh's *Pursued*, Dick Powell in *Stations West*), or the way neo-noir in its Technicolor form began as early as the 1953 *Niagara*, the film that made Marilyn Monroe a true star (some might place this even earlier with the appearance of another 20th Century-Fox *noir en couleur*, the 1946 melodrama *Leave Her to Heaven*). The futuristic neo-noir *Blade Runner* (1982), a key movie in its use of space and architecture, gets a single mention. These authors also ignore foreign examples, though they occur significantly in the period their books cover. In Britain, for instance, there is Alberto Cavalcanti's *They Made Me a Fugitive* (1946) and Carol Reed's *Odd Man Out* (1947) and *The Third Man* (1949).

Most missed perhaps in these books is humour: the wisecrack, the ironic observation, the witty remark in the extended voice-over narration that became a characteristic of the genre. It would have been good to hear something of Bob Hope's clever spoof of the noir thriller, *My Favourite Brunette* (1947), in which noir star Alan Ladd makes an uncredited appearance as the private eye in the next office to Hope's baby-photographer, and Carl Reiner's *Dead Men Don't Wear Plaid* (1982). In the latter Steve Martin plays a 1940s private eye whose investigations ingeniously draw together clips from a dozen or more 1940s noir thrillers from several studios. Apart from their entertainment value, these movies attest to and confirm the way film noir impinged on, and was playfully received by, its audiences.

The Cold War and the American Cinema
(2008)

There was a brief, hopeful interregnum between the end of World War Two and the onset of the Cold War. The hot war was brought to a dramatic conclusion by the dropping of the two atom bombs on Japan in August 1945. Precisely when the Cold War started is less certain, but it is generally reckoned to have begun with a verbal barrage heard around the world, fired off by Winston Churchill on 5 March 1946. Speaking after receiving an honorary degree at Westminster College, a small, fairly obscure university in Fulton, Missouri, he expressed his continuing respect for his wartime colleague, Joseph Stalin, and the brave Russian people, then made this grave statement:

> From Stettin in the Baltic to Trieste in the Adriatic, an iron curtain has descended across the continent. Behind that line lie all the capitals of the ancient states of Central and Eastern Europe … and all are subject in one form or another not only to Soviet influence but to a very high and increasing measure of control from Moscow.

This speech was to make Fulton forever famous. Hitherto the town was known outside Missouri, if known at all, as the model for the nasty Midwestern community featured in *King's Row*. This was the 1942 Warner Brothers movie that provided the future president and Cold War warrior, Ronald Reagan, with his most famous role and with the celebrated line 'Where's the rest of me?' It was spoken on seeing that his legs had been amputated, and he used it later as the title of his autobiography.

'The Cold War and the American Cinema' began life as a lecture, delivered at the Victoria and Albert Museum, 8 November 2008, to accompany the exhibition *Cold War Modern: Design 1945–1970*.

Reagan was to play a key role in bringing to an end the Cold War during his second term as US president, and in 1989, the year the Berlin Wall came down, he was asked whether he still thought of the Soviet Union as 'the evil empire' (a term which evoked or invoked the *Star Wars* movies). He said, 'No, I was talking about another time, another place.' The year Churchill delivered his Fulton speech, Reagan was the vice-president of the Screen Actors Guild. The following year, as the Guild's president, he appeared as one of the group of friendly witnesses who went from Hollywood to Washington to testify when the House Committee on Un-American Activities (HUAC) opened its first post-war investigation into communist subversion in the film industry. Appearing after a number of rightwing figures, among them the actors Gary Cooper and Adolphe Menjou and the producers Louis B. Mayer and Jack Warner, Reagan, a registered Democrat, spoke of his abhorrence of the communist philosophy and its adherents. Then he added:

> But at the same time I never as a citizen want to see our country become urged, by either fear or resentment of this group, that we ever compromise with any of our democratic principles through that fear and resentment. I still think that democracy can do it.

Reagan was later revealed to have become around this time a secret informer for the FBI.

The friendly witnesses were followed by the unfriendly ones. Their number was in the teens and included the composer Hanns Eisler and the playwright Bertolt Brecht. But these two leftwing émigrés slipped away to resume their careers in Eastern Europe, and the hearing focused on the so-called 'Hollywood Ten'. They were all American filmmakers – writers, directors, and one producer, all of them male – whom the Committee knew to be, or recently to have been, card-carrying members of the Communist Party. In a rowdy couple of days they stood on the First Amendment to the Constitution, guaranteeing Freedom of Speech, and were dragged from the hearing room by court officials after challenging the Committee's authority and refusing to answer the question, 'Are you now or have you ever been a member of the Communist Party?' Over the next decade this question was to become a mantra of the era. Their appeals to the Supreme Court against the charge of Contempt of Congress were rejected, and three years later in

1950 they served sentences in federal penitentiaries of between six months and a year.

Meanwhile, Hollywood's principal figures led by Eric Johnston, the president of the Motion Picture Association of America, gathered in New York at the Waldorf Astoria Hotel. After their meeting, held in private, they issued the co-called Waldorf Declaration on 25 November 1947, just three weeks after HUAC had held the Ten in contempt. Johnston had told the Committee he would uphold freedom of speech. 'We insist on our right to decide what will or will not go into our pictures,' he said. But the Waldorf Declaration was a total capitulation to HUAC and the beginning of the blacklists, loyalty oaths and the concept of guilt by association that were to characterise so many branches of American life. The Hollywood Ten were all fired by their employers, and a statement declared: 'We will not knowingly employ a communist or a member of any party or group which advocates the overthrow of the government of the United States.'

Eric Johnston was to lecture the industry on producing more positive representations of American life in a speech that began 'We will have no more *Grapes of Wrath*, we will have no more *Tobacco Roads*, we will have no more films showing the seamy side of American life.' But an iron curtain did not immediately fall on Hollywood, and indeed the Un-American Activities Committee turned their attentions elsewhere for the next three years.

Something emblematic happened in May 1948. On 1 May, the RKO studio released Jacques Tourneur's political thriller *Berlin Express*, produced by the liberal Dore Schary and set in the immediate aftermath of World War Two. Burying their various differences, an American, an Englishman, a Frenchman and a Russian get together to frustrate a neo-Nazi plot aimed at abducting and killing a German liberal statesman, whose project is to lead a united Germany. The film is notable for being shot on actual locations in France and Germany (thanks are given at the end to the British, American, French and Soviet occupying authorities for their cooperation), and it concludes in the shadow of the Brandenburg Gate as the American and the Russian part on a note of what would very soon be regarded as gravely misplaced optimism. A week later, on 12 May, 20th Century Fox released the first Cold War movie produced by a major studio, *The Iron Curtain*. In this semi-documentary drama, Dana Andrews, an A-list star at that time, plays the real-life Igor Gouzenko, an intelligence clerk at the Soviet Embassy in Ottawa. Encouraged by his wife he defects to the West, taking with him valuable evidence of Russian espionage activities.

From this point on the cinema was to be affected by the Cold War and to reflect the issues of the conflict between East and West more than any other art form, though the burgeoning television industry was, along with radio, to be on the receiving end of the same super-patriotic organisations pursuing suspected subversives and other threats to orthodox opinion.

Two questions immediately arise. The first: why did Hollywood capitulate so readily to HUAC? The second: what was HUAC so determinedly after? The answer to the first question is that ever since the first images were thrown up on the big screen in 1896, there were demands for censorship, and once Hollywood was established as the centre of film production in the second decade of the twentieth century, the film industry was targeted by protectors of public morality across the nation. The major studios, that rapidly came to dominate the industry, were created by Jewish immigrants or the sons of Jewish immigrants, uncertain of their identity as Americans and devoted to the protection of their lucrative enterprises. A typical instance of the pressure put upon them by anti-Semitic groups was this report in a 1920 newspaper: 'The lobby of the International Reform Bureau, Dr Wilbur Crafts presiding, voted tonight to rescue the motion pictures from the hands of the Devil and five hundred un-Christian Jews.'

As a result of these demands for censorship and the bad publicity created by a number of sex and drugs scandals within the California movie colony, the Hollywood moguls created the Motion Picture Producers and Distributors of America Inc in 1924 and invited Will H. Hays, a Presbyterian elder from Indiana and postmaster-general in President Warren Harding's cabinet, to be its first president. A code of industrial self-censorship was set up, and morality clauses were written into performers' contracts, so both the products themselves and the private lives of those involved in their making were subject to official scrutiny. For all their personal goodwill and honest protestations of combining popular entertainment with artistic ambition and social criticism, the movie moguls had one thing in mind above all: self-preservation.

The second question – what was HUAC so determinedly after? – has several answers. The House Committee on Un-American Activities was created in 1938 largely through the insistence of Samuel Dickstein, a New York Jewish Congressman, who intended it to investigate the activities of pro-Nazi organisations. It was immediately taken over by the rightwing Texan Martin Dies, who conducted a brief, ineffectual series of Hollywood sessions. His successor in 1945, when the Committee became a permanent institution, was Representative J. Parnell Thomas, an Irish-American Republican from New Jersey. He presided during the 1947 hearings that resulted in the Hollywood Ten being held in contempt. In 1950 Thomas was found guilty of serious fraud, including paying non-existent workers from federal funds, and found himself serving 18 months in the same federal penitentiary as the distinguished screenwriter Ring Lardner Jr, one of the Hollywood Ten. Dies and Thomas had a close associate on the Committee in John Rankin of Mississippi, the most virulent rightwing racist and anti-Semite ever to sit in the House of Representatives. For Rankin the terms foreigner, Jew and communist were virtually synonymous, and in 1947, when a group of prominent Hollywood liberals calling themselves the Committee for the First Amendment flew to Washington to protest against HUAC, he made this statement in the House:

> They sent this petition to Congress and I want to read you some of the names. One of them is June Havoc. We found that her real name is June Hovick. Another is Danny Kaye, and we found that his real name is David Daniel Kaminsky. Another one here is John Beal, whose real name is J. Alexander Bleidung. Another is Cy Bartlett, whose real name is Sacha Baraniev. Another one is Eddie Cantor, whose real name is Edward Iskowitz. There is one who calls himself Edward G. Robinson. His real name is Emmanuel Goldenberg. There is another one here who calls himself Melvyn Douglas, whose real name is Melvyn Hesselberg. There are others too numerous to mention. They are attacking the Committee for doing its duty to protect the country and save the American people from the horrible fate the Communists have meted out to the unfortunate Christian people of Europe.

There were of course communists working in the movie industry who'd become party members for a variety of reasons – among them idealism, the desire to oppose fascism, guilt over their privileged, well-paid jobs. And there were liberals who'd joined various organisations to lend assistance to the properly elected government in the Spanish Civil War and other anti-fascist causes. We now know from KGB archives and elsewhere that Soviet agents were at work in the movie industry. One of the most colourful, notorious and seductive of the Comintern's operatives, Otto Katz, a man of many aliases, crossed the Atlantic and, posing as an anti-Nazi German, moved into the social life of California's movie community. 'Columbus discovered America,' Katz said. 'I discovered Hollywood.' He worked on raising money for the Party, using glamorous celebrities to throw themselves behind the Popular Front, lending their names to high-sounding organisations and helping to make communism acceptable. The communists never believed they could take over the industry, though they worked through the newly created craft unions. Dedicated leftwing writers attempted to influence the content of pictures, quite openly and honestly as anyone would expect them to do. Dedicated Stalinists, acting like their contemporaries in Russia, attempted to whip fellow communists into line. Budd Schulberg, for instance, an idealistic party member, dates the beginning of his disillusionment with communism from the moment he was called before a disciplinary tribunal in 1940 to discuss ideological changes in *What Makes Sammy Run?*, his novel critical of the film industry.

There had been considerable bitterness between left-liberal factions after the signing of the Nazi-Soviet pact in 1939, but an uneasy political truce was achieved when the United States and the Soviet Union became allies in World War Two. Various Washington agencies urged Hollywood to make movies sympathetic to Latin American countries and to support the alliance with Russia. Over the next three years each of the leading studios made one or two pro-Soviet movies, most celebrating resistance to the Nazi invaders. But one, the Warner Brothers production *Mission to Moscow* based on William Davies's book about his term as Ambassador to the Soviet Union in the late 1930s, went rather further than the others. It made a hero of Joseph Stalin and endorsed his pre-war show trials. The film was to provide prime kindling for HUAC to burn Hollywood at the stake. As late as 1983, *Mission to Moscow* was considered sufficiently dangerous for Arthur Koestler, in the week he died, to sign a letter to the press demanding that the film be withdrawn from a Channel Four season of movies about World War Two.

But HUAC had a broader project that was shared across the conservative wing of the Republican Party and points right. This was to bring into disrepute the political initiatives and achievements of Franklin Roosevelt's New Deal, and to set about dismantling the structures he had created. The man most associated with this movement was Joseph McCarthy, the junior Republican Senator from Wisconsin, who emerged on the national scene in 1950 when he made a speech at Wheeling, Virginia, claiming that he had the names of 205 members of the Communist Party working for the State Department. An exponent of what Joseph Goebbels called 'the Big Lie', he gave his name to the process of guilt by association, and what was dubbed on the left as a witch-hunt. McCarthy, however, was never personally involved in the pursuit of the entertainment industry. His targets were politicians, civil servants, top military brass and academics. The McCarthy era came to encompass the period extending from HUAC's initial attack on Hollywood, which occurred before his arrival, to the 1960s, years after his censure by fellow senators and his pathetic, alcohol-soaked death in 1957.

The three years between HUAC's first descent on Hollywood and its second onslaught in the early 1950s were a traumatic time for the United States. Communist regimes were established throughout Eastern Europe. The Soviet siege of Berlin in 1948 made war seem imminent. China fell to Mao Tse Tung's Red Army. The Soviet Union tested its first atomic bomb in 1949, and the general belief was that this could only have resulted from espionage. Then the Cold War turned hot when North Korea, emboldened by the communist victory in China, invaded the South, and President Truman led the United Nations into a so-called police action. This was when HUAC called dozens of people to testify, resulting in a massive extension of the blacklist. Many went into exile rather than accept the Committee's subpoena. Those who appeared either took the Fifth Amendment against self-incrimination (which automatically resulted in dismissal or blacklisting) or confessed to their former party membership and went through the ritual of naming fellow communists (and quite a number who were not), even though virtually all of these were known to the Committee.

Only one member of the Hollywood Ten emerged from prison and sought reinstatement within the film industry by appearing before HUAC, admitting his party membership, renouncing his past, and providing a token list of former comrades. This was Edward Dmytryk, a gifted director, noted for hard-hitting noir thrillers like *Farewell My Lovely* and *Crossfire*. He had only stood by the other members of the Ten out of personal loyalty and was later to reveal that the Communist Party had been manipulating the Hollywood Ten as a means of exposing the hypocrisy of bourgeois democracy.

Shortly after America entered World War Two, the Office of Strategic Services (the OSS) was created by the Wall Street lawyer Wild Bill Donovan for purposes of espionage. It was disbanded when the war ended, then reconstituted in 1947 to coordinate government intelligence activities, with infinitely greater powers and an ever-expanding budget, as the Central Intelligence Agency (CIA). It was far more sophisticated and much less regulated than the FBI, with which it regularly collaborated. One branch of the CIA had a creative aspect of a liberal intellectual kind that was not concerned with intelligence and espionage. It brought together the New England Wasp establishment and the largely Jewish New York intelligentsia that had experienced both Stalinism and Trotskyism and elected to be anti-communist liberals.

Just as the communists had worked through front organisations, so this coalition siphoned money through charitable foundations that disguised the source of their funds. The idea was to publish periodicals, promote movies and stage exhibitions (largely of abstract art as that was considered most representative of artistic freedom and free enterprise). And the aim was to rally leftwing and liberal opinion in two related causes: anti-communism of a carefully reasoned kind, and a positive but not uncritical pro-Americanism. The most famous of these fronts was the Congress for Cultural Freedom, set up by the CIA in 1950 to hold international conferences of anti-communist intellectuals, and to create a series of high-powered, well-produced journals of opinion around the world, most famously *Der Monat* in West Germany, *Preuves* in France and *Encounter* in Great Britain. Hollywood was also targeted, though more to make films offering a positive view of the States than to produce straightforwardly anti-communist films.

The two most significant, and yet ultimately ineffectual, interventions the CIA made in the cinema were produced in Britain, and few people at the time were aware of their provenance. Both were adaptations of novels by George Orwell, *Animal Farm* and *Nineteen Eighty-Four*. The rights to both were acquired shortly after the author's death by people close to, or actually involved in, the American espionage establishment. The CIA operative and thriller writer Howard Hunt, later notorious as one of the leading figures in the Watergate break-in, persuaded Orwell's widow to entrust him with a film of *Animal Farm*. Via a CIA front it was made into an animated film by the company run by the Hungarian émigré John Halas and his British wife, Joy Bachelor, and the CIA arranged for its international distribution. Meanwhile, again through the auspices of Hunt, *Nineteen Eighty-Four* was put into production, again using US government finance. The film brought in two Hollywood actors, Edmond O'Brien and Jan Sterling, to play the rebels, with Michael Redgrave as the totalitarian heavy, thus conforming to a post-war Hollywood pattern by which British actors played the suave villains and Americans the deceived innocents. In the case of both films, another branch of the CIA, the Psychological Strategy Board, advised on the scripts. As a result Orwell's more comprehensive visions of a totalitarian world that criticised both communism and capitalism were shaped into directly anti-Soviet allegories, and Orwell's downbeat endings were replaced by positive statements about the ultimate victory of Western democratic values.

I've mentioned the first major studio Cold War movie, *The Iron Curtain*, produced by 20th Century-Fox. This was followed by a succession of propagandistic pictures, mostly fairly crude, which continued over the next decade. In 1950 for instance, MGM, Hollywood's most opulent studio, commanded by the rightwing Louis B. Mayer, drafted some of its most powerful stars into the movie *Red Danube*, a hard-line anti-Soviet picture about the enforced repatriation of Eastern European citizens from occupied Austria. The previous year, while dealing with the same subject in the same country, the Anglo-American production *The Third Man*, directed by Carol Reed from a screenplay by Graham Greene, managed to avoid the dismissive political response from the liberal intelligentsia that greeted the general run of Hollywood's Cold War pictures. This was partly due to the low-key criticism of the

Russians, and partly to the fact that the two leading characters – the naive author of Wild West novelettes, Holly Martins, and the callous black-marketeer, Harry Lime – were both played by Americans, and neither was presented as acting from an ideological position.

The Third Man is almost the only Cold War movie from the 1940s and 1950s that has attained classic status. Its only equivalent in the theatre is Arthur Miller's *The Crucible*, which has also transcended the political circumstances of its writing to enter the Western theatre's classic repertoire. First presented on Broadway in 1953, Miller's play draws parallels between the Salem witch trials in the New England of the seventeenth century and the McCarthy witch-hunts of the American present. Hollywood showed no interest in Miller's play, which was eventually filmed in France as *Les Sorcières de Salem* (1957), performed by a group of leftwing artists led by Yves Montand, and scripted by Jean-Paul Sartre.

But Miller became a target of the government, had his passport withdrawn by the State Department, and was grilled by the House Un-American Activities Committee in 1956 over his two decades of fellow travelling. Unquestionably his recent marriage to Marilyn Monroe played a part in clearing his name with HUAC and effected his reinstatement. Oddly, he ended up almost making his peace with the Committee when in his concluding statements he said:

> I think it would be a disaster and a calamity if the Communist Party ever took over this country. This is an opinion that has come to me not out of the blue, but out of long thought.

And he added

> We are living in a time when there is great uncertainty in this country. It is not a communist idea: you just pick up a book-review section and you will see everybody selling books on peace of mind, because there isn't any. I am trying to delve to the bottom of this, and come up with a positive answer, and I have had to go to hell to meet the devil.

The 1950s saw the Cold War at its height around the world, and the American cinema in a state of confusion and division. In addition to the various political threats, the major studios were in the process of being broken up by the Supreme Court's judgments that they were in breach of laws on trusts and monopolies. The film industry, in its battle with TV, was trying to hang on to popular audiences by offering what the domestic screen couldn't provide – films in 3-D (a short-lived fad), for instance, and the widescreen, both introduced in 1953. That was the same year that saw one of the most disturbing and controversial events of the post-war era, the execution of the New York couple Julius and Ethel Rosenberg. They were convicted on dubious evidence of being the conduit of atomic secrets to the Soviet Union and sent to the electric chair. Exactly 30 years later Sidney Lumet directed *Daniel*, a film about the Rosenberg case and its effect on the couple's children, based on E.L. Doctorow's novel *The Book of Daniel*.

Fear and paranoia were in the air in the 1950s, resulting in the flourishing of two genres. The first was science fiction, with stories of alien invasions and ecological catastrophes that reflected the nuclear angst and xenophobia induced by the Cold War. Key examples are the 1951 *War of the Worlds*, where the action of H.G. Wells's novel was switched from the English Home Counties at the turn of the century to present-day California, and Don Siegel's low-budget classic *Invasion of the Body Snatchers*, in which emotionless extra-terrestrials take over the minds of a Californian community as a beachhead for world domination. Siegel's film divided critics, not as to its quality, but its meaning. Was it a film about communist subversion or an attack on the corrosive conformity of the Eisenhower years?

The other genre was the western, which instead of fading away, as many had predicted, achieved a new, altogether more exalted life in the 1950s as a way of treating contemporary problems of politics and morality in an acceptable, all-American historical setting. Unsurprisingly there were no films directly attacking HUAC or arguing for mutual tolerance with perceived enemies. But such issues were dealt with in allegorical form in popular westerns like *Broken Arrow* (1950) and *High Noon* (1952). *Broken Arrow*, the apparent theme of which was peaceful coexistence between settlers and Apaches, was scripted by Albert Maltz, one of the jailed Hollywood Ten, but signed by a front, Michael Blankfort, who in 1952 was himself arraigned before HUAC. *High Noon* was the last Hollywood screenplay by the leftwing writer Carl Foreman, who that year went into exile in Britain after refusing to testify before HUAC.

Gary Cooper, one of HUAC's first friendly witnesses, received an Oscar for his performance as a US marshal left to fend for himself against ruthless gunmen by a craven frontier community. It was open to several interpretations, one of the most obvious being HUAC descending on Hollywood and no one standing up for targeted individuals. A leading Swedish critic, however, thought it was a defence of America's involvement in the Korean War, then raging. In 1981 the Solidarity movement in the Gdansk shipyards adopted the iconic image of Cooper standing alone in the dusty streets of *High Noon* as its own defiant emblem against a repressive communist government. In Sydney Pollack's *The Way We Were*, a 1974 movie about an American couple involved in political and social change between 1940 and 1970, a western, which appears to be about a persecuted Native American, is shown at a party attended by leftwing American screenwriters in the 1950s. One of the guests observes, sadly, that this is the only way anyone can make a serious liberal film in Hollywood.

As it happens there was one single attempt to make an openly leftwing picture in the 1950s when Herbert J. Biberman, one of the Hollywood Ten and a committed Stalinist, directed *Salt of the Earth*, about a strike of exploited Hispanic miners in New Mexico. An agit-prop film perhaps, but a humane work of force and conviction, it was made largely by blacklisted artists and financed by the communist-dominated Mine, Mill and Smelter Workers' Union. The union leaders and the film's cast and crew were harassed throughout the production by the Justice Department, the FBI and the local police. When it was completed, distributors throughout the country, backed up by the national union to which movie house employees including projectionists belonged, refused to handle it. One cinema in New York gave it a short run, and it received a limited distribution and a warm reception in Europe. But a decade passed before *Salt of the Earth* was released in the States and became a cult film among 1960s political activists.

Hollywood was a deeply divided town, a place of conspiracy, rumour, surveillance, betrayal, exploitation and arbitrary law. A vigilante group called the Motion Picture Alliance for the Protection of American Ideals, created by rightwing super-patriots in the 1940s, conducted its own private court to condemn liberals or help those who repented their pasts to clear themselves. One of its supporters was John Wayne, who appeared in a succession of red-baiting Cold War films, the most absurd being *Big Jim McLain*. This 1952 film was produced by Wayne, and he himself played a House Un-American Activities investigator routing an attempt by ruthless communists to take over Hawaii by force. A rumour circulated at the time that Wayne was slated for assassination by secret communist cells in Mexico and the United States. Preposterously, the celebrated Hollywood stuntman, Yakima Canutt (who doubled for Wayne in *Stagecoach* and for Charlton Heston in *Ben-Hur*) claimed that in 1955 he got together a posse of fellow stuntmen and captured a gang of communist conspirators as they assembled to prepare their assault on Wayne. They were given the choice of being put to death or bundled onto a plane and flown to Russia. They all accepted the deportation offer.

Apparently Canutt never mentioned this courageous patriotic intervention to the authorities. He would no doubt have been commended by Jack Warner, head of Warner Brothers, who distributed *Big Jim McLain* and produced *Blood Alley*, the Cold War action movie Wayne was making when this alleged incident occurred. Warner is the subject of a famous, probably apocryphal anecdote of the time. He described the liberal writer Philip Dunne as a communist and refused to employ him. 'But Phil's an *anti*-communist,' someone expostulated. 'I don't care what kind of goddamned communist he is!' Warner replied. 'I'm not going to have him working in this studio.'

A major change in Hollywood's approach to the Cold War came in 1960, when the conformist Eisenhower era was nearing its end, and the Democratic hopeful John F. Kennedy was preparing to succeed him. In 1957, the Oscar for best original story was awarded to Robert Rich for the film *The Brave One*. Rich was a pseudonym for Dalton Trumbo, the most prestigious member of the Hollywood Ten. The following year the Oscar for best screenplay was given to the French novelist Pierre Boulle for *The Bridge on the River Kwai*. Boulle spoke scarcely a word of English, and his novel had in fact been adapted by two blacklisted writers, Michael Wilson, who'd written *Salt of the Earth*, and Carl Foreman. As with several other films, their names have been restored to newly struck prints of the film.

In 1960 two producers of major multi-million dollar movies

embarked, quite independently, on challenging the blacklist, in both cases over films scripted by Dalton Trumbo. Trumbo combined leftwing political opinions with a conventionally middle-brow ability to transform literary blockbusters into rousing emotional stories for the big screen. For the past decade he had been receiving half his usual fees for bootleg scripts, for which others took credit. Now the independent writer-producer Otto Preminger hired him to adapt *Exodus*, Leon Uris's crude bestselling novel about the creation of Israel, and the actor-producer Kirk Douglas engaged him to write a screen version of *Spartacus*, a historical epic about the slave revolts in ancient Rome. Both were big-budget films with all-star casts and running well over three hours. Preminger had been battling the Hollywood Production Code throughout the 1950s. Now he was challenging both Hollywood and the legions of rightwing activists.

Trumbo had written a pseudonymous screenplay for a western Douglas had produced and starred in, *Last Train From Gun Hill*, and the actor was taking a further risk in producing *Spartacus*, a movie on a subject that had long fascinated the political left. Indeed the film was based on a novel by Howard Fast, a blacklisted author jailed in 1950 for his political intransigence, though he'd subsequently resigned from the Party and recanted his communist opinions. Both films were in post-production before Trumbo was named as their screenwriter. Both were picketed at their initial screenings. But the public went to see them, and they enjoyed considerable success worldwide. The blacklist was breached but not destroyed. The same year Frank Sinatra announced he'd hired Albert Maltz, another member of the Hollywood Ten, to write a film about Private Eddie Slovik, the only GI to be shot for desertion during World War Two. Joseph Kennedy, the father of Jack Kennedy, told him to drop the film or get off his son's presidential bandwagon. Sinatra backed down. But two years later he was involved in the first of a succession of Cold War films that helped change the nature of political cinema in the Western world.

This movie was *The Manchurian Candidate*, a dark comedy-thriller directed by John Frankenheimer. A box-office failure at the time, though a critical success, it was later to be called, by Pauline Kael, 'the most sophisticated political satire ever to come out of Hollywood'. Its elaborate plot turned upon an upper-middle-class conscript being abducted while on patrol in the Korean War, brain-washed by Russian scientists, and sent back to America as an unconscious tool of the Soviets, ready to kill at any time. His secret control is his mother, a dedicated communist who is manipulating her dim-witted second husband, a McCarthyite senator, with a view to undermining American democracy. The only way this senator can remember the number of communists he accuses the State Department of concealing is by thinking of the '57' on a bottle of Heinz tomato ketchup. In this double-edged film the American right is perceived as the real danger to the nation, as great as, if not greater than, the left.

The following year Frankenheimer made another conspiracy thriller, the deadly serious *Seven Days in May*. A rightwing general (played by the liberal actor Burt Lancaster) plans to lead a *coup d'état* in Washington to overthrow a liberal president thought to be making too many concessions to the Soviet Union. The plot is narrowly defeated by a group of presidential loyalists, notable among them a marine colonel played by Kirk Douglas. President Kennedy gave his support to the film, even arranging to be out of the White House for a few days so Frankenheimer could shoot there, but he was assassinated before the film was released.

Meanwhile in England, Stanley Kubrick, who'd directed *Spartacus*, was making the blackest of comedies, *Dr Strangelove or How I Learned to Stop Worrying and Love the Bomb*, arguably the greatest Cold War movie. Its subject is the arms race and the concept of MAD, or 'mutually assured destruction'. A US Air Force General, disgusted by the cautious diplomacy of his president, unleashes a wing of nuclear bombers on the USSR as a pre-emptive strike, which in turn activates the Russians' Doomsday Machine, a device that will ensure the total extinction of mankind. But not only is this Cold War warrior insane, so in different ways is everyone else in the film – the dithering liberal president, the head of the Strategic Air Command, the president's German-born adviser Dr Strangelove, the Russian ambassador, and the pilot of the chief assault bomber. Though based on *Red Alert*, a serious novel by the British author Peter George, the film was devised by Kubrick and the anarchic comic writer Terry Southern, and it's a potent mix of Fritz Lang and Jonathan Swift that concludes with a lyrical montage of nuclear explosions accompanied by the World War Two hit song

'We'll Meet Again' sung by the Forces' Sweetheart Vera Lynn.

After its release was delayed for a couple of months because of the Kennedy assassination, *Dr Strangelove* was a popular and critical success, one of the harbingers of the Sixties revolution that was to change American life for decades to come. It was, however, viewed with considerable suspicion, indeed hatred, in establishment circles, where it was thought to be undermining Western morale to an extent bordering on the seditious. I had a personal experience of this. In December 1963 when the picture was building a pre-release reputation through special private screenings, I was called by one of the editors of *Encounter* and asked what I thought of it. I said I'd arrange to see it and give them a call. When I reported that, with certain reservations, I thought it masterly and hilariously funny, they told me they were looking for a less conventional response. A couple of months later, the May 1964 *Encounter* published an extremely hostile review by the leading sovietologist and cold warrior, Robert Conquest, denouncing *Strangelove* as anti-American. *Encounter* was one of the most distinguished cultural journals of the twentieth century, and Conquest's piece was tucked away in the 'Notes & Topics' section between an essay on C.S. Lewis and a Gallup Poll on social and economic satisfaction in Western society. Only much later did I realise that word must have been passed down from the CIA through the Council for Cultural Freedom to launch an attack on *Strangelove*.

The CIA was also troubled at this time by the novel *The Spy Who Came In From the Cold*, written by John le Carré, a pseudonym for a junior employee of MI6. It centred on the corrosive effects of the Cold War on the West and saw our own espionage activities as a mirror image of those of the Soviet Bloc. As a result le Carre's name joined Graham Greene's on a list of those regarded by the CIA as, in the words of Frank Wisner, head of the Agency's Office of Policy Coordination, 'dupes' and 'ill-wishing and grudge-bearing types'. A dour, respectful screen version of *The Spy Who Came In From the Cold* appeared in 1965, and over the next 25 years adaptations of le Carré novels for the cinema and television were the most serious and critical movies about the espionage establishment. Other films on the subject were slick, comic or melodramatic, most significantly the Bond movies. Their success at the time, starting with *Dr No* in 1962, and their enduring popularity are due to the elimination of the often virulent Cold War politics embraced in the novels by Ian Fleming, himself a creation of the intelligence community. Amusingly, the screenplays for the Bond film *Goldfinger* and *The Spy Who Came In From the Cold* were written by the British film critic, Paul Dehn. In 1950 Dehn had won an Oscar for the original story of the British movie *Seven Days to Noon*, one of the earliest popular pictures to alert the public to the international arms race and put the case, however tentatively, for unilateral nuclear disarmament.

From this point on, the Cold War more or less ceased to dictate Hollywood's agenda or employment policies, and in 1967 a successful Hollywood comedy called *The Russians Are Coming, The Russians Are Coming*, turned on a middle-class East Coast community ending up protecting the crew of a Soviet submarine accidentally stranded on their New England holiday beach from a paranoid US military force. I say 'more or less' for two reasons. First, the Vietnam War, which Jack Kennedy had helped instigate, and his successor Lyndon Johnson to institutionalise, was a taboo subject, and only one sizable picture, John Wayne's gung-ho 1966 *The Green Berets*, was produced while the war was on. It was, however, dealt with indirectly, in *M*A*S*H*, the 1970s comedy ostensibly about the Korean War scripted by Ring Lardner, another unrepentant member of the Hollywood Ten. Second, the era of the blacklist, the House Committee investigations, the naming of names, the enforced exiles, the perceived treacheries of friends and comrades, left wounds that have yet to heal and scars that remain visible. Elia Kazan, whose membership of the Communist Party in the mid-1930s had been brief, appeared before HUAC as a friendly witness in 1952. He resumed his career – still a tortured liberal – after making the melodramatically anti-communist picture *Man on a Tightrope*. It centred on the manager of a Czech circus, constantly harassed by the communist authorities and escaping with his company into the freedom of neighbouring Austria. When in 1998 the withered 89-year-old Kazan was led on stage by Martin Scorsese to receive a lifetime achievement award at the annual Oscar ceremonies, there were public protests outside the auditorium, and a number of prominent figures in the audience refused to join in the standing ovation.

Hollywood has made a handful of pictures touching on the blacklisting, though only *The Front* (in which Woody Allen plays a writer whose name is used to sign TV scripts by blacklisted authors) compares in frankness with two British films financed by television, Philip Saville's *Fellow Traveller* made in 1989 and Karl Francis's *One of the Hollywood Ten* (made in 2000), which focuses on Herbert Biberman and the production of *Salt of the Earth*. Otherwise the era is rarely revisited and there is no film by an English-speaking director of comparable insight and distinction to Costa-Gavras's *L'Aveu*, a 1970 French film about the Slansky show trials in communist Czechoslovakia starring Simone Signoret and Yves Montand, both former fellow travellers.

It was on a visit to Prague that the conservative American student of Soviet Affairs, Anne Applebaum, was struck by the different attitudes shown by tourists towards Soviet and Nazi memorabilia, the communist sort regarded as comic and chic, the Nazi as repulsive. She reflects on this in the introduction to her book, *Gulag: A History*, which won the 2004 Pulitzer Prize:

> If there is a dearth of feeling about Stalinism among Prague tourists, it is partly explained by the dearth of images in Western popular culture. The Cold War produced James Bond and thrillers, and cartoon Russians of the sort who appear in Rambo films, but nothing as ambitious as *Schindler's List* or *Sophie's Choice*. Steven Spielberg, probably Hollywood's leading director (like it or not), has chosen to make films about Japanese concentration camps (*Empire of the Sun*) and Nazi concentration camps, but not about Stalinist concentration camps. The latter haven't caught Hollywood's imagination in the same way.

This was of course written long before the appearance of Spielberg's *Indiana Jones and the Kingdom of the Crystal Skulls*, in which Harrison Ford as the world's most celebrated archaeologist returned to the fray. The three previous Indiana Jones movies were set in the 1930s, with Nazi troopers as the enemy. In his fourth adventure in the series, set in the United States and Latin America in 1957, the enemy is twofold. First there is a ruthless band of stereotyped Soviet soldiers led by voluptuous femme fatale Colonel Irina Spalko, dressed in a trouser suit, sporting a page-boy haircut and wearing opaque shades. It's camp stuff, parodying characters in anti-communist comic strips and B-movies of the McCarthy era, and it's clear where George Lucas, Steven Spielberg and screenwriter David Koepp found their inspiration. Secondly, but rather less comical, Indiana Jones, the patriotic all-American hero, is investigated and harassed by the FBI. Despite his sterling service in World War Two, he's suspected of assisting the Soviet enemy and possibly of treason. So one part of the film trades in old Hollywood propagandistic fictions, the other in disturbing historical facts of a kind Hollywood once assiduously ignored. This is also part of the legacy.

In the autumn of 2002 I arranged a season of Cold War films at Tate Modern to accompany a retrospective exhibition of paintings by Barnett Newman. Most of the American movies mentioned in this, my V&A, lecture were screened. It had been the intention to include some examples of the handful of Soviet films from the 1940s and 1950s, among them Mikhail Romm's The Russian Question, *in which an American journalist returns home after a tour of duty in Moscow and is destroyed for trying to tell the truth about Soviet life, and Mikhail Kalotozov's* Conspiracy of the Doomed, *a justification of the show trials of politicians and intellectuals in an unnamed Eastern European country, who've been conspiring with Western imperialists. None of these pictures had been shown in the West before, and at the last moment the new guardians of Russia's film archives suddenly seemed to be less than eager for them to be seen now. They imposed absurd conditions and demanded such exorbitant fees that the films had to be withdrawn from the season.*

Victor Fleming: *Gone With the Wind* and *The Wizard of Oz* (2009)

Seventy years ago, on 15 December 15 1939, one of Hollywood's most legendary movies, *Gone With the Wind*, a celebration of what the American South endured as a result of the Civil War, had its whites-only world premiere in Atlanta, Georgia. Its stars were there – Vivien Leigh who played the brave, capricious, head-strong, thrice-married heroine Scarlett O'Hara, and Clark Gable, Hollywood's democratically elected King, who played the handsome, pragmatic hero Rhett Butler. Also present of course was its producer, the 'Boy Wonder' David O. Selznick, who'd been developing the film for three years, ever since buying the rights to Margaret Mitchell's mammoth bestselling 1936 novel. Absent and not especially missed was the man who was to win one of the film's nine Oscars, its director Victor Fleming. He wasn't there partly because he'd had a row with Selznick, but mainly because he'd stayed behind in Los Angeles to attend the funeral of his mentor and hunting companion, Douglas Fairbanks, the great silent star for whom he'd been chief cinematographer 20 years before.

A few months earlier, on 25 August 1939, another legend had its premiere, *The Wizard of Oz*, the magical family movie based on Frank Baum's 1900 novel, also a famous bestseller. It made a major star of the 17-year-old Judy Garland as Dorothy Gale (16 when the film was shot), the rural orphan reared by her aunt and uncle on an impoverished Midwestern farm, who's whisked off by a tornado from monochrome Kansas to the Technicolor world of Oz where she takes a transformative journey with the Cowardly Lion, the Tin Man and the Scarecrow. This film was also directed by Victor Fleming, and like *Gone With the Wind* has become part of the warp

'Victor Fleming: *Gone With the Wind* and *The Wizard of Oz*' first appeared in the *Observer*, 27 December 2009.

and weft of popular culture. Each subsequent generation has added something to the accreting legend by way of song, parody and affectionate tribute, among them Elton John, John Boorman, Robin Williams, David Lynch and Salman Rushdie who called the film 'my very first literary influence'. James Cameron specifically references it in *Avatar*.

In the Reagan–Thatcher years Ronnie and Maggie figured on the walls of students' rooms, standing in for Gable and Leigh in a satirically refigured poster of *Gone With the Wind*. The question, 'Are you a friend of Dorothy?' came to mean 'Are you gay?' The two movies were hilariously conjoined in Steve Rash's cult comedy *Under the Rainbow* (1981), when a riot on the sound stage of *The Wizard of Oz* results in a chase that takes Toto and the Munchkins through an adjoining set where Rhett and Scarlett are performing in *Gone With the Wind*.

Both films have key lines that everyone knows – 'Toto, I've a feeling we're not in Kansas any more'; 'Frankly my dear, I don't give a damn'. They have immediately recognisable melodies – Max Steiner's 'Tara Theme', Harold Arlen and Yip Harburg's 'Over the Rainbow'. Each ends in a strongly affirmative way linking its heroine to her native soil. Scarlett returns to her estate, declaring: 'Tara! Home! I'll go home, and I'll think of some way to get him back. After all, tomorrow is another day.' Dorothy, after tearing herself away from Oz to return to dreary Kansas, proclaims: 'And I'm not going to leave here ever, ever again because I love you all! And Oh, Auntie Em, there's *no* place like home.'

In 1963 Arthur M. Schlesinger Jr, the greatest historian of the Roosevelt era and movie critic of the short-lived glossy monthly *Show*, wrote in an article called *When the Movies Really Mattered* that 'the Golden Age of Hollywood' was the 1930s. 'The combination of the Depression and the New Deal,' he declared, 'gave the Hollywood of the Thirties its particular audience – an audience which was at once demoralised by the downfall of the system, exhilarated by the promise of action and deeply responsive to the image of purpose and freedom.'

Nine years later, in 1972, Peter Bogdanovich wrote in his monthly column for *Esquire* an essay called *The Best Films of 1939*, bestowing on that year a legendary place in American film history. The first two movies he mentioned were *Gone With the Wind* and

The Wizard of Oz, pointing out that Victor Fleming had won that year's directing Oscar for the former, and had 'guided Judy Garland' through the latter. He did not, however, regard Fleming as the director of the year. For him that accolade belonged to John Ford, three of whose pictures appear among Bogdanovich's ten best of '39, a list that excluded *Oz* and *GWTW*. Seventeen years later Ted Sennett wrote *Hollywood's Golden Year, 1939*, described as 'a fiftieth anniversary celebration'. His two longest chapters are devoted to *GWTW* and *Oz*.

Why then is Fleming so little known and celebrated, and why did it take 70 years before we got the first critical biography, Michael Sragow's excellent, scrupulously researched *Victor Fleming: An American Movie Master*?

First of all, a word about Fleming. He was born in 1889 in a Californian tent city in Pasadena, his dirt-poor parents recent migrants from the Midwest fallen on hard times. Oddly, his mother's and father's background united key incidents from *Oz* and *GWTW*. Their home in Missouri had been swept away by a tornado. Fleming's paternal grandfather had fought in the Confederate Army and his maternal grandfather had marched through Georgia with the Union Army, taking part in the battle of Atlanta. His father died when Fleming was four, his mother remarried happily, and he left school early to become involved in the new world of engineering as a motor mechanic, cab driver, competitive racer, and chauffeur, in which role he encountered the pioneer movie director Allan Dwan. Soon he became a cinematographer, working for the greatest action star of silent cinema, Douglas Fairbanks. This led to a commission in the Signal Corps in World War One and a key assignment as President Wilson's personal cameraman at the postwar Paris peace conference. After his return from Europe he was promoted to be Fairbanks's director, had his classical features enhanced by a broken nose (the result of an on-set punch-up), became the lover of the actresses he directed (Norma Shearer, the 'It Girl' Clara Bow and Jean Harlow among them), and with the coming of sound he ended up as a key director at Paramount.

Fleming, often described as more handsome than the actors he worked with, made Gary Cooper a star in the first major sound western, *The Virginian* (1929), and went on to MGM in 1932 to shape Clark Gable's screen persona as the hardboiled expatriate torn between socialite Mary Astor and wisecracking demi-mondaine Jean Harlow in *Red Dust* (1932). He discovered the vulnerable side of Spencer Tracy in *Captains Courageous* (1935), and brought together Tracy and Gable in several hard-nosed pictures. One often feels like telling young directors right out of film school with their diplomas and much-vaunted cine-literacy to 'get a life'. Fleming, his friend Howard Hawks and others of their generation had led colourful lives before coming to Hollywood. The veteran moviemaker Henry Hathaway, one-time assistant to Fleming, observed: 'Clark Gable on screen is Fleming ... Every man that ever worked for Fleming patterned himself after him. Clark Gable, Spencer Tracy, all of them. He had a strong personality, not just to the point of imposing himself on anyone, but just forceful and masculine.'

There are, however, less likeable sides to his character. Many people regarded him as anti-Semitic, but this may well have been a reflection of the coarseness of male conversation in those days. He doesn't appear to have harboured deeply engrained prejudices. The screenwriter Ben Hecht, an ardent Zionist, recalled him as 'aloof and poetic', enjoyed working with him on *Gone With the Wind*, and wrote amusingly about being called in to rewrite the script. When Hecht revealed he hadn't read the novel, Selznick and Fleming acted out the story, the former playing Scarlett, the latter Rhett Butler and Ashley Wilkes. Fleming was also at times vituperatively rightwing and a founder member of the Motion Picture Alliance for the Protection of American Ideals, a witch-hunting organisation that encouraged the House Un-American Activities Committee's investigations of Hollywood. On the other hand he was highly regarded by, and got on well with, the communist screenwriter Dalton Trumbo, jailed as one of the Hollywood Ten.

If Fleming was so clearly admired by his contemporaries, why isn't he an acclaimed auteur with a name as familiar to popular audiences as Hitchcock and Spielberg? There are a number of reasons, the first inevitably deriving from the peculiar way Fleming joined the troubled productions of *Oz* and *GWTW* as MGM's trusted trouble-shooter. He was the studio's safe pair of hands, the man who a couple of year's later was proposed to *Life* magazine by America's most celebrated film critic, James Agee, as the perfect subject for a feature on 'the reliable journeyman director'. *Oz* was stalling under the stolid direction of Richard Thorpe, who was thrown off by producer Mervyn LeRoy. George Cukor, designated director on *GWTW*, took over briefly before the arrival of Fleming, who threw himself into a project on which six writers had worked.

Everything was going well on *Oz* until, early in 1939, George Cukor came into conflict with Gable and Selznick on the set of *GWTW*. Gable thought Cukor, seen as a 'woman's director', was giving too much attention to Olivia De Havilland and Vivien Leigh, while Selznick felt the movie lacked dynamism. So Cukor was fired. As Selznick's own company was co-producing with MGM, Fleming was snatched away from MGM's *Oz*, where he was replaced for the film's final weeks by King Vidor. Working from Fleming's storyboards, Vidor directed the monochrome sequences, but Fleming returned to shape the film at the editing stage.

The similarly troubled *GWTW* had at least eight writers, including Sidney Howard, the Pulitzer Prize-winning playwright who took a single credit, and five directors. Fleming re-shot much of Cukor's material, the film's production designer, William Cameron Menzies, had supervised the burning of Atlanta while the film was in pre-production, and Sam Wood stood in for a week or so when Fleming had a breakdown. In his study of *GWTW*, Gavin Lambert reckoned that Fleming directed 45% of the final product, Wood 15%, Menzies 15%, Cukor 5%, and the film's second unit 18%. So film historians have described it as a group enterprise, a producer's movie, an example, if a rather extreme one, of the studio system at work.

Fleming died in 1949, too soon, as his biographer Sragow points out, to contribute to the oral history of Hollywood the way Ford, Walsh, Lang, Dwan, Cukor and others did. He left no archive of annotated scripts, autobiographical notes or letters, other than the embarrassingly effusive billets doux he sent to his last love, Ingrid Bergman, star of his disastrous final film, *Joan of Arc*. The *Cahiers du Cinéma* critics and future New Wave directors ignored him while propagating their 'politique des auteurs', and the American critic Andrew Sarris, their chief interpreter in the English-speaking world and coiner of the term 'auteur theory', continued the marginalisation. In Sarris's famous taxonomy of American filmmakers, first published in 1963 in the quarterly *Film Culture* and then in *The American Cinema: Directors and Directions 1929–68*, one of the most influential film books ever written, Fleming was assigned to the final, catch-all category 'Miscellany'. Sarris did, however, concede that 'apart from Cukor, he was the only Metro director who could occasionally make the lion roar'.

Having leapt at the chance to make *Oz*, Fleming took on *GWTW* with some reluctance. But he was the man with the versatility, the combination of the tough and the tender, and the decisiveness to bring order to these expensive, drifting projects. No wonder Selznick eventually issued an order that 'Fleming should direct everything, however seemingly unimportant'.

He was able to tell Selznick that 'your fucking script is no fucking good', and to set about reshaping it. He'd tell the capricious, initially uncooperative British star, 'Miss Leigh you can stick this script up your royal British ass.' This was part of a strategy to deter her from making Scarlett too sympathetic too early. On the other hand he was one of the few directors who could convince Gable that it was not unmanly to cry in the crucial scene where Rhett receives the news of Scarlett's miscarriage. He was not as subtle an explicator as Cukor was and upset some actors by constantly saying, 'Ham it up.' But Howard Hughes, a man not noted for the subtlety of his insights, reassured his then girlfriend Olivia De Havilland that she and the other actresses in the film should not be alarmed by the departure of the sensitive George Cukor. 'Don't worry,' he told her, 'everything is going to be all right – with George and Victor it's the same talent, only Victor's is strained through a coarser sieve.'

The question remains, was Victor Fleming more than the reliable journeyman filmmaker doing his job with anonymous efficiency? Sragow's biography suggests that he was in fact a highly emotional man whose commitment to his work was so extreme that he frequently drove himself to a state of extreme physical and nervous exhaustion. The final instance was *Joan of Arc*, the troubled epic he hoped would surpass *GWTW* but which brought about his death in 1949. It would seem that his two 1939 movies became personal projects for him as a result of his second marriage in 1931 that had turned him into a family man and devoted father. He brought great sensitivity to the world of children in *Treasure Island* (1934) and *Captains Courageous* (1937), stories set in the world of men. When he undertook *Oz*, a story seen through the eyes of the innocent young Dorothy, he was thinking of his two little daughters. He told the film's producer, Mervyn LeRoy, that he wanted them to see 'a picture that searched for beauty and decency and love in the world'. It was the other side of the marriage, the increasingly difficult relationship with his wife Lu, that he brought to *GWTW*. Fleming had a very personal understanding of the complex relationship between Scarlett and Rhett and of the problems confronting a confident long-time bachelor and celebrated ladies' man adjusting to a wilful wife and a different way of life.

So perhaps the time has come to re-examine Fleming's oeuvre in the light of Sragow's biography and to give him appropriate credit for his two most famous pictures as we approach the seventieth anniversary of their British premieres. *The Wizard of Oz* opened here in March 1940, *Gone With the Wind* followed in April, and audiences took particular pride in the fact that the former was largely scripted by a British writer and three of the four names above the title of the latter were British. Both films brought hope, happiness, inspiration and respite to an embattled country. There's a particularly poignant moment in Jean-Pierre Melville's film *The Army of the Shadows* when two French *résistants* on a secret mission to meet De Gaulle in London take the chance to see *GWTW* before returning to Occupied France and their probable death.

Index of Films

Index of Names

Film books from Carcanet Press